Catamaran Racing:
For the 90's

by
Rick White
Mary Wells

WITH CHAPTERS CONTRIBUTED BY:

Randy Smyth, Hobie Alter, Jr., Wayne Schafer, Carlton Tucker, Larry Harteck, Roy Seaman, Bob Curry and Dave Calvert

and Preface by:
Eric Sharp

*RAM Press * Key Largo, Florida*

Published by RAM Press, Publishers
PO Box 2060, Key Largo, FL 33037
Manufactured in the United States of America
Designed by Mary Wells
Cover design by Liz Hill
Artwork by Laurent deBernede

Library of Congress Cataloging in Publication Data:

White, Rick
        Catamaran Racing: For the 90's

        Includes index
        1. Catamarans   I. Wells, Mary.   II. title.
        ISBN 1-880871-00-9

Library of Congress Catalog Card No.: 92-60018

Acknowledgements

This book is not based upon the knowledge of a single person or of a dozen people. It is the result of pooling the experience and experiments of hundreds of people, both monohull and multihull sailors, and boiling it down into the basic elements of what makes a boat sail faster and more efficiently and how to win on the race course.

We have been in the unique position, since beginning Rick White's Sailing Seminars in the spring of 1989, of being on the cutting edge of new developments in sailing and racing. Much of the new knowledge in this book we owe to the guest experts who have been so generous with their time, helping us teach others to get better and faster.

Therefore, we would like to thank our catamaran seminar guest experts to date: Hobie Alter, Jr., Bob Curry, Alan Egusa, Jay Glaser, Randy Smyth, Carlton Tucker, and Jim Young; and our monohull experts to date: Brett Davis, Bob Findlay, Scott Kyle, and Ian Lineberger. We have learned from every one of them.

Hobie Alter, Jr., Dave Calvert, Bob Curry, Larry Harteck, Wayne Schafer, Roy Seaman, Randy Smyth, and Carlton Tucker have lent their time for chapters to this book on areas in which they have particular expertise.

All of the above sailors are true sportsmen who share our desire to keep one-design sailing and racing alive. Through the seminars and through this book, they are helping many thousands of sailors. They set a great example for all of us.

We also want to thank turn-of-the-century sailor Manfred Curry, whose wisdom is still being rediscovered today, and modern-day journalist Eric Sharp, one of the few who understand sailing well enough to make it come alive for the readers and who was kind enough to write the preface to this book.

And special thanks go to Bill Wells, my personal mentor on catamarans — if I had not had him to follow around the race course, I probably would never have gotten into second place. And if he had not retired from racing, I probably never would have gotten into first place.

He's 82 now and plays tennis two to four hours a day. I have a hard time beating him at that game, too.

CONTENTS

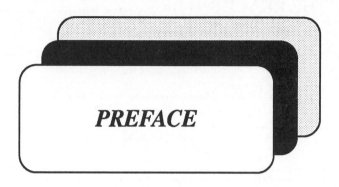

PREFACE

BY ERIC SHARP

In a dozen years of writing about boats for the Miami Herald, Detroit Free Press and a number of magazines, I've had the opportunity to sail with and observe at close range many of the world's top racing skippers, including America's Cup luminaries Dennis Conner, Chris Dickson, Ian Murray and the late Tom Blackaller.

In that time I've met three nearly anonymous sailors who, given equally-matched boats and crews, could hold their own with any of the above, whether it be aboard catamarans or lead mines (keel boats).

Rick White is one of them.

White is one of those characters you run into in most sports, people who are enormously respected by the top players but who are unknown to outsiders. That's mostly because he started racing and dominating catamaran classes at a time when sailing had a much lower profile and was still something you did on the days when you didn't have to earn a living.

He literally wrote the world's first book on catamaran racing in 1972, in the days of the multihull equivalents of the Model A Ford and the rumble-seat roadster — the Hobie 16, Shark, B-Lion, P-Cat and other venerable twin-hullers.

Twenty years later, White's latest book includes chapters by himself and other top multihull skippers who in the past five years have pioneered the latest techniques, such as the "Catamaran Roll Tack," the "Wild Thing," and spinnaker and gennaker use.

It doesn't matter what kind of multihull you sail, or what size — this book will make you better at it. There are chapters on specific boats by people who have won world and national championships on them. But it really doesn't make much difference which boat you put these people on. In fact, if you took White's eight guest contributors and dropped them into any catamaran national championship they'd probably fill up most of the top 10 finish list.

The book lies beside me in manuscript form as I write this, and I guess what impresses me most is how much the reader will get for his money. If you're a beginner, I figure you can take two or three years off the learning curve to reach the top of your local fleet. If you're an experienced multihull racer, there's a ton of stuff in here that will save you a lot of wasted time in experimentation.

The only thing better than reading this book would be crewing for White, which is both fun and enlightening. He races not for money or notoriety but for the thrill of competition and the sheer joy of sailing. His wife, Mary Wells, and I once crewed for him aboard a MacGregor 36 catamaran he had bought a few days before. Our lone headsail had seen better days, the winches were about two sizes too small and we couldn't get the port daggerboard to extend more than 18 inches below the hull.

Our only chance was to win the starts, and White not only won them, he gave the five other skippers aboard newer, bigger and better-equipped boats a lesson in sailboat racing. We did three races that day on Biscayne Bay south of Miami, including one downwind start, and in each White outmaneuvered the competition to place us at the line first and the prime starting position.

White played that MacGregor the way Itzhak Perlman plays a violin. But I have also seen another side of White that I think may contribute equally to his winning ways, and which comes through continually in the countless chapters of this book.

It was in one of the last World 1000 races, a mad-cap endurance event in which two-man crews race 21-or-less-foot catamarans 1000 miles from Miami to Virginia Beach, Virginia. Half of the boats were one-offs (The Nacra 6.0 and G-Force 21 were first built for this race) with compliments of 5-10 sails and were sailed by teams who had budgets of $50,000 - $80,000 for a single, two-week event. White sailed on a modified version of the venerable 20-foot Shark that he built himself. His sponsorship fell through, so he didn't have the stronger, lighter version of the boat that he wanted; he used borrowed, and highly inadequate sails; and the boat was finally finished so late there was virtually no time for testing.

It was a disaster! After hitting something underwater on the first day, the boat started taking on water and soon White dropped back from third to the tail end of the fleet. But each night, while the other crews were getting their needed rest after leisurely dinners, White was working for hours to correct the problems on the boat.

When the boat finally broke up in a storm 400 miles from the start, forcing White and son Dave to make a hairy beach approach through huge surf in an unstable, sinking boat, he was terribly disappointed for a day or so. But then he perked up and announced, "Next year, I'm going to get started earlier and make sure I have the sponsor lined up before I start building the boat."

This is a guy that doesn't give up.

There are chapters in this book by several other great sailors who are as competitive as White. Randy Smyth, Larry Harteck, Hobie Alter, Jr., Carlton Tucker, Wayne Schafer, Roy Seaman, Bob Curry, and Dave Calvert share the attribute of genuinely wanting to see other sailors come up to their own level. If you walk up to these guys on the beach before a race, they will tell you just about anything you want to know (with the exception of the trick they figured out last week). They all thrive on competition.

I remember once asking Smyth about an event where he won with six straight bullets. He grimaced and confessed, "It wasn't much fun. There really wasn't anybody there to challenge us." But then he brightened at the thought of the following week's national championship when "...all the hotshots will be there. That's going to be a hard one."

One final note. Sometimes, when I read a book preface (if I bother to read it), I come away wondering just what qualifications the person had to write it. Well, I can claim to have been beaten in catamaran races by every famous sailor who contributed to this book, sometimes by several of them at once. How many of you can say that?

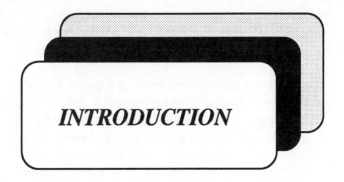

When the earlier edition of this book came out 10 years ago, I thought we had all learned pretty much everything there was to know about catamaran sailing and that there were no more secrets.

Now I know a lot more than I did then, and I realize that there will always be secrets when it comes to sailing — the secrets are things that nobody has yet discovered. New secrets are coming to light every year with advances in both technology and technique.

Whether you are a beginner or a veteran, sailing is a never-ending learning process. For the people willing to reach out and keep seeking new answers and better ways, this is a sport that can never become boring.

And the nice thing about the "secrets" is that anybody can discover them. You don't have to be a world champion sailor to figure out a faster, more efficient way of tacking or create a better jib lead system or devise a way to keep the jib and main sheets from mating. For amateur inventors, sailing is a wide-open field. For sailmakers and boat designers it is an unlimited playground for trying out new theories in physics, aerodynamics and hydrodynamics.

To this point no one has yet found the outermost limit of speed that can be achieved under sail. Even one-designs, with their strict limitations, seem to go a little faster with each passing year, as we learn more about sailing them to their full potential — and as the "limits" of their potential seem to keep expanding.

The revision of this book has been long overdue to catch up with advances of the past decade. Some basic theories have changed, new techniques are still in the process of being perfected, spinnaker poles have sprouted on catamarans, long-distance "drag races" have become more popular, new one-design classes have been created, exotic sail materials are being used.

This book attempts to address all of the new, while retaining all of the basics that have successfully withstood the test of time and change.

But something else has happened in the past 10 years. In the early 1980s catamaran sailing and racing reached a peak of popularity. Fleets were thriving, regattas filled beaches, and dealers were prospering. Toward the end of the decade, the trend took a sharp downturn. Fleets have been dying and dealers have been going out of business all over the country. Rather than dwell on the negative, we prefer to take a positive approach to this what goes down must come back up. To address this situation and give a host of possible solutions, we have included a chapter at the end of the book entitled "Revival."

This may be the most important chapter, because it will profit nobody to learn how to race better if there is nobody to race against.

I would like to explain how and why this revised book became possible. If I had spent the last 10 years sailing with my local fleet, I probably would not know much more than I did in 1983. It takes a while for innovations to filter down through the sailing community.

But I was very fortunate. In 1987 I was invited to serve as guest expert for catamaran week at the Ontario Sailing Centre outside of Toronto in Canada. The Ontario Sailing Centre, since the early 1970's, had been developing a training program for its Olympic sailors, and to support their program, they offered week-long seminars for the public — geared to a different class of boat each week.

During my week as guest expert, I was shocked to find out how much I did not know. And I was also surprised to find how much I learned about what I already know, just by having to teach it to others. I was invited back again the following year, which was almost a disappointment, because I was so impressed with the course, I desperately wanted to take it myself. I had seen how much a week of on-water drills had improved all the sailors there, both beginning and advanced racers.

I began asking myself why there was nothing similar for sailors in the United States. (Although the Canadian program is open to U.S. sailors, Canadian sailors get priority, and the number of boats is limited.)

At my request, the director of the Ontario Sailing Centre agreed to help us put together a similar seminar down in the Florida Keys in the spring of 1989. That was the genesis of Rick White's Sailing Seminars. It was the beginning of the only ongoing program of seminars for catamaran sailors in the United States.

Since then Mary and I have traveled tens of thousands of miles putting on seminars in all parts of the country in an effort to help other sailors improve their skills and, at the same time, we hope, rekindle enthusiasm for sailing.

For most of the seminars we bring along a guest expert. From teaching and from learning what is going on in various parts of the country and from listening to what these various guest experts have to say, we have been in the unique position of being able to stay on the front of the wave, so to speak, of new developments in sailing.

While I am on this paper bandstand, though, I want to stress that what all the experts agree upon is that the tweaks and the gadgets are a very minor part of being a successful racer. Carlton Tucker sums it up well in the chapter on unirigs: "People worry about how tight their diamond wires should be, and then they start at the wrong end of the line...get your head out of the boat."

You've all heard the British term, "Penny wise and pound foolish." In sailboat racing this translates into inches wise and yards foolish.

Some people think nothing of going to a marine store and spending $300 for a little brown bag of goodies that are going to help them go faster. In one-designs, this translates into saving inches on the race course. (Although it will cost you a fortune, I might add.)

Meanwhile, that same person has a slow tack that costs them yards in distance; or starts at the wrong end of the starting line — more yards; or goes to the wrong side of the course — maybe a few football fields worth of distance; or has a bad mark rounding — many yards; or finishes on the wrong tack — more yards; or just plain sails with his mainsail stalled — miles. At this point the inches that you brought home in the little paper bag don't mean diddly.

But perfecting boat handling, starts, tacks, gybes, mark roundings, finishes, layline calls and tactics will save you pounds. (And cost you nothing.)

If you finish a race in last place but only a few hundred yards behind the leaders, chances are you lost those few hundred yards doing one or a combination of the no-no's above.

I think I speak for most of the great racers of the world when I say, don't worry about the pennies until you have the pounds in your pocket.

When you have set your boat up like the others you are sailing against and when you have mastered all the basic principles that will get you around the course in the shortest possible distance, when you have cut off all the yards you can, then start worrying about the pennies — the additional little things that will gain you inches in speed.

This book will help you with both the pennies and the pounds, but we hope you will concentrate on the pounds first.

And while we do not attempt to look into the future, we must all be aware that there are still many secrets to be discovered, and we must all participate in the search.

The most difficult thing about creating this revised edition was the process of "cutting."

The 1983 edition, entitled "Catamaran Racing: Solutions, Secrets, Speed," contained 284 pages. This edition contains 350 pages, despite the fact that we reduced type size, narrowed the margins and eliminated all photographs and nine chapters. Yet, the original version contained 20 chapters and this has 28, along with 58 diagrams.

We ADDED the following chapters: "Boat-Handling," "Strings to Pull," "Telltales," "Pre-Race Prepping," "The Reaching Leg," "The Finish," "Wind Shifts," "Tactics," "Revival," "The Prindle 19," "Spinnakers," "The Hobie 17 (Unirigs)," "The Nacra 5.8," "Distance Racing," "New in Sails," "Wind & Weather," and "Olympic Class."

We did not want to eliminate anything — only add — but the book would have gone on forever, and the cost would have escalated beyond the means of the sailors to buy or of us to publish.

The crewing chapter was one we struggled over eliminating, but our solution was to place "Notes to the Crew" at appropriate points throughout the book, in bold-face type. We strongly believe that any serious crew should know as much as the skipper, but the notes are there for those who want to skim.

Therefore, this book is packed full of streamlined information that we and our guest contributors hope will be helpful to sailors everywhere, whether they race or just sail for the sheer joy of it.

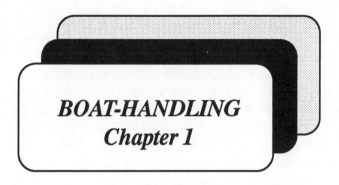

BOAT-HANDLING
Chapter 1

This chapter is the longest and one of the most important in this book, because it is imperative that you understand and master the techniques described here before getting into the fine points of sail trim, boat tuning, racing and tactics.

A boat out of control on the starting line (or anywhere on the water) is as bad as an out-of-control skier on a crowded slope. If you cannot control your boat in all circumstances and conditions, if you cannot put it through its paces with instinctive reactions, you will be doing a lot of 720s, or worse, causing damage to your boat and others, and possibly even injuring someone.

The starting line is the place where you will find yourself in the closest proximity to the most boats, because all the boats in the regatta congregate there before the race. You will have to maneuver in close quarters and heavy traffic. However, some of the maneuvers discussed in this chapter will also be useful at marks where many boats are converging at the same time. And they will make you look like a real pro while pulling in to or taking off from a dock; or coming in to or going out from a beach; or maybe a crowded anchorage.

Going a step farther, being able to control your boat in any conditions could help you to save somebody's life in a man-overboard situation.

Before we start putting the boat through its paces, though, we need to discuss how to steer this sometimes obstinate critter and make it go where we want it to go.

STEERING

Many people first getting on a sailboat of any kind do not realize that the rudder is only one of three major steering elements on the boat.

The rudders are the most obvious steering device. However, they are also the smallest and least effective. The most important steering device is the sail (or sails). Obviously, they are much larger and more powerful than the rudders. When the rudders and the sails work against each other, the boat is trapped in the middle, an innocent victim that is just along for the ride and doesn't know which way to turn.

But there is yet a third steering factor that can help or hinder both the sails and the rudders — the weight of the crew.

Understanding how these three mechanisms work together or against each other is extremely important, because they can not only help you go forward, but also help you to stop or even to back up. As we delve into the mechanics of boat maneuvers in this chapter, it will become clear how the three can work together to make your boat obey your every whim or work in disharmony to make sailing a battle on the water.

Let's analyze each of the steering mechanisms:

RUDDERS

The function of the rudders is the most obvious. Assume you are sitting on the windward side of the boat and the boat is moving forward through the water. If you pull on the tiller, the nose of the boat goes away from you and away from the wind (or down). When you push the tiller away from you, the bows come your way and more toward the wind (or up). That is simple enough — however, the sails can easily overpower simple rudder control.

Also remember that rudders do not work at all if the boat is static, sitting still. There must be movement through the water in order for the rudders to have any effect (whether you're moving forward or backward). The sails are the engine. From a dead stop you must actually begin both movement and steerage with the sails alone until there is enough forward motion for the rudders to be effective. Again, there must be a flow of water across the rudder in order for it work at all.

SAILS

The sails act to balance the boat's power and steering. Given neutral helm (let's pretend the rudders are not on the boat), if the jib is in and sheeted and the mainsail is out and unsheeted, there will be more force on the jib than on the mainsail, tending to drive the bows AWAY from the wind.

On the other hand, if the mainsail is in and sheeted and the jib is out and unsheeted, the predominant power is on the main, pushing the sterns away from the wind, thereby causing the bows to turn TOWARD the wind.

A good example of this is demonstrated by the sailboard *(See Diagram 1.)*, which has no rudder system at all. If the mast is leaned forward, the force is toward the bow (like a jib) and will steer the board away from the wind.

As the mast is leaned aft, the force is toward the stern, causing the bows to turn closer to and even straight into the wind — much like a windvane — because there is no longer any sail forward to push the bow away from the wind.

The power of the sail can easily overpower any rudder steerage you may apply. If the sails are not trimmed properly for the steerage you are applying, the rudders will be overpowered, having little or no effect on the direction of the boat. And by the same token, the sails can be a tremendous asset to the steerage.

We have already pointed out that by manipulating the main and jib, the sails can steer a boat by themselves, without any aid from the rudders. Someday while out playing off the beach, try pulling up the rudders and going in a straight course with just the sails. This is a good way to appreciate both the balance of a boat's sail plan and the steering powers of the sails.

The jib makes a wonderful forward wind rudder. If you are head to wind (in irons) and wish to get out of that position, you simply pull the jib out to one side or the other. The wind hits the curvature of the sail, creating negative pressure on the leeward side. The movement of the bow will be toward the negative pressure side and will swing back onto a close-hauled course again. If you want to end up on starboard tack, you will pull the jib across to the starboard side of the boat. If you want to be on port tack, pull the jib out to the port side.

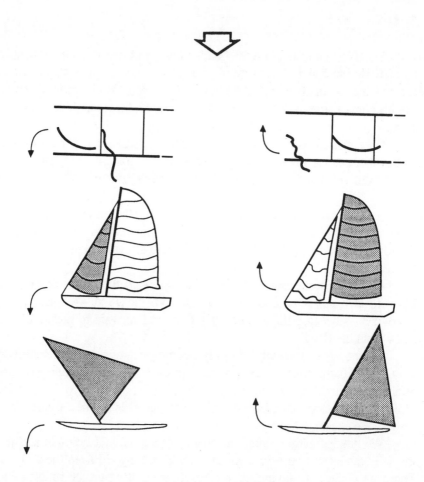

DIAGRAM 1

Going a step further, this same procedure can help you complete a tack in adverse conditions where it is difficult to get the bows to come all the way around. This bit of extra side thrust by the jib ensures that you are not going to have a bad tack. Note: This is not proper tacking procedure — just an emergency "save" technique.

The jib also helps to get a boat moving from a dead stop. Picture yourself sitting dead in the water, with the wind quartering over your bow. You are not in irons, but actually in a position to beat to weather, except that your sails are out and flapping. Now you want to go forward.

If the main is brought in alone, there is a good chance the boat will be overpowered by the main and just round up head to wind. However, if you bring in the jib first, it keeps the bow off the wind, and then the main can be brought in to begin accelerating.

Unirigs do not have a jib to assist in steering, and for them the third steering factor — crew weight — becomes very important.

CREW WEIGHT

Proper positioning of weight on the boat also can help or hinder what the rudders and sails are trying to do.

For the purposes of this chapter and subject, we are only talking about weight distribution in its role of helping to steer the boat. Weight distribution is also a major factor in your boat's speed, but that is covered in depth in Chapter 2.

A catamaran, because of its width, is inherently more stable and less tippy than a monohull, such as a Laser or a Thistle, for example. Because a Laser is so excessively sensitive to weight distribution, let's use that as an example to illustrate.

A Laser is designed to be sailed flat (a difficult thing to achieve). However, if it heels to leeward, the boat's tendency is to head up into the wind and it is difficult to make it bear off until you hike it flat again. If you hike a Laser flat, it wants to go straight, and if you heel it slightly to windward, its tendency will be to bear off.

For similar reasons, weight distribution is also very important in helping to steer catamarans; but it requires much more exaggerated movement and placement of weight to make it happen, simply because cats are more stable.

When you change the angle of the boat on the water by moving your weight — to tilt it to leeward or to windward, tilt it more forward or more back — a number of other complex things happen.

These changes in position of the boat can change the center of effort, the center of lateral resistance, the efficiency of the lateral resistance, the efficiency of the sails, the helm, and the amount of friction or drag. These are interesting subjects for students of hydrodynamics and aerodynamics.

However, as sailors, we only really need to know the EFFECTS of weight positioning on your steering.

WHAT WE DO NEED TO KNOW IS THAT:

If you are going to weather and you get a puff and the boat flies a hull, it wants to head up until you get it relatively flat again.

If you are trying to bear off to go downwind, you MUST have the boat flat when you begin your turn, or the boat will not want to bear off.

When you complete a tack, going immediately forward on the new windward hull will flatten the boat out so you can bear off to pick up speed.

The less wind there is and/or the slower you are moving when you are attempt to change directions, the more valuable weight movement is in assisting the steering.

Just as an experiment, put your boat into irons and, if you have a jib, furl it or leave the sheets loose so it is not an influence. Uncleat the mainsheet and leave slack in the sheet. Now, move to the aft port corner of the boat — the boat will start turning to port. Move to the aft starboard corner of the boat — it will start turning to starboard.

Weight distribution can help or hinder in any maneuvers that involve changing the boat's direction. But by far its most important role is in helping you tack your catamaran with speed many monohulls would envy.

Weight movement is an especially important factor on unirigs, which do not have jibs to help steer the boat.

The importance of weight placement will become more clear in some of the descriptions of specific maneuvers that follow.

THE ROLL TACK

The catamaran roll tack, a modified version of the monohull roll tack, is the most important refinement in catamaran boat handling in the past decade. It is a crucial breakthrough in speeding up tacks and, for those who master the skill, opening up the weather leg to more effective use of tactics.

Here is where weight distribution plays one of its most critical roles, and it is equally effective on sloop rigs and on unirigs, although for the unirig it is imperative for successful tacks. The lesson we learn from how to use weight to turn a boat in a roll tack can also be used to control the boat when stopping, parking, getting out of irons or helping to save a tack when you inadvertently tack into a wave or a header.

The tack is initiated in a normal fashion, with the skipper saying, "tacking" or "hard alee," and beginning to put the tiller over. At this point, as the boat just begins into its turn, the skipper must be moving back to the aft windward corner of the boat, and the crew (on a two-person boat) must immediately move back beside the skipper.

Both people stay in this position as the boat comes through the eye of the wind. At this point the crew goes diagonally across the boat and forward to the main beam on the new windward side. The skipper remains back in the corner of the old windward side until the boat is headed onto the new tack. At this point he crosses to the new side and goes forward.

Let's analyze what this weight distribution pattern is doing.

By moving to the aft windward corner as the boat is turning, you are lifting both bows clear of the water, reducing drag, and making it easier for the boat to turn. As the boat comes into the eye of the wind and the burden is released on the sail, you will actually be lifting the former leeward hull almost completely clear of the water, and the boat is pivoting on the back corner where your weight is concentrated.

The crew crosses to the new side first, pulling in the jib, which helps turn the bows even more onto the new tack.

The skipper stays as long as possible, so his weight can continue to assist the turn. When he crosses, he should switch his tiller behind the mainsheet blocks and immediately go forward beside the crew.

This final action of moving the weight to windward and forward gets that hull back down and flattens the boat, which helps the skipper bear off onto a close reach and get up speed before again heading up to his normal close-hauled angle.

Of course, a lot of other things are going on at the same time.

Let's first talk about the crew. When the turn is initiated, the crew will uncleat the jib and hold it while moving back beside the skipper. As the boat is turning, the crew must watch the jib. As soon as the wind catches on the back side of it, the crew watches the telltales on the jib and eases the jib in unison with the boat's turning so the telltales will continue to flow. As the jib crosses the center line, the crew should be moving diagonally forward across the boat, taking the new jib sheet with him and continuing to ease the old sheet while bringing in the new sheet, attempting to keep the telltales flowing until the jib is sheeted on the new side.

Meanwhile, the skipper is steering smoothly and with steadily increasing pressure throughout the turn, without leaving his position. As the boat comes head to wind, the skipper should release about 2 feet of mainsheet and recleat it, also without leaving his position in that aft corner. After the boat is headed onto the new tack, the skipper comes across, switches his tiller, and moves forward, sheeting in the main AFTER the jib is in.

As you can see, the only thing about this tack that is different from a "normal" tack is the weight distribution.

Timing for this weight maneuvering is very critical. Go across too soon, and you kill the tack. Go across too late, and you will not accelerate out of the tack rapidly enough.

The roll tack works best in light and moderate air. In heavy air it can be done, but the waiting time on the old windward hull is down to a heartbeat for the crew and maybe two heartbeats for the skipper — otherwise, you risk capsize. However, the more practiced you get at this maneuver, the less trouble you will have under any wind condition.

On the Hobie 16 and the Prindle 16, very sensitive boats to fore-and-aft weight, the procedure is the same except that the skipper and crew will not move as far aft (to avoid risk of capsizing backwards).

For the unirigs, it is especially important to stay on the old windward side as long as possible, and then go forward rapidly to the main beam on the new side to help the boat bear off and promote acceleration. Unirigs need to exaggerate their turn more than sloop rigs and bear off a little farther onto a reach to build speed before heading back up. Not having a crew to help get the boat flat, the skipper has to move extra fast when he goes across and forward.

Unirig sailors have a natural tendency to get through the tack, move to the opposite side and sit near the back of the boat while they look up at their sail, trim it and wait for something to happen. Only after the boat starts moving do they go forward. If they stay on the old side until the boat is turned onto the new tack, then go across and forward AS or even before they begin sheeting the main, the boat will accelerate much faster and will have far less tendency to want to turn back up into the wind.

The wings on the Hobie 17, the Magnum, the SX, and the Hobie 21 help them to accentuate their roll tacks even more because of the added leverage. Sit on the wing at the back corner and stay there through the tack.

Remember, the ultimate is to virtually fly a hull briefly while you are still on the old side and then immediately get across and force the new windward hull down so the boat can bear off for a moment to pick up speed before coming back up to a close-hauled angle.

In the traditional tacking method, the crew went almost immediately across to the new side, and the skipper came across as the boat was going through the eye of the wind. Putting weight on the new side too soon keeps both hulls in the water, and the sails have to literally drag them around to complete the tack — a slow way to go.

An additional benefit of the roll tack is that the bows will be somewhat in the air and the wind will catch them and help blow them around to the new tack. For the unirigs, this helps to make up for the lack of a jib to help them through the tack.

The steps for the roll tack, for skipper and crew, look something like this, on a very basic level:

Keys for the skipper (this goes for unirigs, as well):

1. Hard on the wind and mainsheet in tight.
2. Begin turn gently but apply steadily increasing pressure on the helm through the turn and move aft at the same time.
3. As the boat goes through head-to-wind, release approximately 2 feet of mainsheet (a little more for a unirig) and recleat it.
4. After the hulls are pointed onto the new tack, move directly across, transfer your tiller and move forward toward the main beam, heading down onto a close reach and sheeting in at the same time (if the jib is already in).
5. Build speed for a moment on the close reach and head up to closehauled.

Keys for the crew:

1. Move aft with skipper, when he says "tacking" and begins the turn.
2. Take up slack from the lazy sheet (the sheet that is not doing anything on the current tack but that you will be pulling in for the new tack).
3. Uncleat the burdened sheet and grab the lazy sheet with your other hand right at the block.
4. When the wind catches the back side of the jib, begin easing the burdened sheet and simultaneously pulling on the lazy sheet, to keep the jib drawing and telltales flowing all the way through the turn.

5. AFTER the main goes over, cross the deck and go diagonally forward to normal position, continuing to pull the new sheet with you as you go. By pulling directly from the block and crossing the boat with that sheet, you have already pulled in 6 to 8 feet of sheet.

6. Sheet in until the jib is set.

Cautions:

* DO NOT MOVE TO THAT BACK CORNER UNTIL THE TURN IS ACTUALLY INITIATED. Sitting in the back of the boat while you are still going straight will slow the boat down and you will not have speed going into the tack.

* NEVER LET GO OF THE TILLER. For a fast tack, it is absolutely imperative that you NEVER let go of the tiller at any point during the tack and NEVER allow the rudders to straighten out even for a flicker during the tack.

Straightening out the rudders detaches the flow of water from the rudder, dramatically slowing the tack. Because the boat is moving slowly through the middle part of the tack anyway, it is difficult for the water flow to reattach when the rudder returns to its proper turning angle. Remember, when your rudder does not have water moving over it, it cannot steer.

The point where most skippers have a problem with letting their rudders straighten out is the transfer of the tiller extension behind the mainsheet system. However, if you do a roll tack properly, this should not even be an issue.

You see, you will be sitting on the old windward corner and steering all the way through the turn. By the time you head over to the other side and switch the tiller, you will already have the boat pointed in the new direction when you transfer the tiller. By the time you make the tiller transfer, you have already completed a great tack and your rudders are already straightened out.

The folks that get in trouble and let the rudders straighten out during the tack are the ones that are coming across too early. If they do not make a perfect tiller transfer, the rudders will straighten and the tack will slow down considerably, or worse. So don't worry about it. Do a roll tack, staying on the old windward corner until the tack is completed, and the rudders will be carving all the way through the turn.

This does not mean you are free to be sloppy and jerky when making your tiller transfer, however. You always want to keep one hand on the tiller crossbar while flipping the extension around. You don't want to jerk your rudders and detach water flow any more than you want to jerk your sails and detach air flow.

Notes for the Crew:

✔ It is important to remember that both skipper and crew must be back in the corner together. If skipper and crew are sitting side by side on the windward hull, the skipper moves back and the crew moves back beside him. After the boat has come around toward the new tack, go diagonally forward to the opposite windward hull. If it is light air and the crew is on the leeward side of the boat, clear up on the bow, he must go diagonally back across the boat to sit beside the skipper and then, after the boat is around on the new tack, simply moves straight forward to again be positioned on the new leeward bow.

✔ We talked about "sailing" the jib through the tack. You may be accustomed to backwinding the jib through the tack (keeping it cleated until the boat is around and than releasing it and snapping it in on the new side). It usually is not necessary to backwind the jib in a properly executed roll tack. Just watch the telltales and try to keep them flowing as the boat, in effect, turns underneath the sail. Keeping the jib sheeted flat to backwind on the old side is like putting out a brake to slow the boat.

✔ In order to "sail" the jib through the tack, you MUST uncleat the jib BEFORE it backwinds. Once the wind gets on the back side of the sail, it can be very difficult to get the sheet out of the cleat because of the pressure. That is when you end up diving across the tramp and yanking it out of the cleat with both hands.

✔ The Hobie 16 jib, because of its full battens, can be difficult to tack in light air. It keeps getting caught on the mast. One way to minimize this problem is to cut the protruding ends of the battens off as short as possible.

There is a technique for getting the jib across without touching the mast. Grasp the clew of the sail, pull down on it and at the same time push forward to bend the battens to create a bow in the direction you want the sail to go. While holding the sail with the bow in it, pass it across in front of the mast. Mission accomplished. (The secret is in having the sail bow in the right direction. If you are trying to get the sail across to the starboard side, you must bow the battens to starboard.)

✔ The crew is in total control of the success of the tack as it nears completion, because until the jib is sheeted in, the mainsail cannot be sheeted in. If the main comes in first, the boat will head back up into the wind, and you may go into irons. Until you pull the jib in on the new tack, the boat is not going anywhere. Pulling in the jib is the final step in getting the bow around onto the new tack, so the skipper can pull in his main and get the boat moving again.

NOTE: This does not mean more is better. You do not want to sock the jib in flat and hard immediately. You want to bring it in so it is an inch or so looser than your final, close-hauled position. Then as the boat comes back up to its normal course, you will sheet those last few clicks to its final position.

✔ An additional responsibility for the crew is making sure the mast rotates during the tack. In light air, if the mast is hesitant about rotating, the crew should take action to force it around as soon as the boat has gone through the eye of the wind.

THE JIBE

Jibing is much easier than tacking and, when properly done, much faster. You do NOT want to roll tack on a jibe. The skipper and crew should stay forward (unless heavy air conditions), and the skipper should only go to the back of the boat for as brief a time as possible to transfer the tiller and help the mainsail across. The skipper should notify the crew to prepare to jibe and then say "jibing" as he puts the tiller over.

The crew must get the jib across to the new side and set it in downwind position immediately.

The skipper should initiate the turn from his normal position and when nearing the point of the boom coming across, go aft to exchange his tiller extension, throw the boom over and then move directly to his normal position.

Coming out of the turn onto the new tack is very important. The skipper should head briefly higher than the normal course. That will allow the boat to rebuild its speed quickly and then you can resume your normal course.

Timing your jibe is important. If you are already running down the face of a wave, that is an ideal time to jibe. You are half-way through the jibe already, if you are sailing by the jib, and you can allow the wave to keep up your speed while your sails are changing.

So, you always want to initiate the jibe when you have boat speed, if possible.

The most important thing to remember in jibing is to get through the "slow zone" as rapidly as possible. *(See Diagram 2.)* The slow zone is that area where you are relying almost entirely on momentum to keep you going.

To reduce time in the slow zone, carve a smooth turn, with steadily increasing pressure on the tiller and NEVER, NEVER allow the tiller to straighten out

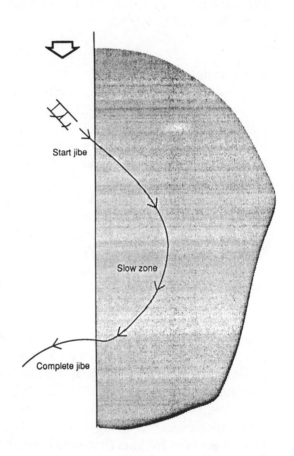

Start jibe

Slow zone

Complete jibe

DIAGRAM 2

at any point during the turn. It takes practice to learn to switch hands on your tiller without letting it straighten out and to learn to never let go of it; but it's another of those little skills that pay big dividends in performance and make up lots of seconds on the race course.

The crew need only let go of the jib clew and go to the other hull and hold it again in its proper set, allowing the skipper to sail by the jib tell-tales once again on the new tack.

The skipper, having set his mainsail as suggested in Chapter 12, "The Downwind Leg," and Chapter 8, "Telltales," will leave his traveler and mainsheet cleated. If they were set perfectly on one side, they will be set the same on the other side.

Notes for the crew:

✔ You have two options when jibing — to get across before the boom or get across after it. The ideal is to get across before it, so that you will have a head start on getting the jib set on the new side. But if you realize your timing is just a split second off, wait for the boom and then go. The reason is obvious (they don't call it "boom" for nothing).

✔ As with tacking, the ideal is to keep the telltales flowing on your jib as long as possible through the jibe. As the boat turns downwind, ease your jib out simultaneously until just before the main jibes. Then very quickly bring the jib over to the new side and try to get the telltales immediately flowing again. If your timing is right, the jib will come across during the most downwind portion of the jibe, and will be initially forward and full to keep it from stalling. You will then bring it in, telltales flowing, as the boat continues to turn, until the jib reaches its normal downwind sailing position. Stop bringing it in at this point and leave it there, so the skipper will be able to look at the jib immediately upon completing the jibe and will know whether he is heading too high or too low.

✔ To make jibing smoother, it helps if you turn off the ratchets on your blocks for going downwind — the jib sheets run through much easier for the jibes (just remember to turn the ratchets back on when going upwind, unless it is very light air).

✔ If you have time, it also helps, when your skipper says "jibing," to frantically pull through, on the back side of the block, a bunch of the sheet on the side you are holding it. This gives you a bunch of slack to help eliminate sheet hangups and make sure the sail will go across with no problems.

✔ If the jib is controlled by barber haulers instead of hand-held, the crew will need to release the barber hauler and sheet on the old side and reset them on the new side. It helps to have marks on your lines so they will be set the same on both sides.

✔ If the boat has positive mast rotation, the crew will need to also release this before the jibe and reset it on the new side after the jibe.

THE HEAVY-AIR JIBE

The S-turn jibe we have described above works in all but heavy-air conditions. Jibing can be a very hairy experience in heavy winds, when there is a danger of pitchpoling. But if you are prepared and use the following technique, it becomes a bit easier. In those conditions, to provide extra stability, just as the mainsail goes across, head the boat straight downwind just before the boom hits the end of its line. This will soften the force and absorb the momentum equally with the buoyancy of both bows. Then head up to your normal downwind course. This is sort of a reverse S-turn.

IN MORE DETAIL:
First, alert the crew of the planned jibe, with crisp commands such as "Prepare to jibe" and "Jibing."

With the crew duly alerted, bring the helm over with steadily increasing pressure until the mainsail is about to jibe, then help the boom across. Be ready to bring the tiller back quickly to head straight downwind again on the other tack as soon as the boom comes across. You should keep all crew weight aft through this entire maneuver.

The power of the sail striking hard on the opposite tack will try to round the boat up. You must stop that action by heading the boat down to stabilize it. Once it is stabilized, return to your normal handling of the boat while on the downwind leg.

Please note that this jibing technique is only to be used in survival conditions, in order to reduce the possibility of capsize. If you were to head up higher than your normal course, as you would ordinarily do, the power of the boom going over could make the boat round up violently and go over.

If you find, after the jibe, that you are beginning to raise a hull, head it down quickly and get all your weight aft in the boat. By heading down, you will be utilizing the buoyancy of two hulls and not just the leeward hull. But the same force that began raising a hull may now try to dig the bows under water and cause a pitchpole. Getting your weight aft quickly should stop that threat.

Usually, however, the jibes should not be quite that violent, because you are getting pretty near the speed of the wind itself. As an example, when a monohull, limited to its hull speed of possibly 8 knots, jibes in winds of 18 knots, the difference between actual speed and wind speed is 10 knots. Therefore, there is a great deal of violence in the boom coming across.

In the catamaran, in the same 18 knots of wind, you may well be nearing the same speed as the wind and the boom is ushered across by a mere 2 or 3 knots difference. Hence, a more docile jibe.

But a caution: If you execute your jibe too slowly and dally too long in letting the stern cross the wind, the stalled sails will slow down your boat speed tremendously, resulting in a proportionately more violent jibe.

STOPPING

While the catamaran has the ability to really scream along, it also has the ability to stop almost immediately, due to its light weight and therefore low inertia, or momentum.

To stop the boat, head the boat up abruptly by jamming over the rudders. This turns your rudders into a good-sized sea-brake off your stern. At the same time let go of the sheets, including the main traveler, while continuing to head up almost directly into the wind. All this braking action stops the light weight of the cat very quickly. That is why it is easy for a cat to go into irons; it has so little weight momentum to help carry it across the eye of the wind in tacking.

But in this case we are stopping exactly when and where we want to stop. In order to maintain control and not go into irons, as soon as the boat has stopped, keep the bows pointed on a close-hauled or close-reach angle, with the sails out.

This maneuver comes in handy when you want to head up and stop beside a dock, another boat or before hitting the beach. It is also a necessary maneuver on the starting line.

You probably will have to approach the starting line with moderate, controlled speed, on a reaching angle. Cruising primarily on the jib with the traveler partway out and the mainsheet slack is not a bad idea, as it ensures you are not going to go into irons (stuck head to wind) on the starting line.

You are moving swiftly along on a close reach and decide to stop. You jam the rudders hard over and bring it up almost directly into the wind, at the same time easing the sails to a full luff. If you still are not stopping fast enough, push the boom of the mainsail out further to the leeward side of the boat so that it begins catching wind on its backside. (You will need to release your traveler for this.) The main will create a tremendous amount of wind resistance to slow the boat even faster.

You probably do not want to tack in the above situation, so be sure not to push the helm over too far, and onto the other tack. This could be disastrous on a crowded starting line — imagine being suddenly on port tack in a crowd of eighty sailors screaming, "STARBOARD."

Now you want to move along farther down the line. Sheet in the jib to pull the bow away from the wind, steer the direction you want to go, and, if you need more speed, sheet in the main a little. Some people use the main traveler for these maneuvers, rather than the mainsheet, since it goes in and out much faster because of less purchase.

Notes for the crew:

✔ **Be prepared for sudden, jerky changes in direction when maneuvering for a start or in any tight quarters, so you don't get thrown off balance — or off the boat.**

✔ **Be aware of how your jib helps steer and control the boat. When stopping the boat or parking the boat (as later described) sit slightly inboard, near the mast, so that if the boat goes into irons, you can grab the lazy sheet and pull the jib toward you, backwinding it to help pull the boat back onto the tack you want to be on.**

GETTING OUT OF IRONS

If the boat goes completely head to wind and you are in irons, you will notice it begin to back up. Assuming you were on starboard tack before you went into irons and you want to remain on starboard tack, simply push the main out to the port side, catching wind on its backside, and push your tiller toward the same side the main is on. *(See Diagram 3.)* The wind on the mainsail will push your stern back to its original tack, and your rudders will aid that turn. You will quickly be back on the original tack and stopped.

You can speed the process of getting out of irons on a sloop rig with weight distribution, but for a unirig it is almost imperative. If you are in

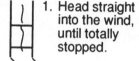
1. Head straight into the wind, until totally stopped.

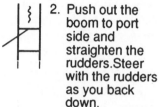
2. Push out the boom to port side and straighten the rudders.Steer with the rudders as you back down.

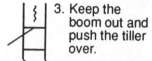
3. Keep the boom out and push the tiller over.

4. When the boat is in close reach position, bring in the jib, straighten the rudders. Sheet in the main slightly, steer to close reach until you gain speed.

5. After gaining speed, sheet in the main and sail close hauled.

DIAGRAM 3

irons and trying to go back onto starboard tack, you have the main pushed out to port, are pushing the tiller to port, and you must also get your weight as far as possible toward the back port corner. This will lift the bows — especially the starboard bow. The wind can then push on the bows much like a backwinded jib and turn the boat back onto its starboard course. When the boat is on course, move the weight back to the windward side AND FORWARD, to flatten the boat so it can bear off and accelerate.

Note that this weight distribution technique is based on the same theory as used for the roll tack. In this case, because you were head-to-wind to begin with, you are using your weight as you would in the last half of a complete tack.

When you are caught in the irons position in a hairy blow, watch carefully that your weight balances the boat fore and aft, as well as side to side. The wind from ahead can get under the trampoline and blow the boat over backward; or if the boat suddenly comes out of irons and you are caught on the new leeward side, it can capsize sideways.

Notes for the crew:

✔ **Again, you can help speed the process of getting out of irons if you pull the jib toward you, letting it become a bag of air pulling the bows away from the wind and back on the proper tack.**

PARKING

Once you have brought the boat up into the wind enough to stop it or slow it to the desired speed, and if you want to "park" it, fall back off to a close reach angle, or about a 50-degree angle to the wind and leave your sails out so the boat does not move forward. The helm will probably be pushed hard over at the same time. You will then be sitting still, with the wind quartering your bow. Anytime you feel

Two ways to approach the starting line

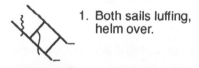

1. Both sails luffing, helm over.

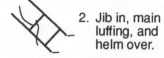

2. Jib in, main luffing, and helm over.

DIAGRAM 4

like moving, straighten the rudders and then it is a matter of simply sheeting — first the jib and then the main — and off you go again. By controlling the sheeting, you can either sit still, crawl forward very slowly or take off at maximum speed.

Another successful way to park is to trim the jib in to a position of soft close-hauled (not as tight as you would normally sail when going to weather). The main and traveler should be released and the helm pushed over. *(See Diagram 4.)* The wind sees the jib in and tries to push it off and onto a reach, while the rudders equally counteract that pressure and force the bow back into the wind. The main does nothing. You now have an Mexican standoff — no one wins, and the boat parks.

To get going, simply straighten the rudders and let the wind swing the boat toward a reach, the main then comes back in, balancing the power and you can steer a close-hauled course.

Note for the crew:

✔ **Take notice that in both parking techniques the jib is required to come in FIRST in order to regain forward motion. If the main is sheeted first, the mainsail will overpower the jib and the rudders, and weathervane the boat high up into the wind, with a good possibility of going into irons.**

On a unirig, the boat must be parked with the bows turned a little farther off the wind to ensure it does not go into irons. The main should be quite loose either by sheet or traveler or both. It can help for the skipper to sit toward the aft-center of the trampoline, keeping the bows up slightly, so the wind will tend to push the bows away from the wind while the mainsail is trying to make it head up.

Note: Keep in mind that when you are parked, you will tend to drift slowly sideways, so make sure you allow for this drift when you pick a parking spot on the starting line.

BACKING UP

You may be raising your eyebrows right now. Backing up? Why?

Actually backing up is a useful trick to learn, and catamarans do it very well. It can come in handy at the starting line or getting into a dock with a wind blowing onto the dock or getting off a beach with an offshore wind.

We discussed backing very briefly in connection with getting out of irons, but that involved merely backing the boats around onto the proper tack. Now we want to know how to keep the boat backing up in a straight line.

Suppose you are forced above the committee boat with only 40 seconds to go. Instead of tacking off to port, finding room to jibe and make another run at the start — all of which will probably take more than a minute, making you very late for the start — you could simply just back up to the line, and proceed in a good starting position.

Randy Smyth tells a story about a race in Germany. There were 80 Tornados and all of them were parked on the starting line at the five-minute gun. There was absolutely no room anywhere to get near the starting line.

Randy sailed out ahead of the committee boat and out in front of the lineup of sailors down to the favored leeward pin, headed up into the wind and began backing down into the starting line.

Needless to say there was a lot shouting at him, for it would certainly seem that Randy was going to cause an accident. But the shouting stopped and the scurrying began, as the parked boats scrambled to get out of the way. They had finally figured out that despite the fact they were sitting still and Randy was backing up, they were the overtaking boat and had no rights. Randy won the regatta.

Well, there are many more war stories, but you get the point — learn to back up.

To back up, you steer the boat head to wind as if stopping. Make sure you go STRAIGHT INTO THE WIND, or it won't work. This is where that telltale on the sidestay or bridle is important to tell you when you are straight head to wind. When you are head to wind, AND NOT BEFORE, push the boom out to leeward, catching the wind in the backside of the mainsail; straighten your rudders and begin steering as soon as the boat begins to go backwards.

Remember that when you are moving backward, the back edge of the rudder is now actually the leading edge of the boat and whichever way that edge is turned, that is the direction the sterns will turn.

If you just want to back up straight, you have to try to hold the rudders straight. Let the jib just flutter — it will probably be smacking the mast.

When the boat begins to move backward, it will start moving quite fast. As it begins to back up, the rudders will want to flop to either one side or the other, so you must hold the tiller very firmly and guide the boat so it does not fall off to either tack.

To get out of the backing mode — and get back onto the tack you were on before you started backing up — simply push the tiller and the bow will swing quickly back to a 45-degree angle to the wind, sheet in the jib first, then the main and off you go.

For the unirigs when you are through backing up, as with getting out of irons or in doing a roll tack, it can be helpful to move your weight to the aft port corner, keeping the main out to the port side, as you steer the boat back onto starboard tack, so that the bows can swing away from the wind. As soon as you are on course, cross to the other side and get weight FOR-WARD while sheeting in. Getting forward is the key to getting any boat to accelerate, but especially so in a unirig.

Notes for the crew:

✔ A caution for Hobie 16 sailors: Whenever the boat is head to wind and the jib is against the mast, it tends to catch and fill on one side or the other, trying to pull the bows in that direction. When the skipper is backing up, the crew has to work hard at keeping the jib free so it doesn't catch any air.

✔ Once the basic technique has been mastered there are some refinements you can make. To go backward faster, move crew weight forward. The skipper is limited by having to hold the boom out to one side, but the crew can move up to the bow. This helps to get the sterns free of the water so there is less drag in going backward — transoms were not designed for efficient "forward" performance.

✔ And if backward speed is really important, after the skipper has control of the main and the steering, the crew can hold the jib out to the side opposite the mainsail, creating a wing-and-wing effect going backward.

A variation on the backing technique is the method for backing away from a beach or a dock when you have an offshore wind. Except in very light air, it can be difficult to get a boat turned completely around, stern to the wind, without it taking off on a reach, possibly leaving skipper and crew behind. This can be doubly dangerous if you are leaving a narrow beach with breakwalls or rocks extending into the water at both sides.

The easy way to handle this situation is to pull up both rudders and pull up daggerboard or centerboards. Leave the main traveler and mainsheet loose. Either furl the jib or make sure both sheets are free. Then, with the boat pointed into the wind, skipper and crew sit on the bows and push off. The boat will move backward downwind. You can alter course to minor degrees, if necessary by dragging a foot on one side or the other. Just keep going backward until you are in open water and have plenty of maneuvering room. Go back to the tramp, get the rudders and boards down, and, using weight, sails and rudders as described before, head off onto your chosen course.

THE 720

The dreaded 720 is the penalty to exonerate yourself for a rules infraction on the race course. Although it seems like severe and unusual punishment when you are attempting to do one, it is far preferable to the old days when you either had to drop out of the race or go to a protest hearing with the deck stacked against you. You can, of course, still take the option of going to the protest committee if you think you are in the right — but even if you really are right, you still have a 50-50 chance of being the one who is disqualified. So why take a chance. Learn how to do a 720 fast, so you can still have a respectable finish in the race.

A 720 consists of two consecutive 360-degree turns in the same direction. It involves executing two tacks and two jibes and ending up on the same tack you were on when you started.

When you are going to weather, you are already close-hauled, so it is much easier and faster to begin your 720 with a tack. When you are going downwind, it is much faster and easier to begin your 720 with a jibe.

Let's say you are going to weather on starboard tack. You would tack to port, immediately release the traveler and mainsheet so the boat can fall off downwind. Go immediately into your jibe, which will put you back onto starboard. Bring in the traveler and the main as rapidly as possible to bring the boat back to a close-hauled position. Go only as far as necessary to build up a little speed. Tack again onto port, again fall off downwind and jibe, which puts you back on starboard. Sheet in and head back to weather. The 720 is completed.

From a downwind position, let's say you are on starboard. Jibe to port. Bring in the traveler and mainsheet and head up to close-hauled. Go only far enough to get a little speed, and tack onto starboard. Immediately dump the traveler and mainsheet to let the boat fall off again downwind. Jibe again to port. Bring in the traveler and mainsheet, head up and tack to starboard. Dump the traveler and mainsheet immediately to fall off downwind on starboard tack. The 720 is completed.

When you are doing a 720 on the weather leg, remember that your goal — the A mark — is upwind of you, so don't sail any farther than absolutely necessary on the jibing portion of your 720, as that will be taking you downwind and away from the A mark. You will have to sail that distance over again when your 720 is completed.

By the same token, when you do a 720 on the downwind leg, don't spend any more time than necessary going to weather before executing your tacks, as that is taking you upwind and away from your goal, the C mark.

Before doing a 720, make sure you are in clear air and out of the way of other boats — you have no rights while you are doing your 720.

If you need to do a 720 on a reaching leg of the course, sail above the rhumb line to do the maneuver, where you will have clear air instead of having a whole line of boats going over you, taking your wind and slowing down the 720.

HINTS TO HELP:

☞ If you ease your mainsheet 2 feet as usual during the tack and cleat it and then immediately release your traveler, the boat will fall off much more rapidly, as the sail load on the rudders will be released.

☞ If you bring your traveler back to center and cleat it immediately BEFORE the jibe, it will help the boat to round up to weather much more rapidly, and all you will need to do is pull in two feet of the mainsheet.

☞ If you have a jib, do not release it too fast when you are falling off the wind; keeping tension on it will help the bows to fall off. When you are heading back up to close-hauled, do not sock the jib in too fast, or it will fight to keep the bows from coming up.

☞ It is easy to become disoriented when you are going in circles and lose track of where you are in the 720. To reduce confusion, it helps if the skipper can talk his way through it out loud. "Okay, tacking.....falling off.....jibing.....hardening up.....tacking.....falling off.....jibing.....hardening up.....we're done."

This works for both unirig and sloop rig boats, but on the sloop rig it is especially helpful to keep the crew oriented as to what is happening next.

Notes for the crew:

✔ **If the skipper is verbally talking through the turns — and if your reactions are instinctive enough — use weight distribution to help speed the turns.**

✔ **When you are turning off the wind, let your jib out JUST A FRACTION slower than the main — the extra pressure on the jib will help the boat fall off.**

✔ **When you are turning back up into the wind, let your jib lag JUST A FRACTION behind the main, so it is not counteracting the efforts of the main when trying to head up.**

FALLING OFF (Turning Downwind)

We are including this under boat-handling, because it is not as simple as it sounds and, if improperly executed, can be dangerous in heavy air.

Let's say the wind is blowing 15-20. We are approaching the weather mark and need to fall off around the mark to start sailing downwind — a 90-degree turn. If you simply pull on your tiller to start the turn without releasing your main, you will have a tremendous fight on your hands, because the boat will try to keep going straight, the bows will dive, the sterns will come up, leaving you even less steerage, because your rudders will be mostly out of the water and will be kicking up roostertails because they are trying to turn and can't. Another word for this is "cavitation," which means the rudders are trying to steer in a pocket of air or bubbles.

The proper way to make this turn is to release both the main traveler and the mainsheet simultaneously with turning the rudders, if not a fraction of a second before. This takes all the load off the rudders and allows them to make their turn. It keeps the bows from diving and keeps both hulls flat on the water for stability. (The jib, of course, should be eased out to its downwind position at the same time.)

If the wind is strong enough that the bows still want to dive a little, move crew weight aft during the turn. This has the dual effect of keeping the bows up for stability and also keeping the rudders in the water for better steerage.

When the sterns begin to come up, you will definitely have a tremendous amount of rudder cavitation — that big rooster tail.

We have given this example in terms of higher wind conditions only because the results of doing it wrong are so much more dramatic and potentially unsafe. The technique of immediately dropping the traveler and mainsheet to leeward must be done regardless of the wind conditions if you want to carve a fast, efficient turn. It will not, however, usually be necessary to move crew weight aft during the turn except in heavier air. This will also vary according to the amount of bow buoyancy your boat has.

Notes for the crew:

✔ **When turning off the wind, help the turn by letting the jib go out A FRACTION slower than the main, but try to keep the telltales flowing throughout the turn. The main was released rapidly to ease the pressure on the rudders. So if you keep the jib pulling, it will help keep up the speed through the turn.**

✔ **On the other hand, in heavy air, pressure on the jib will not only be helping the boat around, it will be pushing the bows DOWN, so be prepared to release that pressure on the jib, if necessary.**

SLOWING DOWN

There are many situations where you may need or want to slow down your boat — for tactical reasons or for safety reasons. In numerous places in this book we will be telling you, for instance, to "slow down to win." Here are some techniques for turning off the speed.

It is relatively easy to slow down going to weather. If you just want to slow down a little bit, pinch up higher into the wind and/or move your weight back so your sterns will drag. If you want to slow down a lot and fast, also let your sails out. (Note that we are not trying to actually STOP — just slow down. If you wanted to stop, you would also jam your rudders hard over, as explained in "Stopping" above.)

On a close reach, you can slow down much the same as you would going to weather — ease the sheets and/or head a little higher, and/or get to the back of the boat.

However, on a broad reach (the wind coming from your aft quarter) if you let the sails out, it will probably do no good. So here you want to stall the sails, instead of luff them. Bring the sails in tighter to stall them, get your weight aft and drag the stern and/or jerk your helm back and forth hard a couple of times.

The beam reach can be the problem. Here you have a choice of either of the above techniques, whichever one works.

———

If all of the above maneuvers are practiced until they become second nature, you will be able to sail anywhere, with any skill level of sailors, because you will have the confidence that you are in complete control of your boat at all times.

WEIGHT DISTRIBUTION
Chapter 2

In "Boat Handling" we have already talked about the importance of weight distribution as it relates to controlling and steering the boat. This chapter discusses how weight is used to maintain the proper sailing "attitude" of the boat in the water when it is sailing on a straight course and how that boat attitude contributes to optimum speed.

"Attitude" is the position of the boat in relation to the water. Where you place your crew weight aboard your catamaran (or any other light displacement boat you happen to sail) is as important as how you trim your sails. If the craft is dragging her sterns, is heeled to windward, or has her bows underwater, she obviously will sail poorly.

Those are extremes. But getting the boat at a perfect attitude for the conditions is not an extreme; it is a necessity.

To make things simple, we can safely say your particular type of boat has one, basic, ideal attitude for maximum performance and that this attitude is basically the same for all points of sail and all weather conditions. Crew weight must be moved wherever necessary on the boat to help maintain that ideal attitude.

The proper attitude for most catamarans is normally leeward bow slightly down or depressed in the water, windward hull just skimming the water, both sterns just clear of the water. The importance of a slight heel to leeward is extreme in the case of the asymmetrical hull — you do not want the windward hull creating opposing lift to the labored leeward hull.

The above concept will help you sail your catamaran quite successfully. But nothing is ever quite that simple. First of all, the ideal attitude will differ from one boat type to another. And secondly, different conditions may require you to deviate somewhat from your boat's basic, ideal attitude.

A better way to determine proper attitude is to use these guidelines:

■ In lighter air, on all points of sail, move your weight forward far enough to keep the sterns from dragging. When they drag, you can hear the noise and gurgling — move forward until you hear the sound of silence.

■ In lighter air, going to weather, try to keep the windward hull "light," by putting the crew on the leeward side, if necessary, to maintain a very slight heel to leeward.

■ In heavier air, on all points of sail, move your weight back just far enough to keep your bows from digging in too deeply. As a rule of thumb, if the water is more than halfway up on the bows, move back a little.

■ In heavier air going to weather, and on close reaches, keep the windward hull just skimming the water.

■ Downwind in all conditions the boat should be sailed flat, with sterns free of the water.

■ Going to weather in chop, you may need to let the bows ride a little higher than normal so the waves do not slow down the boat.

■ Going to weather in flat seas and light air, you may improve pointing ability by keeping the leeward bow more deeply depressed than normal.

■ In general, you want to try to keep your effective waterline on the leeward hull as long as possible without dragging the stern. The longer a boat's waterline, the greater the speed of which it is capable. (Unless you have a planing hull and are, indeed, planing, in which case it is beneficial to actually shorten the effective waterline.)

■ Boats with a lot of rocker in their hull design will need less radical changes in weight distribution than a boat with little fore-and-aft rocker.

All of these factors are relative to your particular type of boat. Some boats like their bows more depressed in the water, and some like their bows to ride higher. Some boats have no problem keeping their sterns clear of the water even when the crew is sitting in the middle of the boat.

The Tornado seems to go to weather quite well with most of the leeward hull underwater.

The new Hobie Miracle sits at anchor with both its sterns and its bows well clear of the water.

Perhaps the following explanation will give you a better understanding of your boat's attitude in the water:

Some boats come from the factory with a waterline painted on them. If you were to moor the boat out in the water by itself, you would see that the water line is horizontal to the water. The bottoms of the transoms will probably be level with or just clearing the water.

However, when you have put 300 pounds of crew weight on the boat, if you maintain that same horizontal position of the waterline, the bottoms of the transoms will now be underwater. When you put up sails, you are adding not only the weight of the sails themselves, but the pressure of the wind on the sails. Most of this sail weight and pressure are concentrated aft of the mast, depressing the hulls and especially the sterns even more deeply into the water.

Therefore, to get the sterns out of the water to the same point they were when the boat was sitting there empty, you now have to tilt the whole boat slightly forward by moving crew weight forward. The painted waterline will no longer be horizontal to the water.

If you now were able to draw a new waterline with the boat at its proper attitude, it would start at a point just below the transom and end at a point partway up the bow (how far up the bow will depend on how much weight is on the boat).

Keeping the picture of this new waterline in your mind will help you determine how and when and where to move your crew weight to keep the boat in the ideal attitude, while also taking into consideration the guidelines given above.

Unfortunately, what looks like the logical place or feels like the most comfortable place to sit is not necessarily the right place to sit to keep your boat balanced properly on the water.

If you want to sit in the comfortable place, you need to, No. 1, not complain if you aren't winning races or, No. 2, get a bigger, longer boat.

Often it is difficult to convince people they are not sitting far enough forward until they see themselves in a photograph or on video, with their bows high and their sterns low.

Another important general rule in choppy seas is to treat the weight of yourself and your crew as though the two of you are one chunk of balance. Don't spread the weight out at opposite ends of the boat.

When on the same side of the boat, you should be side by side. If one is on the trapeze, the ideal would be for the trapezer to be positioned with feet on either side of the person sitting on the hull, or at least as close as possible.

When sitting on opposite sides of the boat, crew and skipper should be placed directly opposite each other and move forward or backward in unison to maintain proper boat balance.

The reason for this Siamese-twin act is that your boat can become a bit of a seesaw out there in waves and chop, and while that is a fun game for children, as a sailor you will find the game intolerable. Waves or boat chop can set off the seesaw game; and if you and your crew are at opposing ends of the seesaw, the fulcrum being located somewhere near amidships, you will continue the game for a considerable amount of time, as you watch the competitive parade of your sailing buddies go by.

If you are both sitting together, as near as possible to the fulcrum point, you will find that after one or two seesaws, the game is over and your seesaw board is back at its original attitude.

Sometimes in flat seas and light air the crew is way out on the leeward bow, trying to keep the leeward stern clear of the water — and here comes boat wake. Before the chop arrives, the crew should move back to the fulcrum, which on most boats is at or slightly behind the main beam, and position himself directly across the boat from the skipper. There will be a lot less hobby-horsing. After the water flattens out again, the crew can again go forward on the bow.

To further clarify weight distribution, let us take some examples.

Example 1

The wind is light, the water is flat.

For the above conditions, the crew will be on the leeward hull, as far forward as practical, and the skipper probably will be sitting on the windward side as far forward as practical.

You will probably notice that when the crew goes to the leeward hull, they also need to get forward. If they hang around the main beam, the extra weight on that leeward hull will depress the entire hull, including the stern. And that causes stern drag. Remember, we want the stern to ride clear of the water. That is why the crew must slide out forward on the hull, if possible.

Example 2

The wind is heavy, the water is still flat.

Under these conditions your weight distribution must be totally different from that dictated in Example 1, but with the same ultimate goal.

In this case you and your crew will need to get your weight outboard and aft on the windward side. (How far aft will depend on how heavy the wind is.)

The reason for the weight positioning in Example 2 is that heavy air will tend to cause the leeward bow to drive down under the water.

This phenomenon is explained through a theory of friction. The hulls have much more friction with the water than does the sail with the air. Since the sail is generating a lot of power and has relatively little friction to hinder it, it can and does go much faster than the hulls.

Down below, the boat tries to keep up with the sails but cannot because of the greater friction it has in its contact with the water. Therefore, it drags behind the sail. *(See Diagram 5.)*

The sail now is being tripped by the hulls and wants to fall flat on its face; and all that power in the sail is trying to help it do just that.

It reminds me of the football player who has had his feet partially kicked out from under him, but keeps stumbling and falling forward into the end zone, his torso continuing on much faster than his feet.

So, you see, the power of the sails drives the bow down, thereby tripping the boat. Your job in getting your weight out and aft is to counteract the tripping effect and still keep the boat balanced in its ideal attitude.

In heavy air the need to depress the bow is not as critical. In fact, for the sake of safety, you might want the bow to be riding a little higher. You will be at a very high speed by then and you will not have to worry about the stern, as the water will rush past and off the stern so fast that it will have no way of attaching and causing drag.

If the seas are choppy, it also may be necessary to let bows ride slightly higher in the water — boats with rolled gunwales, like the Hobies, need to make sure that waves are not hitting the gunwales, as that will create a lot of extra drag.

In downwind sailing there is a mild exception. Rather than heeling the boat slightly to leeward, with the windward hull kissing the water, it can be beneficial to sail the boat flat, with the windward hull in the water. Using the buoyancy of both hulls can give the boat more stability on this point of sail. In fact, in heavy air, having both feet under you, so to speak, can be a deciding factor in preventing a pitchpole.

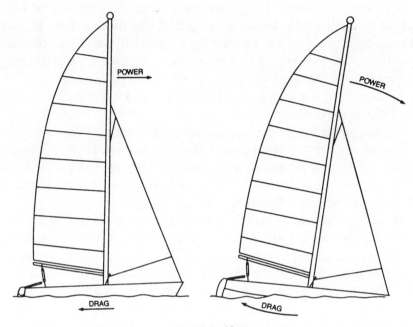

DIAGRAM 19

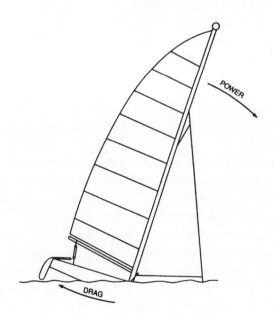

DIAGRAM 5

A word on helmsmanship, along this same line of thought; When you are quartering downwind and a large puff hits, heading down in a cat offers more stability, as you are using the buoyancy of both bows. Heading up presents the possibility of flying the windward hull and simultaneously tripping over the leeward hull if weight cannot be shifted fast enough to compensate. The bonus is that when you head down, the puff is driving you closer to the downwind mark.

Maintaining the proper boat attitude is often most difficult on those screaming reaches that have helped make catamarans so popular. The sail tends to develop its greatest speed and power on this point of sail. In order to harness and use power and prevent tripping (pitchpoling), crew weight must be as far aft and outboard as possible.

On the reach, when you have done all you can as far as weight distribution and the leeward bow still dives, most sailors recommend easing the jib quickly and also easing the main a little, if necessary, and then sheeting the sails back in as the boat's bows start coming back up out of the water. It only takes a few seconds for the boat to correct itself to the proper attitude.

If you have light crew weight in heavy air, you may find it necessary to sacrifice a little sail power and leave the jib in a luff to avoid constant nosediving and keep the boat in its proper attitude.

Being conservative and going a little slower can sometimes pay off in the long run, when you consider how much time you would lose righting your boat after a capsize.

In summary, the principles of weight distribution call for you (and your crew) to move ANYWHERE you have to on the boat to keep it in the proper attitude.

You should try to keep all movable ballast (skipper and crew) together as much as possible, or at least laterally equal in position, to prevent seesawing in chop or seas.

Don't worry if you have to move around a lot, as long as it is aiding the proper attitude. But this movement must not disturb sails or create seesawing. In moderate to heavy air you sometimes find yourself scurrying around like a monkey. But in light air, it's the smooth easy movement of a soft-pawed cat. The inches you gain in boat attitude may be lost in yards by shaking that elusive zephyr out of your sail.

Keeping in mind there are wind puffs, differences in waves, and any number of variations in conditions, you must adjust your crew weight to compensate.

So, be alert and sail with a good attitude.

Notes for the crew:
✔ **The onus of weight distribution rests primarily on you. The skipper is confined to a limited range of positions because he must be able to control the tiller. You, on the other hand, can go anywhere on the boat required to keep the boat in its proper attitude.**

✔ **If it is very light air and you must be forward on the lee-ward bow going to weather, you may not be able to control the jib from that position if you have cam cleats on your blocks. This is not a problem, because usually the jib is cleated and set anyway going to weather. From his position up by the beam on the windward side the skipper can easily make any small adjustments needed to the jib. Weight distribution in this case is much more important than being able to go "click-click" to the jib. Don't feel like you are not doing your job if you are not able to adjust the jib. What you are doing is by far more important.**

✔ **The most difficult for a crew is the light-to-moderate, fluky, puffy, wind condition, which predominates in many parts of the country. In this condition you will be hooked into your trapeze, because you never know when you may have to go out for a few seconds. But you may also be getting far forward on the hull or be hanging out on your trapeze far forward. You will be in and out, forward and back, dancing along the hull to keep the boat in its proper attitude. Put a mark on the bow, if it helps, to know where you want the bow to be entering the water — and then just watch that mark and try to keep it kissing the water.**

✔ **Don't let your trapeze ring slip off your hook when you are forward on the hull, because it will hit the skipper in the face every time.**

To quote famous Hobie-catter Wayne Schafer from Jake Grubb's book *Hobie Cat Sailing,* "Weight trim is elusive; you must constantly shift your position on board to accommodate the conditions. Doing this well is a sensitive art."

THE MAINSAIL
Chapter 3

Prebent masts, exotic sailcloth materials, cascading block systems, multipurchase downhauls — during the past 10 years these factors have contributed to dramatic improvements in the performance of the catamaran mainsail, in a never-ending search for perfection.

Since catamarans first started to acquire a following in this country in the early 1960's, the ribbed mainsail has been an experimental playground for sailmakers. And now with the help of modern computers the boat's "big engine" has been analyzed inch by inch in the effort to gain maximum speed and power from the amount of fabric that will fit in the triangle created by the mast and boom.

Although theories vary from sailmaker to sailmaker and from year to year and from boat to boat as to what is the ideal mainsail shape and what is the best way to achieve it, sailors and experts agree that it has been developed over the years into an extremely efficient, versatile, multi-adjustable wind engine.

In this chapter we will discuss three major conditions — WIND, WATER (Waves) and WEIGHT — that determine whether you want your mainsail to be flat or full or something in between. The chapter, "Strings to Pull," will explain in detail how to achieve those sail shapes and how to change them.

Because it has been well established by history that a full sail works better downwind, we will accept that as a given. Therefore, this discussion relates primarily to the kind of sail shape needed for going to weather; although the three conditions also hold true for determining the relative amount of fullness you need or flatness you can get away with downwind.

The information in this chapter can be used in two ways:

1. If you are in a class that is not limited to the manufacturer's sails, you can determine what basic shape of sail you want cut by a sailmaker according to the conditions you normally sail with.

A good friend of ours on a Prindle 18 once had a sail custom made, and he could not understand why the boat was such a dog. He and his crew were sailing at about 100 pounds over minimum weight, and his expensive, custom sail was cut very, very flat. He simply could not get enough power to move the boat. He should have asked for a sail with a much fuller basic cut.

2. If you are limited to boat manufacturer's sails, you can use this information to change sail shape within the flexibility allowed by the sail.

The two main reasons why sail shape matters are SPEED and SAFETY.

Proper sail shape for the conditions will allow your boat to perform to its maximum potential and speed.

And in heavy air, knowing how to flatten your sail will allow you to sail with greater safety and control — this is as important for the daysailor as it is for the racer.

Let's analyze each of the conditions — Wind, Water and Weight — and how they influence the kind of sail shape you need.

WIND

Take the first of these conditions: Wind. When the air is very light, it is pretty well established that a relatively full sail propels the boat easier than would a flat sail. Some theories try to negate this basic principle, but the age-old, proven fact is that it takes less wind to drive a full sail than to drive a flat sail.

Advocates of the flat sail for light air claim that the full sail will not be able to bend the wind quickly enough, nor allow the wind to attach all the way along the sail to provide power. They further claim that the full sail offers too much friction, while the flat sail offers less resistance to what little air is stirring.

Obviously, the theory goes much deeper than that, but my vote for the full sail is based on much older and more reliable evidence.

Take a look at birds in general. Nature herself shows us the slow-flying birds (light air) have a great deal more arch or camber in their wings than do the fast flying birds (heavy air).

Another good comparison would be the contrast in wing configurations of such slow-flying aircraft as the Ford Trimotor or the DC-3, whose landing speeds are below 50 mph (light air), with their tremendous wing arch, as opposed to the high-speed jet aircraft with flat wings that cannot land at speeds less than 150 mph (heavy air).

Commercial airliners have adjustable wings. If you watch the wings as the plane is coming in for a landing, you can see the front of the wings rotating forward and down and extensions sliding out from the trailing edge to make the wing much fuller, giving it more lift at slower speeds.

In other words, the lighter the wind, the more need for power to get the boat moving.

Another argument for the full sail in light air is in the basic theory of what makes a sailboat go forward.

There are two pressures on the sail. On the lee side of the sail is a negative pressure or a suction effect. That negative pressure can amount to three to four times the positive pressure, which is on the windward side of the sail.

To quote a turn-of-the-century sailor, Dr. Manfred Curry, "We yachtsmen sail, properly speaking, not by means of the pressure which arises from the impact of the wind on the sail, but chiefly by means of the 'suck' which acts on the leeward side of it. A sailboat is sucked, not driven, forward." The deeper the draft or arch in the sail, the more "suck" (and, therefore, power) is created.

Of course, as is true of everything in life, moderation is still the key. Full is a relative term, and if you go overboard and set your sail up too radically full, you will reach a point where the shape does indeed become inefficient.

Using a full sail in light air, I usually start out with the mainsheet not very tight, just enough to keep the leech of the sail in firmly.

Once the boat begins to move forward and pick up speed, creating its own apparent wind, I can slowly sheet in, flattening the sail.

Yet, even though I am using my mainsheet to flatten out my full sail, overall the sail is still relatively full compared to the way I would set it for a heavy air race.

On the other hand, when the air is heavy, you need a flat sail. It is obvious that when you have a lot of wind, you will be overpowered if you have a full sail. You would have way too much "suck" for the boat to handle. Therefore, since you do not need or cannot use the power, you flatten the sail, reducing the negative pressure in relation to the positive pressure.

Between light air and heavy are a vast number of different wind strengths and, therefore, as many different sail settings. If 2 mph of wind is light and 20 mph is heavy, for example, then 11 mph would be exactly moderate. Too bad it can't be that easy, but moderate can run from lightly moderate to heavily moderate. Here we have to make a judgment call.

Axiom for the wind condition:
LIGHT AIR, FULL SAIL; HEAVY AIR, FLAT SAIL.

WATER

The second condition that affects sail shape is water. A lot of judgment and guesswork will be needed for this one, since it is often difficult to determine in advance what the conditions are.

We all know what a flat sea is. If you can comb your hair and shave using it for a mirror, that is flat.

For flat seas you want a flat sail. The reason should be obvious. The water is offering less resistance to the forward motion of your boat, therefore you need less power to get you through it. Take advantage of this lower resistance to go for speed with the flat sail rather than power with the full sail.

At times you may run into large ground swell waves; and, although they may seem huge, particularly as you watch them crash on the shoreline, the surface of the water is smooth. In other words, if the troughs are long and tops are not breaking, you could be dealing with flat water in your judgment of the wave condition.

On the other end of the wave spectrum is the extremely choppy, turbulent sea. This condition requires a full sail to drive through the resistance offered by the rough water. Due to the fact that wave action is attempting to slow you down and knock you around, you need more power to blast through the tough going.

Again, between these two extremes are many other wave configurations which leave you still another judgment call. Let's say the waves are choppy, but not really hurting boat speed much; or say the water is somewhat on the flat side but with a lot of powerboat chop. Then you could refer to the wave condition as being moderate, which would demand a moderate sail — halfway between flat and full.

Axiom for the wind condition:

FLAT SEAS, FLAT SAIL; HEAVY CHOP, FULL SAIL.

WEIGHT

Our third and final condition affecting desired sail shape is weight. In the case of one-design racing, where all boats are supposedly equal, this condition usually refers to crew weight and extra equipment you may carry aboard.

The weight condition is somewhat easier to judge than the other two. Everyone knows what he or she weighs, whereas we usually have to guesstimate wind velocity and wave action. Light weight, obviously, is close to the class's minimum weight, and sailors in each class generally have a consensus of what "heavy" is. You merely have to figure out where your weight falls between those two figures.

On the other hand, we have been to major events where the "equal" boats are weighed, and there have been discrepancies in boat weight up to 50 pounds, and this should certainly be factored in. In fact, in the old Shark class, boat weight could vary by as much as 300 pounds.

In larger cats and monohulls, boat weight is probably more significant than crew weight.

A heavy crew will be depressing the boat more deeply into the water, creating more wetted surface and, therefore, more friction and drag. They will need the additional power provided by a fuller sail to counteract that weight and drag.

A light crew, not needing the power, can go with a flatter sail (which is also a more efficient and faster sail).

Let us assume that you and your crew total up to the minimum weight for your class. Obviously, you have a light weight condition and therefore require a flat sail.

On the other end of this scale we may have "Team Beef," running 100 pounds over class minimum weight. These people will definitely need more power for their weight condition; a full sail.

Axiom for the weight condition:
      HEAVY CREW AND/OR BOAT NEED A FULL SAIL;
      LIGHT CREW AND/OR BOAT NEED A FLAT SAIL.

PUTTING THEM ALL TOGETHER

This is all very confusing and sometimes seems contradictory — at least it used to seem that way to me.

For instance, when you have flat seas, you usually have very light air, as well. Flat seas call for a flat sail and light air calls for a full sail — what do you do? In this case WEIGHT has to be the tie breaker.

For me it used to be sort of like having three county commissioners — a Republican, a Democrat and an Independent — who are voting on the issue of flat or full. Maybe I'd get two votes for flat and one vote for full, so I'd lean toward a flat sail, but compromise by not going all the way.

It was as wishy-washy as government.

While working on my first book, way back in the 1970s, I searched for a simple way to analyze the kind of sail (or sail shape) needed for any of the infinite combinations of racing conditions.

Drawing on my own years of experience, at that time I came up with a great solution. Coining the term "Three W's," for wind, water and weight, I described a method for determining the best sail shape. We decided what shape of sail was needed, independently, for each of the three influencing conditions and then sort of averaged them out to determine what shape sail would best accommodate all three conditions. If two conditions called for a flat sail and the third called for a full sail, you would come up with something like "moderately flat." Still pretty wishy-washy.

Because everything involved with sailing has made big moves toward being more precise, and because I wanted something more specific for myself, I devised a newer version of this aid: White's Three W's Formula for Desired Sail Shape.

My newest formula is an attempt to get away from vague, abstract descriptions. In a sport as infinitely filled with variables as sailboat racing, the more things we can pinpoint, the better.

Therefore, I have now assigned numerical values to sail shape, ranging from a low of 10 for a flat sail to high of 30 for a full sail, and covering all the moderations in between.

The numbers are assigned as follows:

Flat sail 10
Moderately flat sail 15
Moderate sail 20
Moderately full sail 25
Full sail 30

Then we may use White's Three W's Formula for Desired Sail Shape:

$$\frac{\text{Wind + Water + Weight}}{3} = \text{Desired Sail Shape}$$

In place of wind and water and weight, we insert the appropriate numerical value of the sail shape required for each condition (independent of the others). Adding the three figures and then dividing by 3 will give you the average shape that should work best for this particular combination of conditions.

The sail-shape values that are to be assigned for each of the conditions are premised on the following basic theories:

● For light wind a full sail; for heavy wind, a flat sail.

● For heavy waves or chop, a full sail; for flat seas, a flat sail.

● For heavy crew weight (or boat weight) a full sail; for a a light crew (or boat weight), a flat sail.

Nothing can replace experience for knowing whether your sail should be set full, flat, moderately, or whatever. But what we all need, no matter what our degree of experience, is a basic rule of thumb; and that is what the formula is all about.

So our basic rule of thumb for wind conditions looks like this:

WIND CONDITION	SAIL DESCRIPTION	NUMERICAL VALUE
Light	Full sail	30
Moderately Light	Moderately full	25
Moderate	Moderate sail	20
Moderately Heavy	Moderately flat	15
Heavy	Flat sail	10

Our formula ingredient concerning wave condition is determined as follows:

Water Condition	Sail Description	Numerical Value
Heavy chop	Full sail	30
Moderately heavy	Moderately full	25
Moderate chop	Moderate sail	20
Light chop	Moderately flat	15
Flat water	Flat sail	10

Our point scale for determining the best sail shape based on the weight condition:

Weight Condition	Sail Description	Numerical Value
Heavy weight	Full sail	30
Moderately heavy	Moderately full	25
Moderate weight	Moderate sail	20
Moderately light	Moderately flat	15
Light weight	Flat sail	10

APPLYING THE FORMULA

Now we have discussed how to find the appropriate sail shape independently for each of the three conditions that affect it.

Remember, each condition is to be considered entirely on its own merits, without regard to the other two conditions.

Just rate the desired shape at somewhere between flat and full (between 10 and 30) for the wind condition, then for the wave condition, and finally for your weight condition.

Add the three numbers and divide by 3. The result will be the best sail shape for all three conditions combined.

If you are on the beach, do your math with a stick in the sand. Or, if you are on the boat...well, guess you'll have to use the old noodle. But there is another way. We have designed a lightweight, circular, plastic computer and named it the Sail Shaper. It will make the calculations for you. And you can put a lanyard on it and let in hang down under your sailing jacket while you are racing. Keep it right on the boat.

Now, let's take some examples to see how this formula is applied:

Boat A has a crew weight of only 5 pounds above the class minimum. Today they are sailing in San Francisco Bay. As usual, it is choppy, but the air has dropped off to under 5 mph (very unusual for the Bay). What sail shape do they use? Let us apply White's Three W's Formula:

Wind is light, requiring a full sail 30
Water is choppy, requiring a full sail 30
Weight is light, requiring a flat sail 10

Using the formula:

$$\frac{Wind + Water + Weight}{3} = \text{Desired Sail Shape}$$

We have:

$$\frac{30 + 30 + 10}{3} = \frac{70}{3} = 23.33$$

Therefore, the desired sail shape would be 23.33, which on our numeric scale makes the sail almost a moderately full sail.

Let's try still another example:

A good example could be offered by David Rodgers and Mike Christiansen when they competed in the Hobie 18 Nationals in Key Biscayne, Florida, in the summer of 1982. Dave and Mike were pretty light. Although I have no exact knowledge of their weight, I would say they are close to minimum. The seas were choppy and turbulent, and the wind was 20 knots on this particular day. Using our formula, then:

> Wind is heavy, requiring a flat sail 10
> Waves are choppy— full sail 30
> Weight is light — flat sail 10

$$\frac{Wind + Water + Weight}{3} \quad = \quad Desired\ Sail\ Shape$$

$$\frac{10 + 30 + 10}{3} \quad = \quad \frac{50}{3} \quad = \quad 16.67$$

Therefore, the desired sail shape for them in that particular race was 16.67, almost halfway between flat and moderate, so a moderately flat sail.

How about an easy one:

The air has just died, the waves are still choppy, and you and your crew have been getting chubby by overdoing pizza and beer lately. All the W's require full sails (30's), so you just add them up and divide by 3 and you have 30, which means a full sail.

I must keep repeating that all these findings are relative. Who really knows what "moderate" means? How flat is "flat"? Or how full is "full"? Each person's use of the formula and assignment of numbers may very slightly depending on what that person considers to be the upper and lower ranges of wind, wave action, and weight. My "heavy air" could be your moderate.

Alongside other boats, either in or out of race conditions, is the place to figure some of these things out in your mind, when you have a ready measure of boat speed.

White's Three W's Formula simply provides a rule of thumb, a foundation on which to build your sail shape. Use of the formula also will help increase your awareness that every race is unique and conditions are seldom identical; it will get you thinking about what you may really need in sail shape, not just take it for granted.

To really customize the formula, set your own wind speeds, water conditions and weight conditions relative to the 10-30 flat/full sail shape. Keep a log book on performance for every race and for every day. Note the three conditions for each race, the sail shape you selected and the results. After a given period you will see a definite trend toward better overall boat speed.

To make your log more precise, you should put marks on your sheets so you know where you set them for various conditions and points of sail, put numbered marks on the mast so you know how much you downhauled, put marks on lines setting mast rotation, and note what holes you set your forestay and sidestays in for mast rake. Also note how tight or loose you carried your stays and your diamond wires.

Because variables on a sailboat are almost infinite, your log, used in conjunction with the 3 W's axioms, can be your most important tool in helping to narrow down the odds on getting the best sail shape for the conditions.

HIGH-ASPECT-RATIO SAILS

The high-aspect-ratio sail plan was an important breakthrough over the old, large-roach, low-aspect-ratio sails on the pioneer catamarans. To see why the high-aspect-ratio came into being, compare wind designs of some of the best flying birds. *(See Diagrams 6 and 7.)*

The buzzard and the pigeon both have relatively short wing spans, while the measurement from the forepart of the wing to the trailing edge is quite broad. The fore-edge of the wing also is quite thick, and the wing quite arched. These fellows carry a sail plan on each side of their bodies similar to what is found on the pioneer cats. These birds soar at slow speeds and have a lot of lifting power, characteristics suited to their lifestyles.

On the other hand, the albatross has a wing span of nearly 10 feet with remarkably narrow wings, yet still can carry a body comparable to that of a buzzard. The swallow also has a wide span and narrow wings. Both of these birds fly at rather high speeds. Their wings have much greater length in proportion to their breadth (high-aspect ratio).

What this tells us is that the same basic wing area will carry a given body weight, whether the wings are long and narrow or short and wide. The difference is that the long, narrow wings give that bird an advantage in

DIAGRAM 6

Notice the variation in aspect ratio of different types of birds, based on their body size, speed and stability. For an added comparison, turn the drawings clockwise 90 degrees and note the resemblance between the blackened portion of the birds and sailboats.

DIAGRAM 7
Note the similarities between a bird's wing and a modern sail.

speed and maneuverability; while the short, wide wings give an advantage in power and control.

Since the catamaran had already developed much higher speed than had monohull designs, experiments began with the new, high-aspect-ratio sail plan; improvements in performance were dramatic.

For example, the Tornado, before it became a one-design class, tested a number of rigs, including a wing mast. The wing was extremely high-aspect in design and far outperformed the Tornado as we know it today, with its soft rig that has a lower ratio of width to height than did the wing mast.

Wing masts at the time, however, proved unsuitable for general use because it was impractical to leave the mast up when they were not being sailed (When your mast IS your sail, there is no way to luff it, furl it or reef it — all you can do is lower it.) Therefore, the present-day Tornado carries a high-aspect-ratio rig, but a soft-battened sail.

A resurgent interest in the wing mast came about in the late '80s and early '90s after the discovery of new and stronger building materials; however, as of today they are still impractical for everyday use on small one-design cats.

The comparatively high-aspect sails we use today are even more appropriate due to the light weight of modern catamarans, which require less power than did the heavy pioneer classes. And with our ability to control the relative fullness or flatness of our sails, we now have the best of both worlds — power and speed.

CHOOSING A SAIL THAT'S RIGHT FOR YOU

If you have a choice in your sail selection, as is allowed in some classes, choose a full, flat, or medium cut, depending on such things as crew weight, waters in which you normally sail, and general wind conditions.

For example, if the combined weight of skipper and crew is heavy, choose a fuller sail; light, a flatter sail. If you will be sailing on flat inland seas, a flatter sail should do better; if a choppy sea area, you may need a fuller sail. As for the wind, if you sail in an area of steady high winds, you want a flatter sail; but if yours is an area of little air, a fuller sail should do nicely.

You can use the White's Three W's Formula in selecting a sail, just as you do in determining desired sail shape for specific conditions.

The Hobie Class Association permits only the use of sails that were originally purchased from the manufacturer and does not permit modifications — that is, if you wish to race within the class. If you're sailing for fun or on handicap, anything goes.

Keep in mind that when I say "full" or "flat" sails, I am speaking relatively; we are seeking the truly versatile boat.

The way you sail a boat is also a determining factor in sail selection. If you are the super helmsman, never missing a shift, navigating that fine line like a tightrope walker, you may get away with a bit flatter sail than would otherwise be called for. But if you are like the rest of us and make helmsmanship errors, a bit on the full side helps to forgive some mistakes.

A flatter sail will take a little longer to get cranked back up after a tack, or after you stop dead when that huge powerboat blows across your bow. The flat sail is for fast sailing, but the boat needs power (full sail) to get moving to speed again. It takes good sheeting technique with a flat sail to be sure you get it going fast again, once the boat has slowed down. The fuller sail will get you moving considerably quicker.

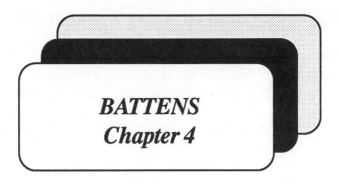

BATTENS
Chapter 4

Time and experience have taught us that a sail with a full draft is superior in light air, chop, or with heavy boat/crew weight; while a flat sail is preferred for heavy winds, flat seas, and light weight.

This again is confirmed by our feathered friends. The slow-flying, heavier birds have the fuller wings, while the swiftest-flying birds have much flatter wings.

Birds are stuck with what nature gave them, but a sailboat has no such limitations. It is for this reason that sailors in many monohull classes have a sail for every reason and every season. Thus, just before a race a major decision must be made: What sail do we use? Flat? Full? Moderate?

It was not until the development of the modern catamaran that someone asked the proper question: Why not use a sail with a changeable draft?

The Egyptians and Chinese have been using full-length battens for centuries. They knew even back in ancient times that full length battens give you: (1) uniform draft where you want it, from top to bottom; (2) a somewhat rigid surface, unchanged by apparent wind; and (3) the potential to change the sail at will to match the prevailing circumstances outlined in Chapter 3.

The fully battened sails developed by the ancients were designed for power rather than speed — they had to pull heavy, cargo-laden boats through the water. In light air the high-arched roaches gave them more power and sail area; while in heavy air the roach would blow open, releasing pressure on the sails. They must have served their purpose well, as they have been modified little over the centuries.

It appears that catamaran sailors are the first to fully explore the potential of full-length battens and use them to get the most possible speed and power out of a sail.

Full-length battens not only improve the performance of the sail, they also make it possible to do without an arsenal of different sails for different conditions. Battens allow drafts to be moved forward or aft at will, simply by planing battens thinner at the areas you want to bend. Making your sail fuller by using light battens or flatter with stiff battens is a much cheaper way to alter sail shape than changing sails.

Of course, a still cheaper and easier, although less effective, way to deal with varying conditions is to either tighten or loosen the batten tie-in tension to make your sail fuller or flatter.

If you have only one set of battens, you probably will want fairly lightweight ones to cover most conditions. Sailors who end up with stiff battens, either by accident or on purpose, have less variance or changeability in their sails than do sailors who have the lighter or more flexible battens.

For all-around use, flexible battens seem to work better, because they are more diverse. When you want a full sail, you simply tie them in tighter, and it is easier to acquire that fullness you desire. When you want the sail flatter, you just loosen them (making sure there are no wrinkles along the batten pockets), and you have a flatter sail. Stiff battens, on the other hand, will not allow you to get much fullness in the sail, even if you really crank on the batten ties.

But remember, the best way to have good sail shape is to have a good sail. Battens can modify problematic sails, but ideally you want that perfectly adjustable sail. To complement that great sail you want light, flexible battens that will HOLD the shape of the sail, rather than having to CHANGE the shape.

A good way to measure a batten's flexibility is to determine the number of pounds of pressure it takes to bend it when you are holding one end of the batten and pressing the other end against a solid object. At home the bathroom scale works nicely — just hold the batten vertically over the scale and press until the batten bends. (You may have to stand on a chair to reach the upper end of the longer battens; holding it in the middle will not give you an accurate resistance reading.) Once the batten bends, the poundage reading may even lighten up, but you are concerned with the initial resistance poundage.

Most people do not have a bathroom scale with them at the beach or sailing club when they are working with their sails. My solution to this problem was to purchase a fisherman's scale for weighing fish. It is a pocket-sized gadget with a hook and weight scale. Just hook it to the top of the batten, stand the batten up straight, pull down on the scale until the batten bends, and read the poundage.

Knowing your battens' resistance poundage doesn't solve all your problems. You have to decide what is light and what is heavy; and if yours aren't what you want, you have to do something about that. At one point in my sailing history, I thought 6 pounds was light in flexibility; I now believe that 3 pounds or less is far better. Also take into consideration that fiberglass battens grow stiffer with age. What may be a light batten this year may be a heavy batten a couple of years later.

Resistance poundage aside, a stiffer batten is usually a heavier batten in actual weight. If you have a whole set of stiff, heavy battens, you are not only adding unnecessary weight to the boat, you are adding it up in the air where it can add to heeling moment.

Even if you have bought a stock boat, don't assume your battens are like everyone else's. Always check the resistance poundage and check to make sure they are pre-tapered (as most are).

Sailboat manufacturers may obtain their battens from more than one source or change sources from time to time. In addition, batten extrusions are not always uniform in shape and weight even from the same supplier. At one Hobie regatta we all sat around measuring batten poundage. They varied from 3 pounds to 12 pounds. Guess who had been doing the worst in the regatta. You win if you guessed the 12-pound battens.

Most catamarans are now delivered with tapered battens. On sloop rigs they taper the second, third, fourth, and fifth battens from the top (give or take, depending on the number of battens your boat has.) The rest are left untapered.

The reason that the battens in the lower section of the sail are not tapered is to keep that portion of the sail flatter and the draft further aft where the jib overlaps. This reduces the possibility of the jib backwinding the mainsail in that area.

You do have the option of custom-tapering your battens. The fastest way is to use a belt sander. Be prepared to itch a lot afterward, however, from the fiberglass dust.

When tapering battens, keep in mind that you may want the draft in your battens a little closer to the mast than where you actually want the draft in your sail. No matter where you taper for maximum draft, the draft probably will move aft from that position when the mainsail is sheeted in.

The tiny top batten is kind of a wild card. It is usually pretty stiff and is very short to do much in the way of tapering. You can leave it the way it is if you are already getting all the power you can handle out of your sail. Or if you need more power — especially on Hobies with comptips — you can shave the whole batten down thinner. This will put shape into that top corner, giving you more power in light air. In heavy air, it will help to reduce power somewhat (when you can't use it anyway) by allowing the leach to blow off and spill wind at the very top.

A great many battens have been and still are being made that, because of the way they are constructed, cannot be tapered; or else they are already tapered for you and modifications cannot be made. The laminated, foam-filled type cannot be modified. They are excellent for some sails because they are lightweight, flexible, and not easily broken.

The location of the draft has been a controversial subject for years. In birds, 33 percent is normal, but in boats the draft may vary to as far back as 50 percent. Remember that while your boat is on shore, not performing, a draft may be at 35 percent, but when sheeted in with the wind in the sails, the draft may be blown 5 to 10 percent farther back.

The mast is an integral part of your sailplan, and that dimension is included when arriving at the percentage of the draft.

With the advent of the newer, exotic sail materials that have very little stretch, battens become of much less importance for moving the draft around.

THE JIB
Chapter 5

W hile the mainsail has continued to evolve and improve, the little sail up front has changed little over the years. It continues to do its job, leading the way and helping to suck the big sail along behind it.

Still affectionately known as "the damn jib," it makes up for its size by being the more challenging of the two sails to control, something any crew or foredeck person can confirm.

While it is not the most important and powerful sail on fractional sloop rigs, which most catamarans are, the jib can either tremendously aid the performance of the main or virtually destroy its effectiveness.

The jib has a much more important function than just filling up that empty fore-triangle space between the mast and the forestay. It also does more than just help the boat to tack or to turn.

In the development of the modern-day jib, man took a tip from Mother Nature. She has donated to us a great deal of knowledge that can be applied to sailing, just as it is to flying. We have simply to observe birds and insects with their varieties of wing styles and flying techniques. Sailing, after all, is merely flying on a vertical plane rather than a horizontal plane.

So what does this have to do with the jib? Birds possess on their forewings a small, narrow leading wing, more fully developed on some birds than on others. Birds of prey generally have much larger leading wings. A great many insects also have this overlapping leading wing.

The most obvious example is the eagle, whose leading wing is quite well developed and thereby easy to study. At closer look, this leading, con- duction wing could be compared easily to the thumb of your hand. Man must have observed this wing section for years, not knowing quite what it was or what it did. But since the eagle is a near-perfect wind utilizer, the leading wing section had to serve some purpose. Man's observation of this characteristic has had an important impact on both sailing and flying *(See Diagram 8.)*

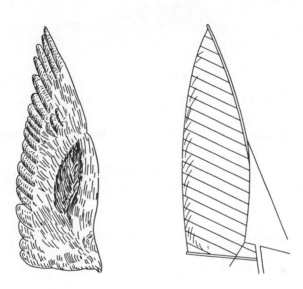

DIAGRAM 8
Birds and sloop-rigged sail plans both have a leading wing.

Aircraft have been using the leading wing effect for nearly as long as planes have flown. In the 1920s such airplanes as the Handley-Page and the Lachmann both had pre-wing sections. *(See Diagram 9.)*

In the modern STOL craft (short takeoff and landing) and in modern jet airliners, a preceding wing is cranked out for takeoffs and landings. The mechanical birds that now fill the skies are all, in effect, using a jib.

The purpose of this leading wing is the same, whether it is on a bird, an insect, an airplane, or a sailboat. In all cases, it is acting as a jib.

The purpose of the jib on a sailboat is to create an accelerated flow of air across the leeward side of the mainsail. *(See Diagram 10.)* That appears to be its only job. It is a complementary sail to the main and is never to be treated as a primary. The bird cannot fly on its small leading wing, nor

DIAGRAM 9
Wing cross-section of a Handley-Page biplane.

could a Boeing or Douglass take off on its leading wing. The jib is there only to make the mainsail more efficient.

Just as the leading wing gives a bird or an airplane more lift, so it gives a sailboat more "lift," which in this case translates into motion forward rather than upward.

DIAGRAM 10
The drawing at left shows a cat-rigged boat, and the drawing at right is the same boat with a jib added. Note the difference in air circulation patterns on the two sails, as indicated by the arrows. The even, aft flow across the mainsail in the right drawing is caused by the slot effect of the jib.

THE SLOT EFFECT

Most of you know why a sailboat is able to go forward through the water. In simple terms, the wind flows more rapidly across the convex curve of the leeward side of the sail than it does over the windward side. This difference in airspeed causes a lower or negative atmospheric pressure on the leeward side of the mainsail. The sail is sucked into this negative pressure area. But because its hull shape or its daggerboards prevent the boat from sliding sideways, it is instead "sucked" forward through the water.

The jib's function is to increase the velocity of the air across the leeward side of the main, thereby increasing suction and the consequent forward speed of the boat.

This increased velocity of air is achieved through a valve effect. Wind striking the concave side of the jib is forced to compress and thereby speed up as it forces its way through the comparatively narrow slot between the jib and mainsail.

Some might argue that the jib-slot flow would eliminate or blow away the negative pressure developed on the leeward side of the main and thereby reduce the suction that pulls the boat along.

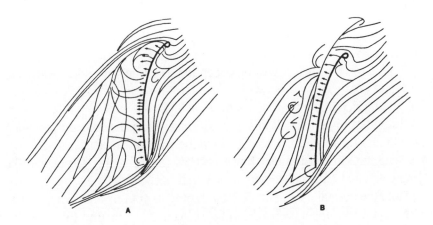

DIAGRAM 11

Figure A shows a cat-rigged boat and the wind's actions upon its sail. Figure B shows the same sail with a jib added.

To better understand the situation, look at drawings A and B in *Diagram 11*. Figure A, a cat-rigged sail plan, shows the action of wind eddies on the leeward side of the mainsail, which involves two sets of forces: One is the negative pressure or suction (indicated by the small arrows pointing to the left); the other, the retarding forces or returning eddies of air (the arrows pointing to the right) on the leeward side of the main.

Drawing B is the same sail with a jib added. Now the air currents take on a totally different pattern.In this drawing the return eddies (arrows pointing to the right) are nearly non-existent, and the wind flows through the slot, down the leeward side of the mainsail, toward the leech.

What is happening is that the retarding flow of returning eddies is stopped from reaching the leeward side of the mainsail by the current of air off the windward side of the jib and across the leeward side of the mainsail. However, the negative pressure forces that are coming off the main are not at all influenced by the air flow off the jib. Only the hindering return eddies are blown away.

The funnel, or slot, has contracted or jetted the air between the two sails and increased the velocity between them; so actually, the negative forces are even greater; and the main will be sucked into the vacuum with even greater force. In other words, the greater the velocity of this current of air between the sail, the less atmospheric pressure and thus the greater the negative pressure.

For proof of the suction theory, try this very simple easy-to-do experiment. *(See Diagram 12.)*
1) Take a piece of heavy writing paper and fold it in the middle *(drawing 1)*.
2) Cut one side in the form of a sail *(drawing 2)*.
3) Take the tip of the scissors and perforate along the fold by punching small holes *(drawing 3)*. This will allow the sail to swing easier.
4) Bend the sail around your finger until has a nice shape, somewhat like your catamaran sail, arched with a nice draft *(drawing 4)*.
5) Hold the normal paper part directly in front of your lips horizontally and blow along its upper side *(drawing 5)*. You will see that the sail part moves upward dramatically, toward the air current.

If you wish, you may hold the paper vertically as it would be on your boat, but holding it horizontally proves even stronger the forces of negative pressure or "suck" that lifted the paper.

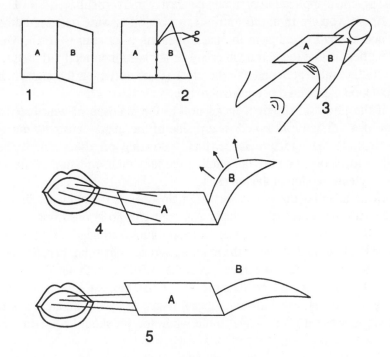

DIAGRAM 12

In this experiment you have been creating an air current across the leeward side of your sail. Now, if you blow on the under side of the paper, or the windward side of the sail, it will only lift up the sail to the horizontal plane, not beyond *(drawing 6)*.

This simple demonstration, designed by Dr. Manfred Curry, should prove to you:

1. The correctness of the theory of suction.
2. The tremendous effect of the wind off the jib (simulated by your blowing across the upper side of the paper, or the leeward side of the sail), which accelerates the air current over the lee side of the main, thereby increasing the lift of the mainsail.

Understanding this jib-and-main relationship is not all that difficult, but the practical application of it may be elusive and difficult.

Again, you are trying to form a valve action: a wide opening in the front and a small opening in the back, creating a jet stream of air. The problem here is that the valve can easily be adjusted incorrectly. If the setting for the small aft opening (the slot) is too loose or too tight, the phenomenon is hindered or even destroyed.

If the jib is set too tight in relation to the mainsail, it will throw a stream of air directly into the leeward side of the main, causing tremendous backwinding and turbulence, totally choking off the main. If the setting is too loose, you are not gaining the maximum pressure available across the leeward side of the mainsail.

Keep in mind that whatever the main does, so should the jib, to complement the power of the main. Although the jib is out front all the time, it definitely is not the leader in determining sail shape. It must always be the faithful copycat of the mainsail. To get maximum benefit from the jib and the slot effect, wherever goeth the main, so goeth the jib.

If the main should be twisting off at the top, so should the jib. Whether it is a beat to windward, a beam reach, or even a broad reach, if the main is set at a given angle to the wind, the jib should be set at the same angle and conform to the main's shape.

The jib is a complementary sail and, if not set the same, will hinder the power of the main, destroying what the mainsail is trying to provide.

If you were to look at the leech of the jib in its perfectly trimmed position you would see it taking the same shape as the mainsail at the point where the jib leech overlaps the main. Obviously, if the belly of the main is very full at the point where the two sails overlap, then the jib leech should clone that fullness at that point. If the main is flat, the jib leech should simulate the flatness, too.

When you first start sailing or even when you first start sailing a new boat or type of boat, the only good way to get a handle on how the jib looks when it is set to conform properly to the main is to put someone else on the tiller and position yourself on the leeward side so you can look at the slot between the main and the jib. Experiment with easing the jib a little and tightening it a little to see how it affects the shape of the slot and how it changes the curve of the back edge of the jib in relation to the back side of the main. Play with it until the sails look as perfectly matched as you can get them. Then go back on the tiller and get a feel for what that look is from where you are sitting. To maintain that perfect relationship, if you ease the main a little, you also must ease the jib a little. If you harden up the main, you also must harden up the jib to the same degree.

The adjustments you can make to control the shape of your jib are explained in Chapter 7, "Strings to Pull."

In summary, remember that the jib is the sail that complements the mainsail — sort of a straight man, as Abbott was to Costello, Martin to Lewis, Laurel to Hardy. Its only purpose is to let the mainsail excel, to create between itself and the mainsail a perfect air valve that jets a winning stream of air through a perfect slot to accelerate the suction of the mainsail.

Use every device at your disposal to mold this little guy to the image of his big brother.

On your jib handling ability may rest your racing success.

RULE OF THUMB: WHEN IN DOUBT, OVERSHEET THE MAIN AND UNDERSHEET THE JIB.

MAST RAKE
Chapter 6

Mast rake is the single most complicated, confusing, and controversial subject in the world of catamaran sailing.

And yet, when you talk to some of the world-class sailors, they make it sound very simple. If they sail a boat with boards, they say, "It really doesn't make too much difference — just keep it fairly perpendicular." If they sail a boat with asymmetrical hulls, they say, "Just rake it back and forget it."

In the monohull world mast rake always has been a simple concept. The mast is designed to stand perpendicular to the boat, and the only reason for changing the rake of the mast is to balance the helm. If you have weather helm, you rake it farther forward; if you have lee helm, you rake it farther back until the problem is corrected.

But catamaran sailors, always in search of the winning edge, couldn't let it go at that. They had to start experimenting, and now mast rake is in a fuzzy area of ifs, ands and buts.

In addition to balancing the helm, it has been discovered that mast rake also can have an effect on the boat's power, stability, speed, leeway and/or pointing ability.

The popular theory in recent years has been that if you rake your mast back, you will point better and go faster to weather, even if you have a weather helm. How did this idea get started? More important, does it really work?

ASYMMETRICAL HULLS & MAST RAKE

This mast rake theory came into being shortly after the arrival on the scene of the Hobies and Prindles, with their asymmetrical hulls, and as other boats of similar design followed.

The idea behind the asymmetrical design was to create a boat without the nuisance of daggerboards or centerboards — one that could be beached easily and yet sail very nicely.

Whether by accident, ignorance, or intent, some sailors began raking their masts back farther than the directions called for on this type of boat. They found their boats going faster and pointing better to weather, even though they had increased their weather helm.

These suddenly hot skippers with their aft-raked masts knew that what they were doing worked, but perhaps they didn't know the whole theory behind why it worked.

The concept involved is actually nothing particularly new. It is a logical extension of a theory that was developed back in 1922 by Dr. Manfred Curry and C.A. Bembe of Germany. They conducted experiments with arced-surface centerboards, that is, concave on one side and convex on the other (the same idea as the asymmetrical hull). *(See Diagram 13.)* They discovered that a traditional centerboard, flat on both sides, would allow a drift to leeward. The drift was not as great as with no board at all, but certainly significant.

Their arced board, however, with the humped or arced side toward the weather quadrant, created lift in that direction. When its angle of attack was straight through the water, the arced board created a lift toward its arced side. Surprisingly, they discovered also that this board presented very little water resistance or friction in its forward movement.

It is much the same as the wing of a bird, sailing against the wind with motionless wings: The lift is upward, or in the direction of the arc.

These old experiments probably were instrumental in the development of the modern asymmetric hull. And they indicate that what keeps these boats from drifting sideways without centerboards is partially that the outer flat side of the hull inhibits sideways motion to leeward, but more significantly, that the curved side of the hull promotes lift to windward. (This is especially true, of course, when the leeward hull is depressed in the water more than the windward hull.)

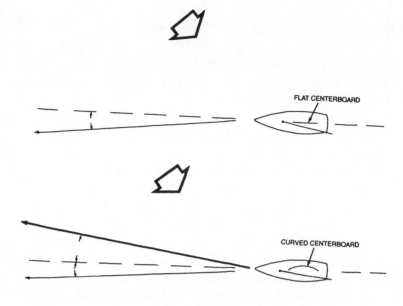

DIAGRAM 13

The boat with the flat centerboard has a 5-degree drift to leeward (solid line) below its axis (dotted line).

The boat with the board arched to windward lifts 10 degrees higher (dark solid line) than its axis (dotted line), and 15 degrees higher than the course with the flat board (light solid line).

Curry and Bembe also found that it helps the lift if you can elongate the curve by attaching the rudder immediately behind the centerboard or keel and accentuating the curve somewhat by sailing with a bit of weather helm. This has been proven by the weather performance of certain designs of fin-keel racing yachts with the rudder attached directly behind the keel.

In an asymmetrical hull we have, in effect, an elongated version of Curry and Bembe's experimental centerboard, flat on one side and arced on the other. *(See Diagram 14.)* And attached directly behind this arced shape is the rudder.

When we rake the mast aft on such a boat, we accomplish three things:

1. We bring the power of the boat back so that the aft portion of the hull is somewhat more depressed in the water closer to the rudders, so the rudders can also act as centerboards in resisting leeway.

2. We also create a weather helm. This makes us angle our rudder in such a way that it continues the curve on the arced side of the hull, smoothing the water flow along that side and thereby actually reducing drag, increasing speed, and increasing lift to weather.

3. It also gives the boat more fore-and-aft stability, which is a very helpful feature for Hobie 14's and 16's, Prindle 16's and 18's, and other boardless boats of similar design which have little buoyancy in their bows and sterns.

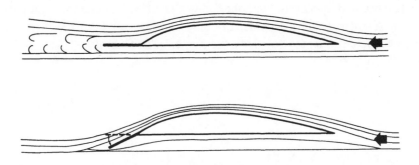

DIAGRAM 14

With neutral helm (rudder straight aft), it actually causes more drag or exit turbulence.
With the rudder corrected for weather helm, the arc of the asymmetrical lifting hull is elongated, allowing for a smoother exit as well as more lift.

With all these benefits, it's no wonder that aft-mast-rakers were cleaning up on the race course.

And naturally a lot of sailors jumped on the bandwagon and started raking their masts back, regardless of the type of catamaran they had.

SYMMETRICAL HULLS AND MAST RAKE

At first glance, it would seem that this theory is out the window when we are talking about daggerboard and centerboard boats, such as the

Hobie 17, 18, and 21, Nacras, Prindle 18-2 and 19, Tornado, and a host of others. They have symmetrical hulls and do not have the underwater, hydrodynamic lift created by the asymmetric hulls. There is no lifting curve of hull for the rudder to elongate, and their boards and rudders are widely separated. They have boards that are more efficient going to weather and should not need the help of the rudders. And, finally, it would seem that on these boats weather helm would cause exactly what everyone thinks it causes: DRAG.

But despite the fact that it seems to go against the laws of physics and logic, there is another school of thought. Rather than use your boards as the only underwater lift, with the rudders just free and steering, you rake the mast aft to bring the center of resistant effort aft from the board to somewhere between the board and the rudder. *(See Diagram 15.)*

DIAGRAM 15

By raking the mast aft, and moving our center of resistant effort aft and between the board and the rudder, both of these underwater structures share the resistance to leeward and share the lift to weather.

Obviously, as the center of resistance moves aft, the boat will want to weathervane into the wind. To stop the boat from trying to head up to a weathervane position the helmsman must turn the rudders to force the bows back away from the wind, resulting in weather ruddertrack. (See Special Section entitled Helm v. Ruddertrack.)

So, we now have a battle between the rudders and the tendency of the boat to turn the opposite direction. This battle should cause drag, but proponents of the theory claim the benefit of the lift outweighs the detriment of the drag. At this point it is believed that the helm should not be more than 1 or 2 degrees in order to be efficient. Any more angle than that and the drag exceeds the lift.

Now, keep in mind, you are only raking the mast within the limitations of your rigging, which is probably not a lot — we're talking inches here, not feet.

There is, of course, another reason for raking the mast back on board boats — to depower the boat and give stability in heavy air.

STABILITY VS. POWER

Raking the mast aft can indeed improve the boat's fore-and-aft stability in heavy air. But by the same token, it may somewhat reduce its power. Raking the mast perpendicular, on the other hand, can increase the boat's power.

The principle of stability is illustrated again by our best teacher, the birds. To quote from Curry:

> *We notice that Nature gives most wings a backward slope; swallow wings are an extreme in this point. But the more the bird tends toward being a quiet soarer, like the gull, the more the wings are placed at right angles to the body. We came to the conclusion in our former observations on birds that no advantage was gained with regard to power by a backward slope of the wing, but that this property of the bird's wings served only to ensure the stability of the flyer.*

Evidence of the power principle was garnered in the early 1900s by Professor Prantdl of Gottingen, Germany. *(See Diagram 16.).* He set up a wind tunnel to measure the lift of two wings. "A" had its wings set at right angles, while "B" was set with wings raked aft 23 degrees. His results showed the lift developed by the right-angle wing to be 11 percent greater than the raked wings.

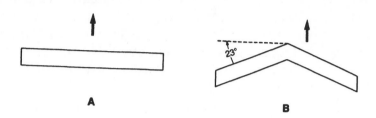

DIAGRAM 16

Professor Prandtl's wing tests showed that wings angled back (B) developed 11 percent less lift than the wings at right angles (A).

Mother Nature knows best; and so fast-flying or acrobatic birds tend to have their wings angled back for stability, while birds that have a great deal of power in their wings are more likely to have their wings perpendicular to their bodies.

And the same rule applies to aircraft. Those with high lift and power have nearly perpendicular wings, while those with less lift have their wings angled aft, such as jet aircraft.

All this evidence relates directly to the mast on your boat. You will definitely find more power with your mast perpendicular, as opposed to aft.

Here is one explanation for the lessening of sail power with the mast raked aft.

If you sail with your mast perpendicular, the leading edge of your sail plan strikes the wind at a right angle, and the wind then proceeds back through the sail plan on a fairly horizontal plane; whereas, the aft-raked mast is struck by the wind at its base first and on up to the top of the mast in a staggered progression.

In addition, the wind usually comes off the water and strikes the sail in an upward direction in the first place; with the sail tipped back, the wind will tend to skip diagonally across the sail and battens rather than flowing more parallel to the battens.

With an aft-raked mast, the boom section, or lower aft portion of the sail, is lower toward the deck than with a perpendicular mast. This can cause that lower, aft section of the sail to be blanketed from any wind effects by the hull and trampoline itself. Add to that the possibility that the boat is heeled, and you may be blanketing the sail nearly a quarter of the way up.

Thus, you are reducing the power in your main by raking the mast aft.

In downwind sailing the same principles hold true for power vs. stability — the perpendicular mast will have more power, but in heavy air conditions raking the mast somewhat aft will give the boat more fore-and-aft stability.

MAST RAKE AND HELM

And finally we come to the traditional role of mast rake on boats — neutralizing helm.

The boat's balance depends on several factors. A number of pressures are at work on your boat. In the sail, you have pressure developed in the pocket of both the jib and mainsail, while below the waterline, you have resistant pressures upon the centerboards, the rudders, the hull and bow.

Somewhere is an axis, an absolute center point for all these pressures. And when all are balanced perfectly on either side of this axis, you will have neutral helm. This means your rudders will be tracking straight forward through the water and you will have no feeling of helm through the tiller.

You can change the balance of your boat and, as a result, change your helm, in a variety of ways, including moving your weight forward or aft, raising or lowering your boards, putting up a larger or smaller headsail or raking your mast forward or back. Any of these things can change the relationship between the center of effort and the center of lateral resistance, which, in turn, changes your helm.

If, when sailing to weather, you must keep the tiller pulled slightly toward you to make the boat go straight, you have weather helm. Most experts agree that 1-to-2 degrees of weather helm is desirable on most boats for best performance.

The farther back you rake your mast, the more weather helm you will have. Helm is neutralized by standing the mast up straighter. If the mast is raked forward too far, you will reach a point where you will have lee helm (the rudders are angled slightly toward leeward in order to keep the boat going straight). This is undesirable for two reasons: 1) it is hindering your efforts to sail to weather and 2) it is dangerous because if you let go of the tiller, the boat will bear off to leeward and pick up speed or capsize instead of heading up into the wind and stopping, as it will with weather helm.

Too much weather helm (beyond 1 or 2 degrees) also is undesirable, because it will cause drag when the rudder is turned at too great an angle to the water.

It seems fairly straightforward and simple: To balance your boat's helm, you just change the angle of your mast until you have the helm the way you want it.

However, the waters have been muddied somewhat by adjustable rudders that can be raked forward or back. Many people have the impression that helm can now also be neutralized by raking the rudders forward somewhat. NOT TRUE. Changing rudder rake DOES NOT affect the overall balance of the boat to any appreciable degree and, therefore, does not change the helm.

What is achieved by raking the rudders forward is that it makes the boat easier to steer — if you have weather helm, raking rudders forward will help reduce the pull on the tiller. If you rake the rudders farther back, on the other hand, the pull on the tiller will be increased. You can easily demonstrate this by cocking your rudders partway up while sailing to weather. If you have any weather helm at all, you now will have a tremendous pull on your tiller.

THE DANGERs of thinking you are changing your helm by raking your rudders are:

1. If you think you have too much weather helm and, as a result, too much drag and that you will eliminate the drag by raking your rudders forward, you are wrong. The boat will steer nice and easy, but the rudders will still be angled to weather to the same degree they were before and causing the same amount of drag. You think you have corrected the problem, but you have not.

2. If you have very excessive weather helm and you try to overcompensate for it by raking the rudders too far forward, you can produce erratic and potentially dangerous steering problems in which the boat may try to dive off to leeward at unpredictable moments. This is in spite of the fact that your boat still actually has the same weather helm it had before you raked the rudders forward.

3. If you have eliminated the "feel" of weather helm, you have also eliminated your communication line to the rudders — you will not be getting strong feedback as to how much helm, and how much drag, you have and you will not feel the changes in the helm as strongly when other factors, such as weight distribution or sail trim, change the balance of your boat.

If you can neutralize both helm and the feel of your tiller with mast rake, why bother adjusting the rudder rake at all? Good question! However, there are a couple of possible reasons.

Rudder rake is useful for reducing the feel of the helm in two situations:

1. If you have a boat that needs weather helm to sail efficiently to weather (especially boats with asymmetrical hulls), but you don't like the resultant pull on the tiller, you can make your life easier and reduce that pull by raking the rudders forward a little.

2. If you sail in heavy air conditions a lot and for stability you need to rake your mast back farther than the boat normally needs for good balance, you again can reduce the pull on the tiller by raking the rudders forward.

Keep in mind that the leading edge of foil-shaped rudders must meet the water on a vertical plane for maximum efficiency. Therefore, raking rudders forward to reduce the pull on the tiller should only be done in very small increments. If you rake forward a fraction too far, your steering can become erratic.

HELM vs. RUDDERTRACK

Weather helm historically has been measured in how hard you have to pull on the tiller. For example, if your rudders are perfectly balanced and are slicing through the water with no angle and there is no pull on the tiller, then you have neutral helm.

If you have a very slight weather helm, 1 to 2 degrees, you also will have to pull slightly on the tiller to keep the boat going straight.

Take that same slight helm, and partially kick up the rudders. You will find you now have tremendous pull on the tiller. If weather helm is judged and defined by the pull on the tiller, we might assume that our weather helm, and consequent drag, has increased. But that is not possible, because the rudders are still going through the water at an angle of 1 to 2 degrees.

By the same token, we can actually reduce the pull on the tiller by raking the rudders forward, even though they are still going through the water turned at a 1 or 2-degree angle. (See Diagram 17.) We now can take away that ever-tiring pull on the tiller we call weather helm.

BUT REMEMBER! The degree of attack by the rudder through the water has not changed by cocking the rudders either forward or aft.

Let's take an example. You have your sidestays set at half way down the chainplate and your have neutral pull on the tiller, which we are calling helm. The rudders are tracking through the water at an acceptable 1 degree of turn to weather in order to make the boat go straight.

You decide to rake the mast all the way back to the bottom holes of your sidestay chainplate, and you notice that you now have weather helm and the rudder is tracking through the water at an unacceptable 5 degrees. You don't want to pull that hard on the tiller, so your next step is to adjust the rudders so they are cocked under the boat. Now you have no weather helm. That is, you don't feel any pull on the tiller.

However, the rudder is still tracking through the water at 5 degrees in order to keep the boat going straight, and that is detrimental to boat speed.

The problem? It's all in nomenclature! What you call what!

Some say "helm" is the angle the rudder goes through the water and the pull on the tiller that is adjusted by raking the rudders under or aft is called "power steering."

Keep in mind that no matter what you call these two things, they are separate issues, and probably should be called two different names. Up until recently we called both subjects "helm."

Since most folks are like old dogs and don't want to change, let's just keep the term "helm" as the definition of the pull on the tiller. Most people don't want to let go of concepts they have held since they can remember.

The subject that we really want to handle, however, is the angle at which the rudder goes through the water, so let's invent a word. Let's call that "ruddertrack."

By using these definitions the example boat above would have neutral "helm" and "weather ruddertrack." You see, the rudders are cocked under the boat, so there is no feel on the tiller — neutral helm. The rudders are constantly turning at an angle of 5 degrees in order to keep the boat going in a straight line — it has a 5 degree weather ruddertrack. (See Diagram 17.)

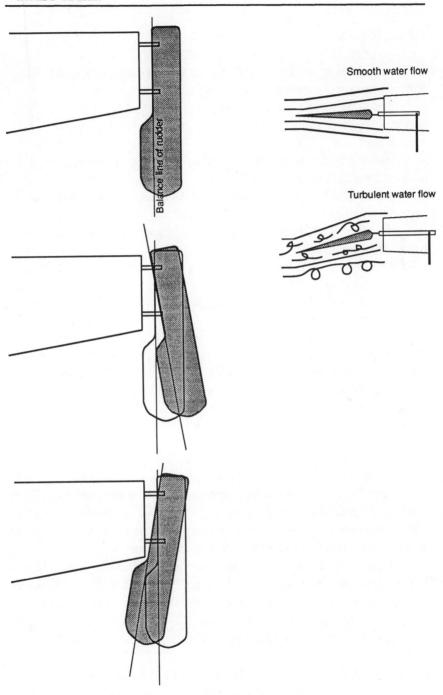

Balance line of rudder

Smooth water flow

Turbulent water flow

DIAGRAM 17

TRADEOFFS

Now let us try to analyze the advantages and disadvantages of sailing with a perpendicular mast or an aft-raked mast.

The upright mast seems to do better in lighter wind conditions, in heavier chop, and with heavier crew weight — all conditions that require more power.

The aft-raked mast seems to excel in heavier wind conditions and in situations that require more stability.

Before making your decision on mast rake, keep in mind that, as mentioned earlier in this chapter, you are striving to get as much power as you can safely, efficiently, and fully use while keeping the boat as well balanced as possible.

But before conditions get to the point where you cannot hold the boat down, the bows are diving constantly, and your crew weight is as far back as it can efficiently be, then, much like the swallow or the jet airplane, you seek stability and reduced lifting power.

For each increment aft you rake the mast to gain stability, an increment of power could be lost. In a "stink" situation, as Jack Sammons points out in his book *Welcome to A-Fleet,* you may forget all about retaining much power. In that case you need stability. There are times when simply finishing a race can win you a regatta.

So, in summary, aft mast rake on an asymmetrical hull is very desirable, despite the fact it does create weather ruddertrack. That very weather ruddertrack is also adding to your underwater lift to weather.

As for boats with symmetrical hull and boards, no one has yet made a hard-and-fast case for either the perpendicular or the aft-raked mast. Both have their advantages and disadvantages. But overall, it appears that in light air the perpendicular mast has an edge; while at the heavier end of the weather scale, an aft-raked mast is most advantageous.

In listening to the guest experts we have had in our Rick White's Sailing Seminars, masts have gone back and forward a lot. Many formerly staunch advocates of aft-mast-rake-at-all-times are now saying it is not that important, particularly on a symmetrical hull. Others who have advocated a straight-up stick on the symmetrical hulls are now raking aft a bit.

In review of the factors that determine your mast rake:

1. In boardless boats with asymmetric hulls, always rake the mast back so the rudders can help to prevent leeway. Whether to just rake it

"back" or "all the way back" depends upon wind, water and weight conditions, similarly to the factors that influence sail shape.

> Heavy air — mast more back
> Light air — mast more forward
>
> Flat seas — mast more back
> Heavy chop — mast more forward
>
> Light weight — mast more back
> Heavy weight — mast more forward

Just as with your sail shape, you can determine each of these factors independently and then divide by three to average them out as a rule of thumb on whether you want your mast relatively farther back or forward for the three conditions.

2. In daggerboard or centerboard boats with symmetric hulls, the same factoring applies for the three conditions of wind, water and weight; HOWEVER, the range is from perpendicular to all the way back, rather than from back to all the way back. As board boats do not necessarily need to use their rudders to prevent leeway, the ONLY real reason to rake the mast aft of perpendicular is stability. Again, whether you want your mast perpendicular or raked aft is a matter of power or depowering and can be determined by applying the rule of thumb above for the wind, water and weight conditions.

3. A third consideration in making the judgment on mast rake is how it affects upwind sailing and downwind sailing. Raking a mast aft will improve pointing ability upwind, although lessening power somewhat. Raking a mast more forward will improve downwind performance, increasing power, but at the same time it will reduce fore-and-aft stability in heavy air.

4. If you have excessive weather ruddertrack on your boat, rake the mast farther forward. If you have any lee ruddertrack at all, which is very undesirable, rake it farther back.

Note: When we talking about raking forward or back, we are referring to the limits imposed by the lengths of the stays and by the holes on the adjuster plates. All the way back on the Hobie 16, is achieved by taking the sidestays to the bottom holes and then pulling them up tight with the jib luff tension. On most boats, you are limited in how far back or forward the mast can go by the amount of adjustment at the bottom of the forestay.

Also keep in mind that not all stays are exactly the same length, even though they may be from the same manufacturer. Settings that work on another boat may not work on yours.

We have tried to present all sides of the issue so you can make an educated decision for yourself on mast rake.

However, keep in mind, extremes of any kind will produce poor results, so do not overdo your mast setting in either direction.

What do I do on my daggerboard boat? I stand the mast straight up most of the time.

STRINGS TO PULL
Chapter 7

You have been introduced to boat-handling techniques and the importance of weight distribution. You have learned what kind of sail shape you need for the conditions of wind, water and weight. It's finally time to talk about what strings to pull to create that perfect sail shape and change it at will.

This chapter is divided into two primary sections: Shaping the Main and Shaping the Jib, followed by a discussion of blocks and cleats.

SHAPING THE MAIN

It is impossible to discuss the mainsail without including that big stick that holds it up. Since those early days of catamarans in the U.S., the mast has matured and become more sophisticated right along with the sails — and, in fact, must be considered an integral part of the sail. Without the modern, tapered, bendy mast, it would be impossible to take advantage of the sail's flexibility — bending the mast is what flattens the sail.

The "strings" to control the mast and the mainsail come in two classifications: standing rigging and running rigging.

Standing rigging refers to the forestay and sidestays, the diamond wires and spreaders — or things that hold up the spar and are permanently attached to the boat.

Running rigging refers to the sheets, the travelers, the downhaul, the outhaul, the barber haulers, and the mast rotation control lines — or things that control the trim of the sails.

All these wires and lines can be used separately or in combination to shape your sails.

Adjustments you can make on the beach:

THE FORESTAY AND SIDESTAYS

These stays can be adjusted so your rig is either tight or loose, and they can be used to rake the mast forward or back; but they do not in any way affect the sail shape of either the main or the jib, with one exception:

If the rig is too tight, it will prevent your mast from rotating freely because there will not be enough slack in the stays to allow them to wrap around the mast when it is rotated.

Inability to rotate your mast to at least 90 degrees and preferably 110 degrees (20 degrees forward of the main beam) definitely can affect your sail's shape and performance. (See "Mast Rotation Adjuster" in this chapter.)

Don't think that by tightening the rig your forestay will be tighter and therefore allow the boat to point higher. The tightness of a forestay is the consequence of a tight mainsheet. No matter how hard you tighten your rig, when the wind blows, you can look over and see the leeward sidestay flopping around. So, don't try to harden up the forestay with the rig — that is the job of the mainsheet. That is one of the reasons we insist on never easing the mainsheet while going to weather in heavy air —in addition to making the main fuller, it will loosen the forestay, making the jib fuller, as well.

There is no good reason for having a tight rig, and there are some good reasons not to.

However you also do not want to go to the other extreme and have a loose or sloppy rig that allows your mast to flop around and shake air out of the sails in chop.

The next question related to the stays is whether to stand the mast up straight or rake it aft. How do you decide? Well, we dedicated Chapter 6, "Mast Rake" just for that question. And since mast rake, per se, does not specifically affect the shape of the sail, please refer to that chapter.

However, as with rig tightness, one thing to consider is that on some boats if the mast is raked too far back, it can inhibit mast rotation, which, in turn, can affect sail shape and performance. In addition, you also do not want a mast raked back so far that the main is sheeted block to block and the sail is not yet flat.

THE DIAMOND WIRES

Should they be tight or loose, and what do they do?

Most modern masts have spreaders and diamond wires that allow you to control mast bend for the lower two thirds in order to affect the sail shape. They also keep the mast from bending too far and breaking.

Loose diamond wires:

The more you loosen the diamond wires, the more the middle or lower two thirds of the mast can bend out sideways, on its minor axis, when the mast is rotated. That bending will flatten the fullness in the middle and/or lower third of the sail. (desirable in heavy air...and/or flat seas...and/or light crew)

This bending action of the mast and flattening of the sail can be enhanced by mast rotation. the closer the mast is rotated to 90 degrees, the easier the mast will bend on its minor axis and the more it will flatten the sail. If more fullness is desired, rotate the mast less than 90 degrees — the mast will bend less, putting more fullness back into the sail.

Although this overrotation technique satisfactorily does the job of flattening out the sail, it has always had two disadvantages: Number one, if you do NOT rotate the mast to 90 degrees, you get less flattening effect and the mast bends into the slot between main and jib, interfering with air flow; and, number two, if you DO rotate the mast to 90 degrees to achieve maximum flattening, the mast is presenting too blunt an entry into the wind, causing drag, as well as creating turbulence along the windward side of the sail.

Another problem with loose diamond wires is that you are limited in the amount of fullness you can put back into the sail if the wind lightens up. You will have to underrotate quite a bit to keep the mast from bending and make the sail fuller, but if you underrotate too far, you will lose the smooth transition between mast and sail, causing a "dent" on the leeward side that will keep the air flow from attaching properly to the back side of your sail.

Tight diamond wires

Tightening the diamond wires makes the mast stand straighter with less bend on its minor axis and makes the sail stay full. (desirable in light air...and/or choppy seas...and/or heavy crew).

But tight diamond wires severely limit your ability to flatten the sail when the wind picks up. They will prevent the mast from bending on its minor axis even if you overrotate.

Until recently, we have had to make a decision before we go on the water as to whether we want tight diamonds or loose diamonds for the wind conditions we expect — and the decision has always involved compromises.

But something new has happened in mast theory that makes these compromises unnecessary.

THE PREBEND THEORY

For years the Tornado class has been experimenting with pre-bent masts, and this technique is now filtering down to the beach cats.

This experimentation has led to a major breakthrough in speed and pointing ability as well as sail-shape control.

Here is how it works: By raking the spreaders aft and over-tightening the diamond wires to an extreme degree, you force the mast to bend on its major axis rather that its minor axis. The minor axis is that measurement across the narrow breadth of the mast from one side to the other, while the major axis is that measurement from fore and aft through its thickest portion. *(See Diagram 18.)*

The diamond wires are actually bending the mast only to a small degree; they are "pre-bending" it. They just seem to get things started bending in the right direction.

What really causes the bending to happen is downhauling and sheeting. And it is no longer necessary to rotate your mast to 90 degrees to facilitate bending to flatten your sail. You can set your mast rotation so the trailing edge of the mast is pointing in the vicinity of the sidestay at the angle which gives the mast the best entry into the wind and at the same time retains a smooth transition between mast and sail.

So, without touching your mast rotation, to flatten your sail, all you have to do is downhaul. If you want your sail fuller, ease the downhaul.

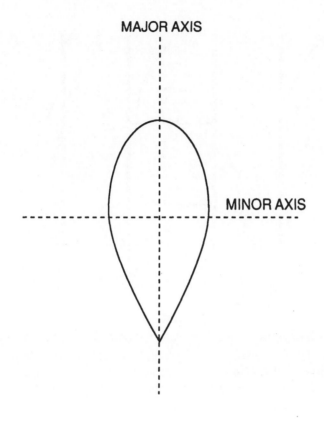

MAJOR AXIS

MINOR AXIS

DIAGRAM 18

This technique not only takes the fullness out of the sail, it takes it out where the jib overlaps, thereby helping the slot effect. But the best part is that no matter how much you bend the mast, it will not bend into the slot. The bowing of the mast is to windward, away and out of the slot — this allows the jib to come in slightly tighter and allows the boat to point somewhat higher. *(See Diagram 19.)*

We tried this in the Hobie 18 Nationals at Daytona Beach and found it very effective, and safe. The first thought that crosses everyone's mind is that the mast will break. So far that has not been a problem.

In summary, the important virtue of the pre-bent mast is that it allows you to make your sail flatter or fuller just with the downhaul. And you can flatten your sail while at the same time keeping the jib slot open and keeping the mast at its most efficient angle to the wind.

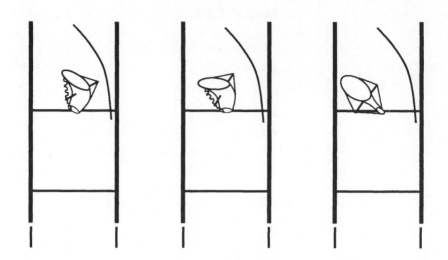

DIAGRAM 19

The two boats on the left are using slack diamond wires to put bend into their masts. The boat on the far left rotates his mast so that the rotation preventer points a little behind the sidestay. Notice that when the mast bends, it bows into the slot, thereby closing it off. The middle boat has the same mast setup, but rotates his mast to nearly 90 degrees. Now the mast bows straight ahead and not into the slot. However, this mast configuration will cause drag because of the blunt entry to the wind and also an eddy that will result on the windward side of the main. The boat on the far right has prebent his mast by tightening the diamond wires until there is the beginning of a curve on the major axis of the mast. Notice that when the mast is rotated, the mast now bows to windward and actually opens up the slot.

Adjustments you can make on the water:

THE DOWNHAUL

As we mention in various places through this book, downhaul is a major factor in flattening out the mainsail, regardless of what other adjustments you have made and regardless of whether you bend your mast on its minor axis or its major axis. When trapezing will no longer hold the boat down, the first string to pull is the downhaul line.

Because downhaul is such an important factor in flattening your sail or making it full, it is extremely important to be able to make this adjustment during races. Ideally, you want to be able to loosen your downhaul for going downwind and tighten it again before you go upwind. You may also want to change it if the wind conditions change. Unfortunately, this can be a difficult adjustment to make, unless you have enough purchase on this particular string.

Most open classes have 12-1 purchase on their downhauls, and they have long enough lines that they can actually be controlled by the crew from the trapeze. Restricted classes usually allow far less purchase — but use as much as is allowed and make it as easy as possible to adjust.

THE OUTHAUL

On sloop rigs, the outhaul should be as tight as you can get it while going to weather. You want to reduce any possibility of the lower section of the mainsail being backwinded by the jib.

On some unirigs, the outhaul can be eased a little since there is no jib to contend with. However, again you need only ease it off a little in situations where you feel you need more drive.

Off the wind, on the other hand, the outhaul should be released on all boats. This will allow the lower section of the sail to get fuller. Most experts agree, however, that the maximum camber you should allow is 9 inches. In other words, the foot of the sail should not be more than 9 inches away from the boom.

This is a line people too often forget to take care of. Either they forget to release the outhaul for going downwind or, even worse, they forget to tighten it again for going upwind and wonder why everybody is pointing higher and going faster than they are.

THE MAST ROTATION ADJUSTER

There are two reasons for rotating the mast. One is that rotation can help create the most aerodynamic possible entry into the wind, both upwind and downwind. The other is that when the mast is rotated when going to weather, it can more easily bend to flatten the mainsail.

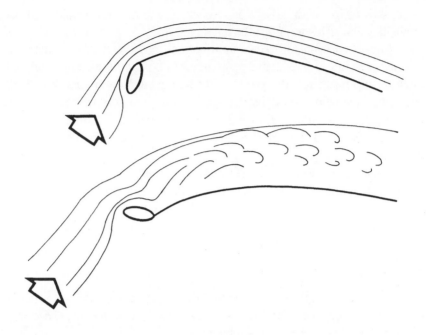

DIAGRAM 20

In the top example the mast is rotated to about 70 degrees, allowing a smooth entry and even flow of air on the leeward side of the sail.
In the bottom example the mast is drastically under-rotated, causing an indentation between the mast and the sail and resulting in turbulence along the leeward side.

The question is how far to rotate on a given point of sail. The best way to determine the ideal rotation is to lay your head right at the base of the mast with your mainsail rigged and sheeted the way you want it. Now, look straight up the leeward side of the mast. You probably will see where the mast-sail junction has an indentation. Slowly rotate the mast around close to 90 degrees and then back again. You will see the indentation disappear and reappear as you rotate back and forth. *(See Diagram 20.)* You want to set your mast rotation so that the indentation is totally gone and the entire mast and sail appear as one piece — like the leading edge of a DC-3, an old cargo plane that developed more wing lift than most airplanes past and present. Then mark where you have it set.

The rule of thumb upwind is: For the flattest possible sail, rotate to 90 degrees; for a fuller sail, rotate only until the trailing edge of the mast points to the side stay or just forward of it, making sure you keep a smooth transition between mast and sail. (For a mast with prebend, rotate no more than necessary to keep that smooth mast-sail transition, and leave it in that position for all conditions upwind.)

Downwind you are looking for that same smooth transition between mast and mainsail. That usually means that the mast must rotate to a position forward of the main beam, around 110 degrees.

POSITIVE MAST ROTATION

Unfortunately, it is very difficult to get your mast rotated ahead of the main beam to 110 degrees without a positive rotation system to force it to that position and hold it there; and positive rotation is not allowed in many one-design classes. So we have to do what we can.

If you have a rotation preventer bar, the crew, when sitting on the leeward side of the boat, may be able to push it forward to force more rotation. Sometimes the skipper can sit by the mast, reach around it and pull the rotater bar toward him. If your mast is difficult to rotate even to 90 degrees, it may be because your stays are too tight or your mast is raked too much to allow the mast to rotate freely.

If you are in a class that permits positive rotation, there are a number of different systems people use — some commercially available and some home-made. This is one of those creative areas where the door is still wide open for people to come up with better, easier ways.

THE MAINSHEET

Rule of thumb: The heavier the wind, the tighter you sheet, to flatten the sail in conjunction with the downhaul. In less air, sheet less hard — just enough to keep your leech tight.

The mainsheet controls the upper part of your sail, and it works hand in hand with that upper set of telltales on your main. When you ease your mainsheet, the upper half of the sail will start to twist off to windward more than the lower half. This means the upper half of the sail will be seeing the wind at a different angle than the lower half. If the backside telltale begins to stall, you can stop it by easing your mainsheet a little to give the top more fullness. If the top telltale is luffing, you can correct it by sheeting in a little, making the top of the sail flatter.

Upwind and downwind, you will normally be setting your sheet at one ideal spot and steering the boat by the telltales (as explained in Chapter 8, "Telltales." However, on a reach you will be adjusting your sail constantly. Now the mainsheet is your primary tool for keeping the telltales flowing at the top of your main. When they luff, sheet in; when they stall, sheet out.

THE MAIN TRAVELER

The main traveler is the primary, basic setting for the angle of your sail to the wind on a given point of sail. It is more a factor of sail trim than of sail shape, per se. Once it is set in its ideal position, it is seldom adjusted except when necessary going to weather in heavy air.

It is also the last ditch resort for controlling the boat and keeping the sail flat when the wind picks up while beating. If you are double trapped, have downhauled to full maximum and are sheeted hard and having to dump armfuls of sheet to keep from flying a hull, move the traveler out in small increments until you find the spot where you are only making small adjustments with the mainsheet.

Understand that moving the traveler out does not in and of itself make the sail flatter — it simply makes it possible to keep the main sheeted hard so the sail will stay flat and you can control the boat.

A good way to look at the traveler and sheet adjustments for heavy air would be to think of your television channel adjustment knobs for UHF. You may have an inside dial wheel that zips quickly through channels 13 through 83, and you can quickly see glimpses of pictures as you pass through. Suppose you want channel 43 and dial close to that number. The picture does not necessarily snap clearly into focus on UHF.

Now, you must adjust the outer circular dial and fine tune the picture and sound to your perfection.

Think of the traveler as the inside dial wheel that gets you in the neighborhood, and the sheet as the outer fine-tuning dial.

And this technique works with unirigs as well as sloop rigs.

The rule of thumb for the traveler going to weather is: Keep it centered unless all other depowering techniques fail. Then ease it down to leeward and set it where the boat is under control.

Off the wind the traveler is eased off, normally, to just inside the lee-ward hull for 8-foot-wide boats. However, the best way to set the traveler off the wind is to sheet in the traveler until the backside, lower telltale stalls (acts up), then ease the traveler until the telltale flows, then cleat it.

Then the mainsheet is brought in until the backside upper telltale stalls, then ease it out. Now you are at optimum power!

MAINSAIL SHAPE SUMMARY

FOR FLATTER SAIL	FOR FULLER SAIL
Tighten downhaul	Ease downhaul
Tighten outhaul	Ease outhaul
Stiffer battens	Softer battens
Loosen battens	Tighten battens
Loosen diamond stays	Tighten diamond stays
Rotate mast more forward	Rotate mast more aft

For prebent mast, point mast toward sidestay and
flatten sail by tightening downhaul; make sail
fuller by easing downhaul.

The above summary relates primarily to adjustments of the mainsail for going upwind. But what about off the wind? That is easy. In general, you want a flatter sail for going to weather and a fuller sail for going downwind. Using the summary above, simply make the adjustments required for making the sail fuller. There is one exception. When sailing downwind, the mast must be ro-tated at least to 90 degrees and ideally to 110 degrees, i.e., for-ward of the main beam.

Any or all of the above adjustments can be used. There may be times when you just do not have enough time on the beach to accomplish everything

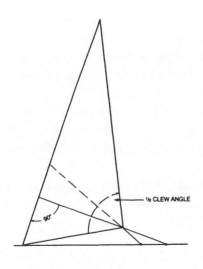

½ CLEW ANGLE

90°

DIAGRAM 21

that must be done, so get the major share of changes made and use on-the-water measures to correct the rest as best you can.

SHAPING THE JIB

JIB LEADS

Tension on the jib sheet is the most obvious part of the mechanism for achieving proper jib shape. But equally important is placement of your jib leads (the points on the boat from which you loosen or tighten the sail from its clew point by means of the jib sheet).

There are some age-old theories on jib lead placements, and there are some "ironclad" rules. I would suggest, however, that these are not so much rules as they are starting points to find where indeed you must set your lead to get the most power from you jib and best contour to complement the main.

One rule is to take one-half the angle at the clew *(See Diagram 21.)* and extend a line down through the clew to the deck. That setting should give you equal pull on both the foot and the leech.

But that may not be what we want. A good deal of our sailing demands us to have the leech fall off or have the top twist off. To do this we must sheet on the foot more than the leech. Therefore, that particular rule does not quite answer all the questions.

The second rule is to measure a line at a 90-degree angle from the luff wire, draw a line from there through the clew, and the extension of that line where the jib lead should be placed. With this rule you should be pulling harder on the foot of the sail, allowing the leech to be looser and thereby falling off more. *(See Diagram 21.)* (This may not be possible if the sail has a radical cut or the forestay has a radical angle.)

Of the two rules, I would lean toward the latter, preferring to err on the side of the leech that is a bit loose rather than one that is too tight. A tight leech causes backwinding of the mainsail, and a backwinded mainsail will perform very poorly.

The bad and sad thing about backwinding is that you do not always know it is happening until it is too late — as your competitors disappear over the horizon. You simply will not go as fast, but there will be no apparent reason.

You probably have read or heard that you can tell you are backwinding the main if the cloth section near the mast is luffing or the mast is counterrotating. But by the time you have noticed these symptoms of backwinding on a fully-battened main, you already are and have been disastrously backwinded for some time.

Even the slightest backwinding can slow your boat, and slight backwinding gives no clue. The mainsail telltales will be streaming back because there is still the flow of air across its leeward side. The sailcloth along the mast will not show signs of luffing, and your mast will not radically counterrotate. If your backwinding is so severe as to give visible signs, you are far beyond being in trouble — you are in the tank.

In addition to determining the ideal angle in relation to tightness of the foot or the leech, you also need your leads set at different positions for different points of sail. Going to weather, when you want a narrower slot between jib and main, the lead needs to be inboard and back. Off the wind you need to get the jib lead forward and outboard.

So, obviously, the ideal would be to have the jib leads on a track that angles outward and forward. Unfortunately, the trampoline decks of most trampolines usually make this impossible, so we have to come up with more creative arrangements.

Sometimes understanding a theory can make the practical application easier. Perhaps it is now more obvious why the jib block sheeting point on the boat can be so critical.

JIB LEADS FOR RESTRICTED CLASSES

In a good many classes you are restricted by the factory-installed travelers, with class rules that outlaw any modifications for inhauling or barberhauling.

First, let's talk about the restricted cat classes. The setting of the jib lead should be directed by the present theory: Do not choke off the slot, and do not slow down the power of the jet stream by allowing the sail to fall off away from the lee of the mainsail too much.

Off the wind, you want your jib leads forward and outboard, far beyond the limits of most travelers. On some boats this is done with the help of barberhaulers. On many one-design classes, however, barberhaulers are forbidden.

The best substitute is your crew, who, while hand-holding the jib clew, is usually sitting in just the proper position (forward and on the leeward side of the boat) to view the entire leech and its complementary relationship to the mainsail.

Note: Make sure your crew does not sit right in the slot, as this simply acts as a wind brake right smack in the middle of your slot's jet stream.

Some designs like the Hobie 16 have an inboard-outboard traveler, but no fore-aft adjustment per se for the jib leads. The same fore-aft effect can be achieved, however, depending on which of several holes the jib sheet is attached to on the clew plate. The same theories apply when determining the best setting.

The best way to pinpoint the ideal jib lead setting is to have your crew take the helm while you are going to weather. Lie with your head in the middle of the trampoline and look at how the leech configuration fits the mainsail. Move the lead around with your hand and play with different settings. You may come up with some ideas to allow the jib to better complement the mainsail.

JIB LEADS FOR NONRESTRICTED CLASSES

On to the boats with no restriction on the jib settings. Use the same technique of lying down on the trampoline or deck and hold-holding the jib while going to weather. See where it best complements the mainsail, and then simply rig your boat to place your jib lead in that position.

"Simply" is the key word here, but it can be a real, creative challenge to find a simple way to do this without turning your deck into a spaghetti factory.

If you happen to have a hard deck, you can have the ideal traveler, as described earlier, angled aft and inboard and forward and outboard. But since most boats have trampoline decks in this day and age, we must find other ways of achieving the same goals.

You have three basic options:

■ Put a straight, fore-and-aft track on the hull of the boat or the support for the trampoline along the inside edge of the hull. You want this track as close inboard as you can put it and on the strongest place. And then use a barber hauler system to pull the jib farther outboard when off the wind. A barber hauler is a separate system of lines that can be controlled from the windward side to pull the jib out to leeward. Although this option does not allow you to place your jib lead inboard enough to be ideal for going to weather, it does give you some flexibility in fore-and-aft adjustment.

■ Sew a plastic or noncorrosive metal reinforcement under the trampoline at the ideal sheeting point for the jib when going to weather. This allows you to have perfection on at least one point of sail, but you have no flexibility of movement either fore-and-aft or outboard, and a barber hauler becomes even more important for sailing off the wind.

■ Plastic-coated cable is available that can be strung across your boat from hull to hull at the point farthest aft that you would want your jib set for going to weather. The jib leads can then be attached to this cable at the ideal in-or-out point. You can make the attachment points permanent, or you can have adjuster lines that let you move the jib leads in or out on the cable. But again, you have no fore-and-aft movement to control the leech, so a barber hauler still becomes a necessity for off the wind.

(Note: Everything is a compromise. If you string cables across your deck, you are adding things that can trip the crew and foul your sheets.)

Just an additional note on barber haulers and the concept of simplicity. If you want to be able to outhaul your jib occasionally but don't want to bother with barber hauler lines, you can attach an open hook at the outermost part of each end of your main beam. When sailing off the wind, simply put the jib sheets under the hook. It will hold the jib out there almost, but not quite, as well as a crew could.

JIB LUFF CONTROL

Luff control is an adjustment of the jib that certainly must not be overlooked, but it is probably the least important. It should be tensioned just enough to remove the wrinkles along the front edge of the jib. If the wind starts blowing harder and you again have wrinkles, tighten it a little more to remove them.

A dacron sail may need more attention to luff tension than a less-stretchy, mylar sail. When the wind picks up, a soft sail will tend to stretch a little, and the draft may blow farther back on the sail, making it fuller. By tightening the luff, this draft can be moved forward again to where it belongs, flattening the sail somewhat.

The degree of tension required can be related directly to the downhaul tension of the mainsail. It can also be related directly to White's Three W's Formula, as discussed in Chapter 3. Therefore, in heavy air (flat sail), flat seas (flat sail), and lightweight crew (flat sail), you should have a tight luff control. For those same conditions, jib leads should probably be set aft.

If the case calls for a fuller sail, the luff tension should be eased and the jib leads may move forward, as long as they do not cause a backwinding situation.

Ideally, the luff tension should be changed as you go around the race course. Off the wind, the luff should be let off to the point just before it wrinkles; then, upon approaching the leeward mark, tightened to give better weather performance.

However, in most classes changes of this nature are difficult to make even between races, and impossible in race conditions. Therefore, most us set the luff control basically for going to weather and just live with it downwind.

Set your luff tight enough so that when sheeted and going to weather in a given wind condition there are no scallops along the luff, but so that at the same time, when you are sailing downwind, the luff is still allowed to fall off and be free without an uncooperative bend or vertical wrinkle.

For you lucky souls who have the availability of adjustment on the race course, use it if you can. If you presently do not have a cockpit-operated luff tensioner in your boat and your class allows it, then by all means install one.

There are two basic types; halyard and downhaul. The halyard type allows the sail to be set permanently at its lowest position and then tensioned off the top of the jib and controlled from one spot on the mast.

The downhaul-type tensioner can usually be set up to control from both sides of the boat (making it easier to get at) but will change the sail set. In other words, it will either raise or lower the entire sail, including the clew, thereby changing your jib lead setting.

JIB SHEETING

Although we have talked on and off about sheeting, let's go over it as a subject in itself. Going to weather is where you are most likely to find problems with sheeting. Or you may have problems and never find out what they are unless you understand the crucial difference that can be made by one tiny click on the ratchet block.

Here is what happens. The more aft you set your jib leads (tensioning the foot more than the leech), the more radical the effect of your trimming will be upon the leech. Ease off the sheet a notch or two, and that may loosen the foot of the sail by an inch, but it may at the same time loosen the leech by several inches.

And much worse, tighten the sheet a notch and suddenly your leech is inches tighter; you are badly overtrimmed, closing your slot dramatically and horribly backwinding the mainsail.

Again, maybe the cloth on the main won't luff, and I am sure the mast will not counterrotate, but you nonetheless will be backwinding the main.

So next you ease it. Ease it too much and you will have lost your pointing ability and power.

☛**If you must be overzealous in sheeting, make sure it's the mainsheet, not the jib sheet. If anything, you want the main oversheeted and the jib undersheeted.**

BLOCKS

High-aspect-ratio sails are more efficient than the old-style, low-aspect sails. It takes a lot more power to pull in the mainsheet than ever before, and pure people-power is no longer enough. As a result, not only have blocks become more sophisticated, with better holding power and cleats, there are a lot more of them, as most boats have 6-1 or 8-1 purchase for their mainsheets.

Blocks also are very important for controlling outhauls and downhauls. Without good equipment, there would be no way to adjust the modern sail to gain the flatness you want to weather, or the fullness downwind.

By use of heavy downhaul procedures, one can actually bend the mast to create sail flatness and it is probably the most important set of blocks on the boat.

The outhaul is also important to get the bottom of the sail flat for the weather leg.

You can increase power with more blocks, but there is a trade-off for increased power — and that is decreased speed. For example, a mainsheet system that is 4:1 will be harder to pull in, but it will pull in faster, and it will play out faster after it is released than an 8:1. With the 8:1 it will take longer to pull in the sheet and it will take longer to let out sheet, although it will be able to pull with twice the power.

Another problem with too many parts in the block-and-tackle assembly is that it requires a tremendous amount of line. On a simple 4-to-1 system, you would have to pull one foot of line to pull the boom in only three inches. An 8-to-1 would require two feet of sheet to be pulled to gain three inches.

However, on downhauls there is no real emergency on easing or tightening the line; so power is more important. At this point, many of the Tornado sailors are using a 16-to-1 downhaul system of blocks.

Of course, some of the one-designs are restricted by class rules from increasing their downhaul purchase. The Hobie 18 Class Association recently approved use of a 6-1 downhaul system, doubling the purchase that boat allows.

Inherent in all tackle systems is friction. Every block sheave rolls around its axle and the line has to bend around the sheave. The more blocks, the more friction. The modern sailor tries to minimize this friction by using ball bearing blocks with large diameter sheaves and the smallest line possible.

One way of increasing power with fewer problems than standard tackle is the cascading system. A cascade is a series of interconnected tackles that each serve to increase the power of the other tackles in the series.

Although the cascading system is not yet seen very much, it effectively can use smaller blocks and produce high power. For example an 8-to-1 tackle would require eight blocks. However, if you hooked up a 4-to-1 tackle onto a 2-to-1 tackle you would have the same power with only six blocks — much less friction, yet same power.

There could be a real future in cascading systems for small and large multihulls. The reduction of load we see downstream in a cascade can be used to save friction, weight and money.

An interesting thing to remember about ratchet blocks is that the farther the sheet wraps around the block, the more pulling power and holding power you will have — the easier it will be to pull in the sheet or to hold the sheet (or any other line on the boat, for that matter).

The ideal jib block will not have a cam cleat mounted on it. Then the line can wrap around the block to the maximum degree possible. Read the following section on "Cleats" to find out how to handle this situation.

If you must live with jib blocks that have the cam cleats mounted on them, set the cleats as high as possible to allow the sheet to get as much grip on the block as possible.

CLEATS

Cleats have been the cause of considerable cursing and many a capsize. They have a disconcerting habit of uncleating and dumping you in the water to windward or NOT uncleating and dumping you in the water to leeward.

The cleat that is on most mainsheet blocks can be adjusted so that it angles farther up or down. Make sure it is set so that it is a little difficult to cleat, but very easy to uncleat.

Many's the skipper who has gone sliding down the trampoline, snapping futilely on his mainsheet all the way, and taking the boat over with him.

Many catamarans have their jib cleats right on the blocks —a very poor system. Most of the high performance cats now have cleats mounted either on the deck or on the side stay on each side of the boat so the jib can be cleated and uncleated from the windward side, close to the crew position in heavy air, which is the only time cleats are really needed for the jib.

Those who must suffer with cam cleats on the jib blocks should, as noted in the section on "blocks," set the cleats as high as possible. This accomplishes three things:

1. It wraps the line farther around the block, making it easier to pull in the sheet.

2. It helps to reduce slightly the annoying habit of those jaws to keep clamping onto your sheet when you don't want them to.

3. It makes it easier to uncleat the jib.

With most such blocks, even at the cleat's highest setting, it is easy to cleat the sheet from anywhere but the back of the boat — if you are back there, you are on a reach and you never want to cleat the jib on a reach anyway.

At this point we have gained great versatility in the sails of the modern catamaran, a versatility which is needed to exact the ultimate performance from the boat.

The concept of getting your sail flat, full, or anything in between is now with us. We have the tools to achieve the flatness or fullness desired and we know how to use those tools; but WHEN to use each of these tools is a matter of even greater import. Consequently, Chapter 3 on my Three W's Formula and the use of the Sail Shaper become very valuable.

TELLTALES
Chapter 8

We now know what sail shape we want and how to get it. But how do we know how to trim the sails to make them go fast? The answer is in those little ribbons that flutter on the sails.

Telltales were aptly named because that is exactly what they do — in fact, they actually are tattletales, because they warn us about what we cannot yet see.

Before telltales were invented, we had no warning that our sail was about to luff or stall. The only way to tell what your sail was doing was to let it out once in a while until the sailcloth visibly luffed and then pull it in until the cloth was smooth. And there was no way to tell if your sail was stalling.

But we're getting ahead of ourselves.

Let's talk about where to put telltales on the sails, and then we will explain how to understand what they are telling us.

WHERE TO PUT THEM

On your jib, place a pair of telltales (one telltale on each side of the sail) on each vertical third of the sail, approximately 9"-12" back from the luff. *(See Diagram 22.)*

On the main, place telltales on the first panel above the hounds, or the area where the sidestays and forestay join on the upper portion of your mast. (The reason for this position is that you want these telltales above the jib so they will get undisturbed air.) Place one telltale on each side ap-

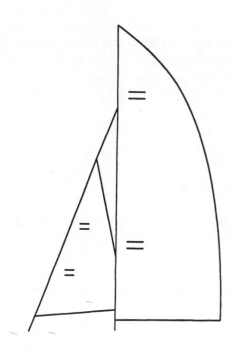

DIAGRAM 22

proximately 12 inches aft of the luff. From that position go about halfway down to the tack and place another set of telltales approximately 12 inches aft of the luff. *(See Diagram 22.)*

You really do not need any more telltales then that on your sails. I highly recommend that you place a telltale on each sidestay and telltales or a windvane fly on your bridle wires — they are helpful for orientating yourself with the true wind angle if you have a slow tack or go into irons or need to back up your boat. If it rains and your sail telltales are all plastered to the sail, you can use these additional telltales to keep yourself heading in the right direction. In the days before sail telltales, those telltales on the side stays were all we used to sail our angle to weather. It was hard on the neck, but it worked.

WHAT THEY TELL US

Okay, now we have telltales on our sails — what do they do and what do they mean?

Their only function is to give us information about what the air flow across the sails is doing. This, in turn, tells us whether to sheet in or sheet out or head the boat down or head the boat up. Think of them as a little voice in your ear.

Some people put telltales all over their sails — that is too many little voices to listen to, and it can be more confusing than helpful.

Let's assume you have the four sets of telltales, placed in the positions recommended — two sets on the jib and two sets on the main.

We will call the telltales on the leeward side of the sail (the side away from you, assuming you are sitting on the windward side of the boat) the "back" telltales. We will call the telltales on the windward side of the sail (the side toward you) the "front" telltales.

The back telltales will tell you if you are stalling; the front telltales will tell you if you are luffing.

LUFFING AND STALLING

Let's define the terms "luffing" and "stalling."

Luffing is easy, because it is something you can physically see, especially on the jib. If you head the boat up too far or let the sail out too far, the cloth along the luff of the jib will start to cave in toward you. This is called "luffing." If you let the sail out all the way or head way up into the wind, the jib will not just cave in, it will start flapping like mad —that is called a "full luff." Another word goes hand in hand with luffing, and that is "pinching." When you are trying to sail a little too close to the wind going to weather and are close to luffing — the cloth is looking a little "soft" along the luff — you are pinching. You are pointing high, but going relatively slow.

Stalling is not as easy, because it is invisible. It means you are sailing too far off the wind or that the sail is in too tight. There are no physical signs of it on the sail itself — you just keep going slower and slower. The stall is insidious and it is also the most disastrous thing you can do as far as killing boat speed. It is easier to recover from an occasional slight luff than from a stall.

The word "stall" is borrowed from aeronautics, where it means, "to lose the amount of forward speed necessary to maintain altitude and be controlled." For an airplane to stay in the air, it must have a certain minimum speed of airflow over the wing, or it will crash.

In the case of a sailboat, if the sail is too tight in relation to the wind angle, air flow diminishes over the "wing," (the back side of the sail), and the sail immediately loses power.

It is the danger of stalling that makes telltales on sails so invaluable, because they can warn of what we cannot see.

Here is how they work.

READING YOUR TELLTALES

When a telltale on the front side of the sail (the windward side) acts up, it means you are on the verge of a luff. The sailcloth may not yet show any signs, but the telltale, being lighter than the sailcloth, is the early warning signal. And it is actually showing you graphically what the wind is doing. It means one of two things is happening: Either you are pointing too close to the wind or your jib is not in tight enough.

To correct for the luff, you will either fall off the wind a little or pull in the sail a little.

When a telltale on the back side of the sail (the leeward side) acts up, it means you are stalling. Sirens should go off and signs should flash: "Take Corrective Action Immediately!" If your telltale indicates a stall, it means you are heading too far off the wind or your sail is in too tight. It also means you are going slow. The telltale is showing you what the wind is actually doing as it passes around the back side of your sail. In this case it would be blowing all over the place. What you want to see is a steady flow of wind across the backside of the sail. When the wind doesn't flow smoothly across the backside of the sail, then the sail is stalled and immediately loses nearly half of its potential power.

To correct for the stall, you have the choice of either heading up closer to the wind or easing your sail a little.

This is the basic principle of the telltales, and it would be easy except for one thing. We are not dealing with just one set of telltales — we have two sets on the jib and two sets on the mainsail, and they all must be tuned to each other — like a barbershop quartet.

TUNING THE SAILS BY THE TELLTALES

For going to weather:

When the jib is sheeted closehauled for going to weather, the upper and lower telltales should be doing the same things — the back ones should both be streaming back and the front ones can be acting up just a little. If they are not doing the same things, it probably means your jib traveler is not set in the right place — your sheet may be pulling down too hard on the leech or back too hard on the foot, causing the top of the sail to do different things than the bottom of the sail. (See "Strings to Pull" for how to adjust your jib leads.)

Once your jib telltales are both breaking and flowing in unison, look at your mainsail telltales. For going to weather, you only need to worry about the upper set of telltales, above the jib (the lower ones are going to flow no matter what, due to the air flow caused by the jib). Again, you want the upper back telltale flowing and the front one can be acting up a little.

If all three sets of telltales are doing the same thing, all the skipper needs to do is watch the lower set on the jib, because whatever that set does, the rest of them are doing.

Caution: If the front telltale on the mainsail is acting up and the front telltales on the jib are not, ease the jib a little — it means the jib is set a little tighter than the main and could be backwinding the main or closing off the slot. Or perhaps, if the jib is set properly, the mainsail may need to be sheeted tighter.

Now that we have telltale harmony, all the skipper needs to do is watch what those lower telltales on the jib are telling him. If they luff too much, he should fall off a little; if they stall at all, he should head up a little. Keep it out of a stall at all costs.

For going downwind:

For going downwind, just as in going to weather, you are going to set your sails, leave them in one position, and steer by those lower telltales on the jib. Now, of course, your sails are set very far out. The jib is held out with barberhaulers or hand-held by the crew, but it is still important that the sail be held in such a way that the top and bottom sets of telltales do the same things. If the top telltale is luffing before the bottom one, you need to pull down harder on the leech; if the top telltale is stalling and the bottom one is not, you need to ease up on the leech to let out the top of the sail a little.

As for the telltales on the mainsail, get the apparent wind at approximately 90 degrees to your direction (the bridle-fly or windward sidestay telltale pointing perpendicular to the boat). Then use the bottom set of telltales to adjust the traveler. Let the traveler all the way out. Then pull it in until the lower back telltale of the main begins to act up. Ease the traveler back down until the lower backside telltale on the main begins to stream. Cleat the traveler.

Next, trim the mainsheet until the top backside telltale acts up; then ease the mainsheet until that same backside telltale begins to flow. Cleat the mainsheet. Be sure the mast is rotated to 110-degrees or the top, backside telltale may never flow, due to the indentation created between the mast and the sail.

In other words the lower set of telltales is controlled by the traveler, while the top set of telltales is controlled by the mainsheet.

Now, just as in going to weather, the front telltale will be acting up a little, but if it luffs excessively, drive the boat deeper. If the back telltale stalls — well, just don't let that happen, but if it does, head up. Downwind, it is advisable to always keep the front telltale in a bit of a luff, but NEVER, NEVER let it stall.

For a Reach:

For the reach, as soon as you are on course, you will set your main traveler by the bottom set of telltales, just as you did downwind. You will not be "setting" the mainsheet and cleating it, as you would do upwind or downwind. Instead, you will be holding the sheet and playing it in and out to keep the upper telltales flowing.

Your jib lead settings will depend upon how deep a reach it is. If it is a fairly close reach, they can remain pretty much as they were for going upwind. If it is closer to a beam reach, you will want to move your jib leads more forward and out. For a broad reach, the settings will be as they are for downwind sailing.

The reach is the only point of sail where you will be adjusting the sails to the wind rather than steering the boat to the wind. Because of rapid changes in the apparent wind and in wind velocity on a reach, the sails must be played in and out constantly in response to the movements of the telltales, so it is important to know how to react immediately to what they are telling you.

Easy ways to remember what to do:

☛If you are adjusting sails to the telltales, always move the sail TO-WARD the telltale that is acting up or flying forward. i.e., if the back telltale acts up, let the sail out; if the front telltale acts up, pull the sail in.

☛If you are changing the course of the boat in response to the telltales, always turn the bows of the boat AWAY FROM the telltale that is acting up or flying forward. i.e., if the back (leeward) telltale is acting up, head the boat up; if the front (windward) telltale is acting up, steer the boat to leeward.

☛Move your tiller toward the side that is acting up. If the back telltale acts up, push your tiller away from you; if the windward telltale acts up, pull the tiller toward you.

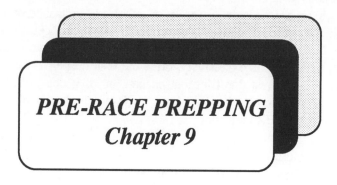

PRE-RACE PREPPING
Chapter 9

B efore you leave the beach for the race course:

1. Have the course information handy on the boat. There is nothing worse than getting the best start, being first at the weather mark, only to discover you don't know where to go next.

The Hobie class developed a stick-on course decal that has been adopted by most classes. It outlines all the courses that are available to be used and assigns each course a number. The race committee simply displays the course number; you check your decal for the description of that course; and you know where to go.

In some regattas, the course may be announced at the skipper's meeting prior to the race. Or if a printed sheet of course designations is given out, try to enclose it in a waterproof, transparent plastic bag to take on the boat with you, unless you have a photographic memory.

2. A pennant and flag information decal also should be aboard the boat. Again, these are stick-ons, available at most sailboat dealerships. They give you ready reference to the various flags that may be flown by the race committee. These visual signals are often the race committee's only means of communicating to the racers: that life jackets are required, there is a postponement, the course is shortened, the race is being abandoned, come within hailing distance, follow me, individual recall, general recall, etc.

3. A starting watch is a must. There was a time when such a device was extremely expensive and did not hold up for any length of time. But the age of electronics has brought us a wide variety of inexpensive watches, many of which will give you a ten-minute countdown feature. Most of these new watches can also be set for a six-minute countdown, which is helpful because many regattas have gone to the three-minute sequence to speed things up when there are many classes to start.

Having a watch sure beats having your crew count "one thousand one, one thousand two . . ."

4. Be sure to take along a protest flag. You should not look upon it as meaning you have a chip on your shoulder and are ready to protest all who cross your path. Most people don't like having to air out their flag during a race. But on the other hand, if you are flagrantly fouled and you have no protest flag, 90 percent of the time your protest will not be acknowledged, let alone heard.

And if you don't protest, someone else may protest you for not protesting, and you could be the one disqualified. So carry it for your own protection, if nothing else.

Make sure your protest flag measures in and qualifies according to your class requirements. Most classes require a solid red, 10-inch-square flag.

5. Make sure you have aboard all equipment required by the race committee: Sometimes this could include a throwable, an anchor and anchor line, and/or a paddle.

6. Read the race instructions thoroughly — if something is unclear, ask questions at the skipper's meeting prior to the race.

7. If it is not spelled out, ask what point on the race committee boat will be used for sighting down the line for the starts and finishes.

8. Make sure you have water or juice aboard to drink between races so you don't become dehydrated.

9. Have essential small tools, extra shackles and ring pins and small pieces of line aboard for making emergency repairs on the water.

10. Put on sunblock and take some with you.

11. Listen to the weather report.

12. If you are unfamiliar with the area, study a chart or talk to local sailors to learn about currents, tides, shallow areas, sea serpents, prevailing wind conditions and geographical wind influences.

13. If you have some time to kill, wash your boat — clean hulls go faster.

14. Check one last time before leaving the beach to make sure your plugs are in.

15. Get off the beach early and check out the wind, water and race course.

And before you leave the beach, remember the old sailor's proverb: "The speed of your boat increases with your own confidence." I would add to that, the level of your confidence increases in proportion to your preparedness.

THE START
Chapter 10

To non-sailing spectators, the start of a sailboat race probably is the only part that seems to make any sense. The boats are all lined up, a horn or a gun goes off, and away they go — just like in motocross, but less noisy.

Unfortunately, for the sailors in that lineup it is usually the most chaotic part of the race. Sometimes it seems as though the whole fleet is trying to start in the exact same spot that you had picked out for yourself.

Boats come from all directions in an increasingly frantic jockeying for position as the final seconds count down to the gun. Skippers are shouting their favorite word, "Up, Up, Up"; sails are flapping noisily; and ratchets are clicking. Boom! The noise stops, and the boats take flight across the water like a flock of swallows after a squabble in the treetops.

Many of the sailors at this start actually went into the melee with a plan of action — for some the plan worked; for others it did not. Unfortunately, what looks great on a nice, smooth blackboard, looks a little different at the moment of truth.

But having a plan that fails is better than having no plan at all.

The start is not an entity unto itself — it is the beginning of the race and therefore your starting strategy is an integral part of the BIG PIC-TURE — your game plan for the whole race.

On the other side of that same coin, the start is ONLY the beginning of the race — so if you screw it up, don't roll over and die; there's still a long way to go, and a lot of things can happen between start and finish.

Before getting deeply into starting techniques, you may want to review some very simple, basic boat handling. While approaching the starting line you may be required to maneuver your boat with precision in very close quarters, and it is imperative to have total control over your boat and have close teamwork between skipper and crew.

Maneuvers you need to master are sudden stops, rapid acceleration, slowing down, parking, speeding up, reaching off, turning in a full circle through a tack and jibe, feathering up, and sometimes all of the above in quick succession. In other words, you should be prepared to put your boat through any paces called for by the circumstances, without having to think about it much.

The mechanics of executing these basic maneuvers are explained in Chapter 1, "Boat Handling."

SOME RULES ON STARTING

While we will not get deeply into rules, a quick review of a couple rules used at the start may be helpful.

First, we all know you are not allowed to barge. If a boat(s) comes crashing in toward the start line from above the layline, that boat(s) is barging.

However, suppose you are perfectly on the layline and and not very close to the starting line. And a boat barges in clear and ahead of you, without touching you or causing you to maneuver to avoid a collision. Then that boat has not fouled you. In other words, your buddy got away with it!

Had you been closer to the starting line where there was no room for him to dive into a hole in front of you, then he would have been caught barging.

And sometimes people get away with it, if there happens to be a hole at the mark and no leeward boats to challenge the interloper. But it is a high-risk move, where you have no rights. And, if you try to nudge in, you will find most sailors are not going to give you an inch.

The other relevant rule has to do with luffing rights.
In order to understand the rule, it is first necessary to understand the concepts of "overlap" and "mast abeam."

Exactly what is an overlap? If you drew an imaginary line to leeward perpendicular to your boat across the aft edge of the rudders and pictured that line, any boat ahead of that line has an overlap. Any boat aft of that line does not.

Exactly what is "mast abeam"? When the skipper of a windward boat sights perpendicularly to leeward from his normal helm position at a leeward boat that is overlapped, if he sees that the mast of the leeward boat is behind that perpendicular line, the windward boat has mast abeam and can hail the leeward boat to either curtail or limit the leeward boat's luffing rights on him.

Before the start a boat can come from behind and once overlapped below you — and not before then — can luff you up to a close-hauled direction. That is when the luffing boat can yell out that favorite phrase of "UP, UP, UP!" Note that he cannot make you come up, nor even call for you to come up until he has established an overlap.

Keep in mind he can only luff you up to a close-hauled course. That does not mean you have to have your sails sheeted in and be sailing a close-hauled course.

Also, that luffing boat must carry out the luff slowly and initially in such a way as to give you the room and the time to make your turn to be on a close-hauled course.

If he gets ahead of mast abeam, then he can luff you all the way to head-to-wind. If he tries before he is mast abeam, be sure to hail, "Mast abeam, close-hauled." He will then have to back off his big luff. By the way, the mast abeam hail is mandatory.

These luffing rights rules apply to boats that have not yet started and cleared the starting line. In other words you must be behind the starting line for these rules to apply.

DOING YOUR HOMEWORK

You will recall that the last item on the 15 Commandments for Pre-Race Preparation was, "Get off the beach EARLY." That is because you have a lot of homework to do before you can devise a starting plan and a strategy for the race.

The primary things you should be finding out before every race are:

1. The favored side of the course, if there is a favored side.
2. Which end of the starting line is favored, or if the line is even.

3. The length of the starting line.
4. The transit for the starting line.
5. The current speed and direction.

THE FAVORED SIDE OF THE COURSE

Getting out to the race course early is a good idea, and it may give you an edge over the beach-clingers. It is helpful to sail up the first weather leg to feel out the shifts, try to figure out the wind patterns — which is a lift, which is a header — and above all, get your tacks smoothed out; get loose.

Use the split-pairs technique to determine if the course has a favored side. Have a buddy of equal sailing speed sail to one side of the course, while you sail to the other side. Designate one of you to tack when near the layline. The other boat will then tack at the same time. Then simply see who is in the lead when the two boats meet. If the boat that went to the right side was ahead, then the right side will probably be the best side of the course to sail. That is not necessarily so, however, and you may want to try it again and swap sides. Try this technique downwind too.

The primary factors that make a side of the course favored are:

1. There is more wind on that side.

2. There is a persistent shift toward that side.

3. There is a geographical shift on that side that can be used to advantage.

4. Same wind but less waves and/or boat chop on that side. (Note, however, waves that are undesirable upwind will probably be helpful going downwind.)

5. The current is more favorable on that side. (Note, however, that current that is desirable upwind will probably not be helpful going downwind.)

(See Chapter 15, "Wind Shifts," for more in-depth discussion of various types of wind shifts.)

THE FAVORED END OF THE LINE

As soon as the starting line has been set by the race committee, try to determine which is the "favored" end of the line. The favored end is that end closest to the direction from which the wind is blowing. If you start at the favored end, you will already be ahead of the boats starting at the other, unfavored end, giving you an advantage right off the line.

So, how do you tell the favored end? There are a number of ways. You can park head to wind on the line and look each way. The end of the line that appears to be farthest upwind is the favored end. *(See Diagram 23.)*

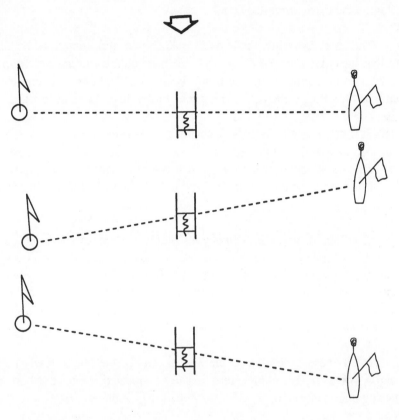

DIAGRAM 23
In the top example, while pointing directly into the wind, both the port and starboard ends are even. This is an even line.
In the center example, the boat again points directly into the wind and sees that the starboard end is closer to the wind and, therefore, favored.
In the last example, with the boat headed directly into the wind, you can see that the port end is closer to windward and therefore is the favored end.

Or you can park head to wind just to the left of the port end of the line and sight down your main beam. Whichever end of the line is farthest ahead of that line is the favored end. However, a caution: If you are not directly head-to-wind, you may be getting a deceptive reading.

Another way is to sight perpendicularly off a telltale on your boat or a flag on the race committee boat.

The race committee boat itself is anchored and, therefore, heading straight into the wind. So if you sight perpendicularly across the committee boat and the port end of the line is behind that sighting line, the line is starboard favored. If the port end is ahead of that line, it is port favored.

Still another way is to sail across the starting line close-hauled on starboard tack and then on port tack. Note which tack took you across the line at the most perpendicular angle. If it was starboard tack, the starboard end of the line is favored. If it was port tack, the port end of the line is favored.

Then again, you could find your buddy and do another split-pairs. Your buddy sails close-hauled from the starboard end of the line on starboard tack, while at the same time (as if you were starting) you sail close-hauled from the port end of the line on port tack. You simply see who has the lead when you meet. If the port starter has the lead, then the port end is favored. *(See Diagram 24.)*

In any case, determine if the favored end of the line is toward starboard, where the committee boat usually is located, or port, where the starting mark is located.

Note: The favored end of the line is not related to its position in relation to the weather mark. If the race course is skewed so the weather mark is off to the right in relation to the starting line, this does not mean the starboard end of the line is favored. The ONLY consideration in determining favored end is which end is closer to the wind. For purposes of determining favored end, pretend the weather mark is not even there. If the mark is over to the right side of the course for some reason, this simply means you will probably want to go to the right side soon after starting and it may be a factor in deciding how far down the line you want to go if the line happens to be port favored.

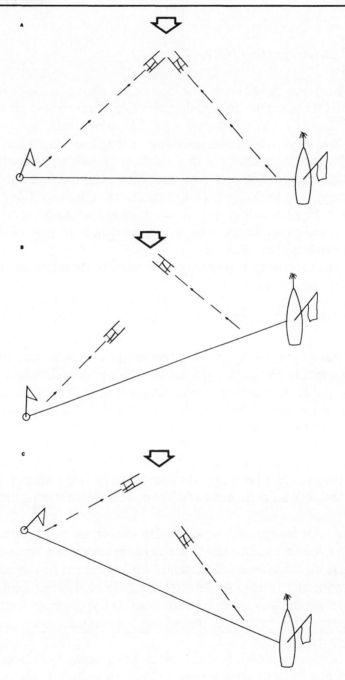

DIAGRAM 24

THE LENGTH OF THE LINE

Next, you should know how long the line actually is. So time it. Start at the RC boat, run the line and time how long it takes you to get from one end to the other. This will pay off big in oscillating winds.

You may have discovered that the starting line was starboard or RC boat favored, but suddenly with a couple of minutes left, the wind shifts counterclockwise. Some of your competitors may not even notice, and some may start to slowly work toward the port (pin) end. However, you know that it takes exactly one minute, thirty seconds to get there. So, you sheet in and go hell-bent and hit the pin end right at the gun, with an awesome lead over the entire fleet.

You see how early preparation can pay off? There is nothing like doing your homework.

GETTING A TRANSIT

But we are still not finished checking the line. Now you need a transit. A transit is a range that you line up with a point on land so you know where you are in relation to the starting line, since there is no dotted line drawn on the water. To get your transit, get several boat lengths away from the race committee boat and position your boat so you can sight across the race committee flag, line it up with the port end of the line and find an object on the shoreline that is on the extension of that same sighting line. *(See Diagram 25.)* Let's say it is a smokestack. That smokestack is now your transit. Your range consists of the port end of the starting line and the smokestack.

As you are approaching the starting line for your start, you can gauge how far you are from the line by watching the relationship between the pin end and the smokestack. If the smokestack appears to be behind the pin, you are behind the line. As the smokestack draws closer to lining up with the pin, you are drawing closer to the starting line. If the smokestack suddenly appears to be ahead of the pin, you are over the line and need to dip back over or back up.

Sometimes the RC boat is as big as a freighter and you can't see over it to line up with the leeward pin, and sometimes there is no land or stationary target over the pin end. Then you may have to shoot your transit in reverse by going down beyond the port end of the line and getting a sight-

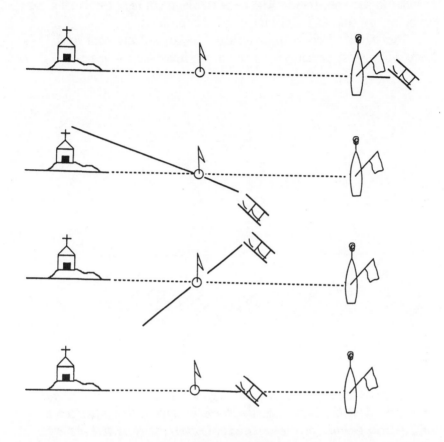

DIAGRAM 25

To get a transit you must sight over the starting flag and across the port end pin to a spot on land. In the top example, you have spotted a church.

With that information, as you approach the starting line, you will simply look over the port end pin and locate the church. In the second example from the top, you see the church behind the pin. Therefore, you are behind the line.

In the third example from the top, you see the church ahead of the port end pin and now know you are over the line.

And in the last example, when you look over the port end pin and see the church lined up, then you know you are on the line.

ing across the pin end and across the committee boat to a landmark. However, when you are coming up to the start, it is harder to look over your shoulder to see your transit. The crew can help out here by looking back just before the start and advising you of your position.

The transit offers a big advantage in large fleets with long lines. There will almost certainly be a sag in the line *(See Diagram 26.)* You

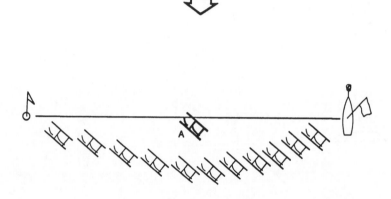

DIAGRAM 26
Here, Boat A has done his homework, gotten his transit, and is the only one of the fleet that knows exactly where the starting line is located. He will get a huge jump on the fleet and be in clear air. Note, it is easier for the boats toward the ends to know where that line is, but it is very difficult to know if you are in the middle of the line.

will know exactly where that line is and have the entire middle open and free of other boats — giving you a safe lead and clear air.

WATCH FOR SIGNALS AND GET THE COURSE NUMBER!!

While you are doing your homework, don't forget to watch for the ten-minute, white or yellow warning signal (or sometimes a six-minute warning signal). Remember that the shape (or flag) is the official signal, not the gun or horn. The five-minute (or sometimes three-minute) preparatory signal is a blue shape, and the start signal is a red shape.

And be sure to get the course number, normally displayed on the committee boat. You may well have the finest start known to the civilized world, but if you do not know the course, you are lost after rounding the weather mark. Most competitors will be glad to tell you what the course number is if you miss it; but a few cutthroat types will do anything to win, including being unsportsmanlike.

WATCH FLEETS AHEAD OF YOU

If other classes are starting ahead of you, you know that you are not allowed near the starting area until the fleet immediately ahead of you has started. Their starting signal will be your five-minute (or sometimes three-minute) preparatory signal.

In some regattas you will be unconditionally disqualified for being in the start area before your start, and rightly so, as you have no business interfering with another fleet's start.

You should have done all your homework prior to their preparatory signal.

After that preceding fleet is gone, you then will have only five minutes to test the line, hardly enough time to do all that and still make a proper start on time. But you can learn a great deal by watching the fleet ahead of you. Observe which is the favored end. Notice which end seems to have the advantage, which end gets congested the most, etc.; and use all this information in formulating your starting plan and maybe some alternative strategies. It's a rare start that works out exactly as planned.

DEVISING YOUR STARTING STRATEGY

Your starting plan should primarily be determined by where you wish to be AFTER the start. You may want to go off immediately to the right side of the course or the left, maybe up the middle.

Another factor that has bearing on where you want to be is your competition. You may have to cover a certain boat or boats (see the section on tactics in "The Weather Leg", Chapter 11.) That is another important input to your decision on where and how to start.

Nonetheless, it is all part of the same question: Where do you want to be after the start?

The best way to discuss starting is to take a few examples.

THE EVEN LINE

We have an even line (that is, neither the port nor the starboard end is favored); it is a big fleet with excellent competition. Here you have the entire line to use, as all positions will be equal after the starting gun goes off. You may have noticed that there was a geographical header a half mile out on the left side of the course, so you want to be on the left side of the course.

Normally, boats on an even line (as well as a starboard-favored line) will try to be the most windward boat and the most toward the starboard end of the line. That usually creates a jam-up at the race committee boat end of the line.

If you want to be on the left side of the course, you will get there faster if you start at the port end of the line in good, clean air; and at the same time you will avoid the traffic jam at the starboard end of the line, where you could be covered, backwinded, or both, by other boats.

On the other hand, if you had a tremendous desire to be on the right side of the course, you would have to fight for a good spot at the starboard end of the line. If you started at the port end, you would never get a chance to tack out to the right side of the course.

A good trick that can be used, if you have to get out to the right side, is a delayed start (lovingly referred to as the "DFL" start.) This takes a good deal of patience. The situation normally occurs when the line is starboard-favored as well, and all the boats will be perched right upon the RC boat, getting nervous, "upping" one another, and doing lots of shouting.

Meanwhile, just park in a position a bit above the lay line to the RC boat and wait. Do not get impatient, because if you make your move too early, you will find that somebody has fouled or stalled or is going backward right at the race committee boat, creating a roadblock on the line.

When the gun goes off, be ready to dive into a good hole coming in off a reach. Carry the reach up and above the boats that will be five to ten lengths ahead of you by now; then tack off immediately into clear air.

You really are not sacrificing as much as you think with this start, for it is getting you to the side of the course you think will "pay," and though you are five to ten boat lengths behind, you are off in clear air, while the rest are backwinding each other terribly.

Sometimes you may get really lucky. A bunch of folks may get there too early and not be able to hold their position, forcing them to drive off down the line, leaving you a big hole to dive into just as the gun goes off. But beware, make sure no one can head higher and cut you off at the RC boat or you will most certainly be the cause of a barging foul.

Let us say you just want to be in the middle, as neither side appeals to you, and you see no obvious advantage. The middle offers a bit of security, for if a big shift comes, you are closer to whichever side of the course has become favored, and you can quickly get into the thick of things.

If you want the middle of the course, you can either be at the starboard end or any position down to the middle of the starting line. The closer you get to the starboard end, the less restricted you will be to tack off to the right side of the course whenever you want. But keep in mind also that you want clear air, and the jam-up at the starboard end may dictate getting on down the line into clear air.

THE STARBOARD-FAVORED LINE

The second example is with the starting line favored toward the starboard or RC boat end. This a line poorly set by the race committee in nearly all cases. The race committee is asking for damage to their boat, for every competitor wants to be at the starboard end with a big lead over the entire fleet. *(See Diagram 27A.)* However, only one boat can be there, and all of them are going to be fighting for just such a position.

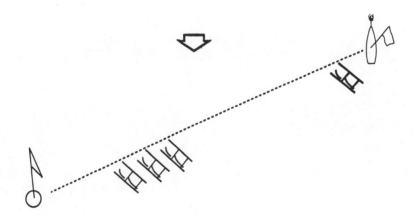

DIAGRAM 27A

One boat will win that berth. All the others (which could be as many as eighty boats or more) will lose it. This may be a good place to use the delayed or "DFL" start, as explained earlier. The delay would give that top position to one boat, maybe two or three; but you will still be right in there and not far behind a few of the lead boats, yet well ahead of most of the fleet.

However, if you want or need to hold onto the starboard tack, you must work up and out of the wake and backwinding of the leading boats' safe leeward position. (See Chapter 16, "Tactics.")

Another possibility is to give the one boat his position and get on down the line and into clear air where you can drive the boat well and keep moving. The boats jammed up near the starboard end are going to play havoc with each other's air. Meanwhile, you are trucking along without any disturbed air. You could continue to drive until such time as a header comes along, and you could easily be right back amongst the leaders.

THE PORT-FAVORED LINE

The third line you will have to deal with is the port-favored line. If the line is not set at an extreme angle, this usually is an excellent line, as it disperses most of the boats pretty evenly all the way down the line from the RC boat to the port pin. The most advantageous place to be in this case is the port end, for it automatically puts you ahead, and in a safe leeward position on the boat and/or boats above and aft of you. *(See Diagram 27B.)*

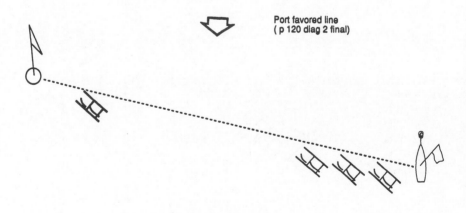

Port favored line
(p 120 diag 2 final)

DIAGRAM 27B

Assume you want the left side of the course; then you want to be most port boat on the line and on starboard tack. That puts you ahead and also has you heading for the side you think will do the best for you.

If you desire the middle of the course, you will want to be at the port end, but you do not have to be number one boat at the pin. In fact, the closer you are to the pin, the worse your chances of staying in the middle of the course; you may not be able to tack for the weather pin at all until the lay line or, worse, beyond the layline, when everybody else decides to go for it.

A word of caution here: many sailors tend to overstand the layline on purpose and that is a major "NO NO" for winning. Those folks are simply sailing more distance than their competitors that do not overstand laylines. The winning boats sail the shortest course, the fastest.

By starting up the line a ways, you are less likely to be trapped over on the left side of the course; however, you are giving the boats to leeward a head start. It is a decision that must be made.

If you want to get to the right side of the course, there are two ways: Stay up the line more and tack off quickly; or try a port tack start.

You know you want to tack off to the right side of the course quickly and, chances are, so do all the boats toward the starboard end of the line. You can probably be as far as halfway down the line and still be able to get to the right side.

Most of the boats will tack to port fairly soon; and for those that don't, you will just have to duck their sterns, although there probably will be only a few.

We all know that a port-tack start is very risky business. The bigger the fleet and the better the competition, the worse are the odds you will be able to pull it off. If you are going to give the port-tack start a try, do not tip everyone off beforehand. Be sure you definitely have a port-favored line, however. Make sure you can indeed beat the starboard boats, if all is equal.

Then make a timed start. For example, reach out from the port pin with one minute fifteen seconds remaining to the start signal. Sail for thirty seconds, gybe, using up no more and no less than fifteen seconds, and reach back to the pin. You must hit the pin on a reach with a head of steam and then, upon rounding the mark, head up and sheet in quickly; the speed of the reach will shoot you way up to windward and have you really moving. Keep it there; you must maintain speed.

If on your approach back to the line you see a good many boats heading for the pin on starboard, be prepared to duck their sterns. This probably will not hurt you unless there is a steady wall of starboard boats. Then you have blown it. If there are only a few starboard boats, then a hole, dive for the hole, head up and sheet in, again gaining and keeping that speed.

Even though you may not have pulled off that awesome-looking port tack start and you have to duck most of the fleet, you will still be no worse off than had you started at the RC boat end and then tacked to port.

THE OSCILLATING LINE

In the next scenario we have what appears to be a port-favored line, but you are aware of a good deal of oscillation in the wind. If you commit early to the port end of the line and wind clocks, you will be in the tank.

Here is a case where it is imperative to know the length of the line by timing it, as explained earlier. You need to know exactly how long it takes to get from the starboard end of the line to the port end. Let us assume it takes a minute to cover that distance. Make your approach to the starting line from the starboard end by at least two minutes before the start. Be prepared to make a dash for the favored port end of the line; or if the wind clocks right, be ready to park and wait for the starboard end start.

If the line goes back to port-favored with only a little time left, head on down as far as you can go and, with as much speed as possible, hit the line at the signal. Here is a perfect time to use your transit that we discussed earlier to make sure you are neither over the line nor way behind it.

If the wind is still holding to port, tack quickly, as you are sailing a header in oscillating wind. With wind oscillating this much, you probably will want to take it up the middle, anyway. If you think the wind is going to continue to clock to the right, you probably will want to get to the right side of the course

The safe place is the middle in oscillating winds: You can tack out easily and are near the rhumb line if there are any major shifts.

GENERAL PRINCIPLES

A couple of general principles should be applied at most starts:

☞ As you are approaching on your lay line to the start, and very near starting time, keep luffing up the boat above you, without allowing the boat below you to do the same thing to you. *(See Diagram 28.)* What you are trying to accomplish is to provide a space below you. This is called "digging a hole" — a hole into which you can drive off and get speed just before the start.

Thus, when there are five to fifteen seconds left — or whatever it takes to get to the line — you quit luffing, bear off into the hole, and drive out into clear air with speed, leaving the chap above you in a backwinded position. That boat won't be able to drive off until you are out of his way.

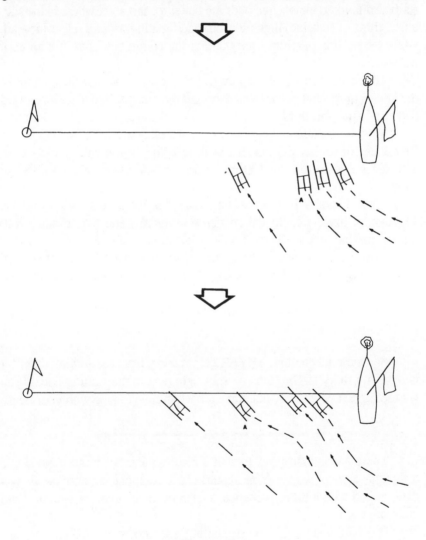

DIAGRAM 28

☞ Often clear air is more important than getting the perfect position on the line. If you have determined the line to be starboard favored, only one boat is going to get that perfect spot at the committee boat. If the line is port favored, only one boat is going to get that spot at the pin end of the line. Instead of joining the mob that is gambling on getting the perfect spot, think of the starting line as being divided into thirds. If the line is starboard favored, maybe the odds are better to start somewhere in the starboard third of the line, digging a hole and getting a good, clear-air start, while the mob is piled up back there at the committee boat in a mess of bad air.

The same thing would apply to the port end favored line. Think of the line in thirds and even if you can't get the pin, get into clear air toward that end in the port third.

Most of the time the boat getting that exact port end or starboard end start does not necessarily fair that well. Imagine, if you will, a track meet. You are going to run the 100 meter dash but the lanes are all different lengths.

Lane 1 is only 100 meters long, Lane 2 is 105 meters long, Lane 3 is 110 meters long, etc. So the runner starting in Lane 5 is running 120 meters, instead of just 100 meters like the runner in lane 1.

However, in Lane 1, there are ten runners; lane 2 has seven, etc, while you have Lane 5 to yourself. The race starts, and while they are bumping shoulders and elbows in the first few lanes, you are running clean and fast in good old Lane 5. Sure, you are running a little more distance, but you may be better off.

☞ One final caution: NEVER get far away from the starting line. If it is light and fluky air, be sure you stay right next to the starting line. If you get too far away, you may not make it back in time to race with your fleet.

There are as many way to start a race as there are starters. No single technique always works. You should show as much aggression as you dare, mixed with a bit of prudence, a dash of logic, a cup of planning and grain of luck.

If a particular technique of starting does not work for you, try another; be inventive. A good start can win races for you; and even if you finish dead last, there is something about a good start that is rewarding.

Notes to the crew:

✔ Before the start the crew should always note the course number, if it is posted on the side of the committee boat, and make sure the skipper knows what the course is. He will probably check it, too, but better both of you getting it than neither of you.

✔ Some skippers require the crew to carry the starting watch and do an audible countdown from the five-minute signal to the start. If this is the case, know in what increments the skipper wants the countdown.

✔ Ideally, the skipper should let the crew know what the starting plan will be so the crew can be prepared. You don't want to make yourself "comfortable" on the leeward hull at the start, only to find your skipper plans an immediate tack to port.

✔ During the five minutes leading up to the start, the crew should be concentrating full attention on the jib. Timing is crucial at this point, and the skipper will need to move the boat forward quickly, stop suddenly, make abrupt course changes, park temporarily, or creep forward slowly. The jib should not be cleated at any point during these maneuvers and must be played contantly, as it is an important tool for changing course as well as speed.

✔ If it is necessary to luff the jib to stop or park, keep a close eye on the sheets where they go through the blocks. The commotion of the jib jerking the sheets and blocks can easily cause the sheet to tie itself into a knot or wrap itself around the block, preventing you from sheeting in the jib.

✔ Listen carefully for the skipper's commands. It is difficult to hear when sails are flapping — both yours and those of other boats around you. The skipper will tend to speak in a lower voice when in close quarters with competitors, because he doesn't want them to know what his next move is going to be.

✔ Try to sit inboard on the trampoline near the mast so that if the boat starts to go into irons, you can reach around in front of the mast, grab the clew of the jib and pull it toward you to pull the bows back to their proper angle.

✔ Somewhere between 20 seconds and 10 seconds before the start, you will assume your normal upwind position, hook into your trapeze and, on the skipper's command, sheet in so your boat will hit the line with speed at the gun.

WEATHER LEG
Chapter 11

O nce upon a time, the weather leg was truly where races were won or lost. Reaches and downwind legs were basically parades, punctuated by a few luffing matches. For monohulls, this is still basically true. But since catamarans developed the art of tacking downwind back in the late 1960's, the weather leg's relative importance has become somewhat more equal with that of the downwind leg.

Nevertheless, you will be sailing to weather on the two most important segments of the race — from the starting line to the first mark, and from the last mark to the finish line, so it is very important to master this point of sail.

In addition, tactics play a more important role on the weather leg, and these will be covered in depth in Chapter 16.

Let's divide this chapter into four parts and discuss each:

1) Setting the boat up for upwind sailing
2) Helmsmanship
3) Shifting gears
4) Rounding the weather mark

SETTING UP FOR UPWIND SAILING

Here we are dealing with close-hauled settings for your boat. We have already discussed many of these things in previous chapters, but a quick review may be necessary.

While still on shore you determined whether you needed a flat, moderate or full sail for going to weather, depending on the wind, water and weight conditions as you were able to judge them from the beach and from weather reports.

Now you are on the water, and you need to make the following adjustments to get ready to go to weather:

1. Set your mast rotation limiter, remembering that less rotation can increase sail fullness and power and more rotation can flatten the sail and depower it. (See Chapter 7, "Strings to Pull.")

2. Adjust your outhaul so the foot of the mainsail is flat, if you have a sloop rig. You want to keep the main from bellying out into the slot, where it will be backwinded by the jib. Even unirig sailors should not allow much outhaul off on the main.

3. Tighten the downhaul, remembering that less downhaul will give a fuller sail and more downhaul will bend the mast and flatten the sail. Always downhaul at least enough to remove wrinkles along the mast.

4. Put daggerboards or centerboards down all the way.

5. Center the traveler, unless the wind velocity is such that you must travel out to control the boat.

6. Set the jib luff control just snug enough to eliminate wrinkles along the luff of the sail when it is sheeted for going to weather.

7. Set jib leads for going to weather.

HELMSMANSHIP

At last, the boat is ready to beat to windward. Now it is all up to the helmsman. Once you are actually sailing the windward leg there are three more things the helmsman MUST do to sail a fast upwind course.

1. Decide the angle of the course you are going to sail — whether to point or foot.

2. Fine-tune the main and telltales for the angle you have decided to take.

3. Steer the fine line.

THE COURSE TO SAIL — HIGH OR LOW

Of course, when we travel to windward, we are, IN GENERAL, sailing at about 45-degree angles to the true wind. However, this angle will vary a few degrees one way or the other with wind and wave and weight conditions, as well as the type of catamaran you are sailing.

In all conditions boats with deep daggerboards will be able to sail a higher course, in general, than boats with inefficient boards or asymmetrical boats with no boards at all. This basic difference in pointing ability can be very important to know when you are sailing in a Portsmouth fleet, for instance, with a variety of types of boats.

If you have a Nacra 18-square-meter, you don't want to be on the starting line pinned beneath a Hobie 16 that is going to point considerably lower than you — and the Hobie 16 doesn't want to be above you, because he will have to pinch up far above his normal course to avoid coming down on you. It's a no-win situation for both of you.

It is also important to understand these differences when you are calling tactics and laylines. If you are on a Hobie 16, for instance, and you call a layline based on the angle of a Nacra, you are not going to make the mark.

However, what we really want to address here are the differences in sailing angle to weather that can change from day to day, race to race and even from tack to tack for any given class of boat, based upon the same factors that determine sail shape: Wind, Waves and Weight.

Here are the general rules of thumb:

● Lightweight boats/crews will be able to sail a higher course than heavier boats.

● In chop, boats must sail a slightly lower course than they will on flat seas.

● In light air your course may be a little lower; in heavy air a little higher.

And the reasons behind these are the same we saw in the 3-W's Formula:

    Light weight ☞ flatter sail ☞ point higher
    Heavy weight ☞ fuller sail ☞ point lower

    Flat seas ☞ flatter sail ☞ point higher
    Choppy seas ☞ fuller sail ☞ point lower

    Heavy air ☞ flatter sail ☞ point higher
    Light air ☞ fuller sail ☞ point lower

In addition, you may find that you can sail a higher course on one tack to the weather mark than on the other. It could be because you are heading more directly into the waves on one tack than on the other. you may have to shift gears on different tacks to compensate for that factor.

Remember that when we speak of sailing a higher or lower course, it is relative to the "norm" of sailing at approximately 45-degree angles to the wind.

TUNING YOUR SAILS BY THE TELLTALES

We discussed in "Telltales" where to place telltales on both the jib and mainsail and how to set them and sail by them for going to weather.

Remember, both sails are trimmed to close-hauled and set so that the two sets of telltales on the jib and the top set on the main are all breaking the same and so that the back telltale on the main is not stalling.

If the back telltales on the jib are flowing aft but the upper back telltale on the mainsail is stalled, you need to ease your mainsheet a little until the telltale flows aft and matches the ones on the jib. Or else you need to head up a little until the main telltale stops stalling and then adjust the jib to conform.

STEERING THE FINE LINE

By now we have talked about every element on the boat but one — the human element. The most perfectly tuned boat, with the best equipment money can buy, will be no more successful without a good helmsman than will a race car with a bad driver or a horse with a bad jockey. Yep! We're talking again about that "loose nut on the tiller."

Learning to steer the boat with a sensitive touch and sail a fine line between a luff and a stall is a skill that must be developed. However, it is not some mystical thing that just happens. There are techniques to help get you in the "magic" groove where you sail exactly the right angle to the wind for maximum speed and maximum pointing ability.

Remember the chapter on "Telltales." To find that fine line all you need to do is pay close attention to what they are telling you. The jib is the most obvious and valuable guide for steering the boat to weather.

Once you have both sails set to one another, then all the skipper has to look at is the lower set on the jib and sail by them. First, they are in much easier view, and second, they are reacting the same way as are the telltales for the entire sail plan.

Now your object is to trust and concentrate on those telltales to steer the boat on the tightrope between a luff and stall.

As a quick review, if the front telltale (on the windward side) acts up, you are luffing and must steer farther off the wind (pull the tiller).

If the telltale on the back side (the leeward side) acts up, you are stalling and must steer closer or higher to the wind (push the tiller). But NEVER let that back telltale stall. It is far less damaging to keep the front one on just the edge of a luff (the telltale flying up or forward briefly every few seconds).

In lighter air you will be looking to keep both front and backside telltales flowing pretty well. But, as the wind picks up you will do better by allowing the front side telltales to act up a bit. And in heavy air, the front telltales will act up a lot. Usually in heavy air you can steer more by the hull — when the hull rises, you head up; when the hull settles down, drive off. Ideally, you want the windward hull just kissing the water all the time.

Once you find that area of steering that gets the boat going as close to the wind as possible and yet as fast as possible — not luffing, not stalling — then you have found that proverbial "sweet spot" that winning racers just seem to fall into.

With experience, you will be able to feel it when you're "in the groove," but until you get to that point, concentrate on those telltales — they will get you close enough.

I think of it rather like manually focusing a camera — you turn the lens one way, and it gets fuzzy, then the other way, and you get it in focus, but you're not sure it's totally in focus, so you turn too far and it's fuzzy again. Until you get the feel of where it's right on, you're going to be out of focus a little one way or the other.

You must concentrate and find that sweet spot.

The helmsman must also be aware of changes in wind velocity. If the wind suddenly gets lighter, the boat will slow down, and you will want to head a little bit lower and ease your jib a crack to open up the slot. When the wind picks up, you can again point higher and bring the jib in tighter. The reason for this is the stretch of the sailcloth.

If you are sailing along in light air and you get a puff, you will notice that the jib has suddenly become much farther away from the spreader and main than before. You should sheet in the jib slightly to compensate for that material stretching. Soon the wind drops down again. With the jib set in exactly the same spot you will notice that the jib is way too tight and the slot is closed off. Again, you must respond and ease the jib sheet a little.

A WORD ABOUT RUDDERS

It became a fad in 1980s to always pull up the windward rudder at all costs. And for the average sailor it costs a lot.

Advocates claim that the boat takes on a totally better feel, making the boat more responsive. The windward rudder is mostly out of the water anyway, if the wind is up, and therefore not as useful. You have also reduced wetted surface.

It's hard to argue with all that logic.

However, except for a few really awesome rudder-tackers that I have witnessed, most skippers take at least an extra 10 to 15 seconds to tack their boat in this manner.

Take our roll tack, for example. While you are initiating the tack you must move to the aft, windward corner while putting over the helm with steadily increasing pressure, and at the same time put down the rudder while not straightening out the helm. Although that could probably be done with lots of practice, it would be very difficult.

And now you have completed the tack. You should be exchanging the tiller, going forward, sheeting and steering off—all at the same time. Now, throw in the extra task of raising a rudder. You will have really slowed down the tack.

In Rick White's Sailing Seminars we used to get a lot of skippers who were tacking their rudders. They generally took anywhere from 20 to 30 seconds to tack from speed to speed. After we taught them how to roll tack and eliminate the rudder-tacking process, they cut their tacking times to around 5 to 7 seconds.

Just imagine, if a roll-tacking cat was going 10 feet per second, he would have gone 250 feet (25 seconds X 10 ft. = 250 ft) ahead of the rudder-tacking tack.

It just seems that a faster tack is worth more in the big picture than merely reducing a little wetted surface. By the way, the Tornado sailors have done some serious speed-testing on this issue and decided Tornadoes that sail with one rudder up are slower than those with two in the water.

But make your own choice.

SHIFTING GEARS

Here you are, off to a good start and everything is going well. But, the wind velocity changes. The next thing you know you are dogging around the tail-end of the fleet.

You may have noticed that some of your competition, no matter how heavy or how light, can just seem to walk away from most of the boats when the winds change. They probably know how to shift gears.

We talked earlier about flat, moderate and full sails. Well, now is the chance to use these three gears by adjusting sail shape on the water.

In the lower wind velocities you will most likely have your traveler centered, your downhaul just snug enough to have nice sailshape and a tight leech. The outhaul will always be all the way out in a sloop. With a unirig you may not have to have it out tight.

You probably will not be sheeting the main as hard in lighter air — after all, you are merely trying to hold the leech in to get the boat to point to weather better. Since the wind is light, there is very little force trying to push the leech of the sail off.

As the wind picks up, everything can usually stay about the same — you need only to trapeze. The wind will begin to blow the leech off a little, so you may want to sheet a little harder.

But, after you and your crew have both been trapping and the boat is still popping up, causing you to constantly be dumping the sheet and re-trimming, easing and trimming, and you seem to spend more time going up and down then going forward, you know that it is way past time to shift gears.

The best way to depower your sail is to flatten it out — particularly the top of your sail. The only way to flatten a sail is by bending the mast.

And the best way to accomplish that is by downhauling and/or sheeting the main. As the top of the sail flattens out, the wind blows the leech off at the top, spilling air to reduce heeling moment, while not sacrificing efficient shape in the remainder of the sail.

Why not just ease the sheet, causing the top of the sail to fall off? Because if you ease the sheet, the mast stands up straighter, making the sail fuller. This creates even more heeling moment. This also eases tension on the forestay and/or jib luff, causing the jib to sag off to leeward. When the forestay/luff sags to leeward you will definitely not be able to point the boat.

So, you begin the gear-shifting process of depowering by downhauling the mainsail. This bends the mast and loosens the tension on the leech of the sail. Now, when you sheet, the mast bends even more, and the upper leech falls off in the puffs.

Suppose the wind has increased still more and you have downhauled the mainsail to its maximum. Now do you ease the sheet? No! Now you ease the traveler, keeping the mainsheet tight.

You will be honking right along at this point and still flying a hull some. And you may have to ease the mainsheet a little now and then. But if your easing and trimming are in the form of armfuls, then your traveler is still too close to center — ease it out.

When the mainsheet trimming gets down to inches, or at least less than a foot in and out, then you just about have the right traveler adjustment.

Of course, you can still hit some holes in the wind patterns and you'll need to bring the traveler back in to get through them, but be prepared to ease it right back out when the wind comes back.

Through it all, you must keep the mainsheet tight. That is the secret to sailing fast to windward. And when you tack, it is an ABSOLUTE MUST that the mainsheet is tight all the way into the tack, until you are head to wind — and only then do you let out a foot or two of sheet.

So the order of changing gears is:
1) Trapeze, using all the sail power you can
2) Downhaul, flattening the sail to depower
3) Travel out, keeping the mainsheet tight

ROUNDING THE WEATHER MARK

It sounds as though it should be pretty easy to round the weather mark. All you have to do is pull on your tiller and turn the boat downwind. But it isn't always that easy. If your sails are still set for going to weather, the rudders will want to continue to go straight. You must let the sails help you make the turn. The driver must ease the mainsheet and quickly release the traveler as he makes the turn down. This eases the resistant pressure on the rudders and allows the boat to head down quickly. Observe the drivers that don't ease their travelers sometimes, particularly in heavy air — you'll see a roostertail of foam flying off their rudders. That is cavitation. The mainsail is trying to weathervane the boat into the wind, while the rudders are extremely angled to make the turn downwind. The two are fighting each other — it's another standoff.

Sure, the boat eventually turns, but it loses a lot of speed that otherwise could be bled off into a deeper and faster beginning of a downwind run.

A good way to ease the mainsail out quickly is to snap the traveler sheet out of the cleat prior to the rounding and hand-hold it. Then just as you make your final approach, snap the mainsheet out of the cleat and hand-hold both in the same hand. As you go around the mark just let them go and the boat will blast around that turn with great speed and ease.

The easing of the jib is not as critical, as it is helping turn the boat downwind. However, the crew should be reading the sail all the way, making sure there is no stall. Once it is eased to the normal off-the-wind position, then it is set and the driver can steer by it.

Then off you go on the downwind leg, or perhaps the reaching leg.

Notes to the crew:

   ✔ **Because the jib is set and cleated going to weather and only occasionally may need minor adjustments, the crew has little to do on this leg of the course, unless the skipper requires the crew to handle the mainsheet in heavy air.**

   Therefore, the crew is free to watch for wind shifts and puffs, note relationships to other boats, locate the weather mark, watch for boats on the opposite tack, and call laylines. This frees the skipper to concentrate on the telltales and keep the boat going fast. Think of the skipper as the driver and you as the navigator.

✔ Caution: When you are on starboard and a port boat is approaching, you do not want to always automatically hail "Starboard." Ask your skipper if you should hail. There are various situations where you do not want to cause the other boat to tack by hailing. For instance, your skipper may be planning to tack himself before the confrontation point is reached. Or he may have tactical reasons for wanting to actually slow down and pass behind the port-tack boat.

✔ Before getting to the weather mark, the crew should have located the next mark of the course — especially if it is the reaching mark — so the skipper will know what angle to sail after rounding onto the new leg.

DOWNWIND LEG
Chapter 12

It looks like it should be easy, but in actuality this is the most difficult point of sail for catamaran sailors to get the hang of. Most people can figure out how to go to weather respectably, if only by having the right sail shape, sheeting their sails in tight and going at about the same angle as everybody else. And usually boats stay fairly grouped going to weather, so you can see what other boats are doing and how their sails are set.

But once you go around that weather mark and head downwind, everyone spreads out all over the pond and you may not even be near another boat until you all begin converging again on the leeward mark.

Going downwind the tiller no longer has that nice solid feel it had going to weather — the rudder doesn't seem to be telling you anything about which way to steer the boat — you have no feeling of helm — the boat does not respond quickly when you turn the tiller. As a result, you may have a tendency to oversteer in an effort to get the boat to turn faster.

There is a much larger variation as to where you can set your sails on the downwind leg. Upwind you know within a narrow range how tight they should be — but downwind how loose should they be?

To make things easier to discuss, let's divide this into three parts:

1) Setting the boat up for downwind sailing
2) Helmsmanship
3) Rounding the leeward mark

SETTING UP FOR DOWNWIND SAILING

Going to weather, you were sailing with a relatively flat sail compared to what you need for the downhill ride. So now think "full." Your goal downwind is to make the sails as full as possible and eliminate as much wetted surface as possible to reduce underwater friction.

As you turn at the weather mark to head downwind, as discussed in "Weather Mark Rounding" in the "Weather Leg" chapter, you have released both traveler and mainsheet. Let the traveler go out to the inside edge of the hull and let the mainsheet go out until the main is as full as it can be without being indented against the sidestays. In other words, do not let the sail go out so far that there is a big crease where the sail touches the sidestay.

Stop turning at the point where the bridle fly or telltale is pointing at a 90-degree angle to the boat or slightly aft (in other words, pointing FROM slightly forward of 90 degrees).

The jib should be let out smoothly during the turn, keeping the telltales flowing and should then be set in a nice, full curve, without allowing the sail to belly out ahead of the forestay. The clew must be either held or barberhauled out as far as possible, so that the shape of the jib conforms to the shape of the main. (Note: If barber haulers are used, these must be pulled to their outer position DURING the weather mark rounding so the sail can immediately take its proper shape.)

Once the jib is preliminarily set, the skipper can sail by the bottom telltales and orient himself to his direction. The rounding and initial set of the sails and getting on course should only take a few seconds.

Then, and only then — when the boat is stabilized, the sails are set and the skipper is on course — begin making the other adjustments on the boat to improve downwind performance.

Sailing the boat is primary. All the adjustments in the world won't make any difference if the boat is going in the wrong direction or the sails aren't drawing.

For example, when is the last time you raised a daggerboard and went 10 percent faster? Never, I presume! However, if you used your speed around the weather mark and bled it off to a fast downwind direction, you could burst ahead of other boats by 5 or 10 boat lengths.

SECONDARY ADJUSTMENTS TO MAKE

1. Rotate the mast to 110 degrees, if possible, to improve air flow over the back of the main. Just like going to weather, the mast is actually the leading edge of the sail and must be rotated enough to both meet the wind at the proper angle and make a smooth transition between mast and sail.

2. Release the outhaul, to make the bottom of the sail fuller.

3. Release the downhaul, if possible, to make the whole sail fuller.

4. Pull up the boards.

A WORD ABOUT DAGGERBOARDS AND CENTERBOARDS

In most cases downwind you will want to raise your boards to reduce wetted surface. However, this does not necessarily mean you can pull them all the way up.

Most beachcats do not have board gaskets underwater to stop the water from coming up into the board trunk while the boards are up.

For those that do not have gaskets, pull your boards only high enough to reduce wetted surface drag, but not so high as to make a gap of any kind in the board trunk. For example, the Hobie 18 board is shaped so that if you pull the board clear of the water, you create a huge cavity in the board trunk — that produces more drag than you created by reducing wetted surface. In essence, you have created another stern drag — instead of having two sterns dragging and causing a fuss, you now have four.

For boats with gaskets, pull your boards totally clear. Gaskets are wonderful for keeping the bottom of the boat clean for smooth, undisturbed water flow. However, they are a pain in the neck to maintain.

Sometimes in a choppy, troubled sea, you may want a board down to make the steering easier — it provides an axis upon which to turn the boat quickly; and if the sea is slapping you back and forth, to and fro, you can control the yawing of the craft easier with a board down.

In heavy air you sometimes get so busy there just isn't time to get to the boards. Again, with the boards left in the down position, you will find that steering the boat is much easier and rudder helm is better (you have a pivot point on which to steer the boat). But two problems may pop up.

First, at extremely high speeds, the boards may cause air bubbles (cavitation) to hit the rudders. If nothing attaches to the rudder except the air, you will find the steering will go haywire — you may totally loose your steering altogether.

Second, the board offers an underwater resistance that allows the boat to raise a hull more quickly than with the boards up.

The best of both worlds would be nice, so raise the boards halfway, and you have a boat that steers fairly easily but has less tendency toward cavitation or hull flying.

Perfection would be to sail with the leeward board up, the windward board down; but in a really hairy blow, who has time for perfection?

HELMSMANSHIP

The boat is now set up for speed downwind, and it is up to the helmsman to get the most out of the boat. There are four more things the helmsman must do:

1. Decide the angle you are going to sail — high or deep.
2. Fine-tune the main and telltales for the angle you are sailing.
3. Steer the fine line between luff and stall.
4. Steer the wind and waves.

THE COURSE TO SAIL — HIGH OR DEEP

As in going to weather, the variety of winds and waves will make some difference to you in the manner and direction in which you steer the boat.

Also the boat itself will make a difference. You will find that the faster boats, such as the Tornado, Prindle 19, etc., are able to sail a little higher downwind, because they can develop enough speed to compensate for the greater distance sailed. The boats on the slower end of the catamaran scale will need to sail comparatively deeper. (As speed capability is reduced, shorter distance becomes more important.)

In light air and flat seas you have nothing stopping you from getting to the leeward pin, but there is also nothing helping you. You are best advised to head a bit higher than normal in these conditions. You must maintain boat speed.

If the seas were still flat and the wind came up a bit, you would find it is easy to go pretty deep — there is nothing trying to stop you and the wind is trying to help you.

Quite often you will get boat chop on a light air day that is quite disturbing — it stops the boat and shakes the sails. Again you want to sail a little higher than normal.

Still another scenario, when you have seas and heavy air, you should head somewhat deeper. Here you have the sea trying to push you down to the "C" mark anyway, so let it help you.

When the wind really starts blowing past the survival state, your boat cannot handle the speeds the winds are trying to create, anyway; and your best bet is to head extremely deep, nearly dead downwind (but watch out for the accidental jibe), and get way aft on the boat. The deep heading will allow the higher volume of buoyancy of both hulls to be used and will make the boat more stable.

Keep in mind that "relatively high" and "relatively deep" mean relative to sailing with your sterns at 45-degree angles to the true wind (just as upwind the bows sail at 45-degree angles to the true wind).

TUNING YOUR SAILS BY THE TELLTALES

In the chapter "Telltales" we discussed where to place telltales on the sail and how to use them to set the sails for downwind.

Just to quickly review: With your bridle telltale pointing at 90 degrees to the boat (or slightly aft or slightly forward, depending on the course chosen based upon the factors explained above), pull in the traveler until the bottom, backside telltale begins to stall. Then let the traveler out until that telltale begins to flow aft and cleat the traveler. Secondly, sheet the main until the upper backside telltale begins to stall, then ease the mainsheet until the back telltale is flowing aft and cleat the mainsheet.

Note: When jibing, do NOT uncleat either the traveler or the mainsheet. You have gone to the trouble of setting them perfectly on one tack — if you leave them alone, they will also be perfect on the other tack. (Review the jibing technique in Chapter 1, "Boat Handling.")

STEERING A FINE LINE

In the old days when catamarans were going wing-and-wing on the downhill leg like monohulls, this was the time to relax a little and watch the water go by.

But these days, there is no time to rest. All high-performance cats tack downwind, sailing at approximately 45-degree angles to the wind (or actually 135 degrees off the wind direction), just as they do in going to weather. *(See Diagram 29.)*

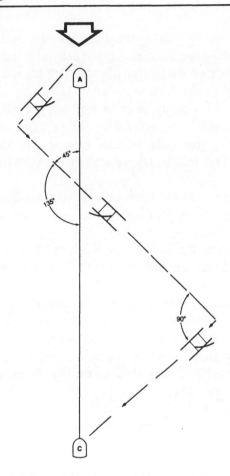

DIAGRAM 29

An example of tacking downwind to get from Mark A to Mark C.

By tacking downwind, you are using the cat's tremendous speed to create a forward-moving apparent wind. While the true wind is coming from a 135-degree angle aft of the bow, the apparent wind moves forward to 90 degrees aft of the bow.

The additional speed is more than enough to compensate for the additional distance covered. A straight line may be the shortest distance between two points, but it is not always the fastest. (Note: The Hobie 14 does very well by sailing straight downwind. And some Hobie 16 sailors will also do the same occasionally in extremely light air.)

Because we are tacking downwind, there is a "sweet spot" or groove that the helmsman must find, just as in tacking upwind. If you head too high, you will certainly be going fast, but you will be covering too much additional distance by not sailing deep enough toward the mark. If you head too low, your sails will stall and you will lose a tremendous amount of speed. You will be taking a shorter line to the mark, but much too slowly.

There is a small, finite line between heading too high and heading too low that makes your boat go fast and, at the same time, deep and toward the mark.

Just as on the weather leg, when tacking downwind you must have some way to tell you how to steer the boat through the fluctuations in the wind and stay in the groove.

The technique we recommend is basically the same as for going upwind: Set the sails for the course you want to steer, tune the telltales to each other, and then just use the jib as your primary guide. If the main is set and everything is properly flowing, and the jib is set to do the same, then all the telltales everywhere on the boat should luff at the same time, or stall at the same time.

Therefore, the driver needs only to look at the lower telltales on the jib and he is reading the entire sail plan at once.

If the back telltale acts up, head up; if the front telltale acts up, head down.

But the challenge is to never let that back one act up.

Here is the big "never" again: NEVER, NEVER let the sails stall! If anything, you would prefer a slight luff to a stall. Even the briefest stall really slows the boat down. I have heard aerodynamic experts say that a stalled sail operates at 100% efficiency — or basically the power you could expect from a barn door. As soon as the flow attaches on the backside of the sail, and the backside telltales begin to stream, the sail creates 180% efficiency. So, never let the sails stall. You want that extra 80 percent of power.

You can closely monitor the backside telltale of the jib and watch for it to barely begin to act up a bit. As soon as it does, head up — do not let it stall. A slight luff is far better than a slight stall.

If it is too hard to walk that thin line I just mentioned, stay toward the side of a small bit of luff. The luff is not nearly as damaging to your speed on the downwind leg as is a stall.

If the air is too heavy for the crew to hand-hold the jib on the leeward side, bring the crew to windward and aft, but still try to get the jib complementing the main as best you can, and endeavor to steer by the jib telltales. To get the jib in the best position will require the traveler to be set to the forequarter and out as far as possible, or barberhauled.

Because you lack other indicators that you have going to weather, like the pressure on the helm and the wind striking your cheek at just a certain angle, downwind sailing demands the skipper to really concentrate on reading the telltales in order to get the boat to perform well, sailing both deep and fast.

Another bonus to this technique of sailing downwind is the ability to pick out wind shifts easily. Since you are walking a thin line, you will immediately notice overall changes in your direction. Despite the oscillation of waves and the fact that you should be heading up for a bit of speed and falling off to drive it as deeply as possible, the overall direction will be much more noticeable than in another popular technique, which we will address next.

Some sailors, instead of setting their sails and sailing by the jib, use a telltale, which can be located either on the bridle or on the sidestay. The most popular device is the bridle fly, a feather or plastic wind vane mounted between the bridle stays and beneath the forestay.

In this technique, they keep the bridle fly or sidestay telltale pointing at 90-degrees to the boat and constantly sheet in and ease off in headers and lifts, puffs and lulls.

Some world-class sailors use this method very successfully; however, most are using the set-sail method described earlier.

We must point out that in the set-sail method, it is still imperative to have a telltale on the bridle or sidestay to make sure you are at approximately the right angle to the wind and for setting your sails to your course heading initially. It provides a general point of reference. But for following the lifts and headers, use the jib.

STEERING THE WIND AND WAVES

If you have waves helping you get down to the leeward mark, use them to your greatest advantage.

Here is where using the telltales on the jib will really pay off.

When you catch the front side of a wave, the boat will accelerate in its descent, and the jib telltales will show a luff, as the apparent wind moves forward. That is a great time to get a whole bunch deeper, by falling off until the jib is no longer luffing. But when you run out of wave and start trying to climb up the next wave, the boat will slow down considerably, and your telltales will show a drastic stall.

Before reaching that point on the next wave, anticipate what is going to happen and begin heading up at the slightest trace of a stall. As you see the bow approaching the next wave, head the boat up to a slight luff and be prepared to go even higher to maintain your speed and keep out of a stall. A stall will kill you! You will have lost all you gained running down the backside of the last wave, and you will sit wallowing in the trough.

ABOUT THE RUDDERS

If you like to sail with only one rudder, there are times you will find that one blade just doesn't cut it — you may try to turn to catch a wave and the rudder will stall. You quite often may require both rudders to gain better steering — and accurate steering is the secret for sailing downwind.

ROUNDING THE LEEWARD MARK

PREPARE FOR THE MARK ROUNDING.

All the things that you did to get your boat to go fast downwind will hinder you while going to weather, so they must undone. And you certainly don't want to wait until you are rounding the mark to do these things. And you most certainly don't want to do them while you are going to weather.

Depending upon the wind conditions and how fast you are traveling, when you are 10 to 20 boat lengths from the mark, you should put down your daggerboards, tighten your downhaul, tighten your outhaul, move your jib leads back (if they were moved forward), release your barber haulers, set your mast rotation limiter for going to weather, and hook up your trapeze. The last thing to do is center the traveler.

By the time you enter the two-boat-length circle, the crew should be on the windward side, both skipper and crew should be hooked to their trapeze wires. There should be nothing left to do but steer and sheet in.

Taking care of all the adjustments well before the mark is not going to slow you down enough to matter for that short a distance, and it pays big dividends in assuring a good mark rounding. Can you picture making a good mark rounding amongst 10 shouting competitors — and here you are still putting down boards, pulling the downhaul, and the outhaul — all while trying to steer and sheet? There is no way!

ENTER WIDE; EXIT CLOSE

This caution is explained more in depth in the downwind leg tactics section of the "Tactics" chapter. However, we repeat it here, because although it is a tactical rounding, it is what you should strive to do every time you round the leeward mark.

Instead of heading directly at the mark, try heading for a point 20 feet to the right of the mark and start your turn there, so that when you pass the mark, you are already hard on the wind. This tactical rounding gets you closer upwind and puts you in a better position tactically on the boats ahead of you and behind you.

Hint for a Faster Rounding:

Just as the key to making a fast turn onto a downwind course is to release the main quickly, the key to making a fast turn up to weather is getting the mainsail in fast — the faster it comes in, the faster the boat can round up and go to windward. You must sheet hand over hand, which means you do not have a hand for the tiller. Most people deal with this by tucking it under their butt while they are pulling in the sheet.

☞**CAUTION: DO NOT sheet in tight BEFORE you get to the mark. What happens if the sail is brought in tight? You stall the mainsail — you lose 80% of your power. You must sheet in as you are heading up to the close-hauled course.**

Notes for the crew:

✔ **Once the mainsail is set, the crew should hold the jib in a set position, complementing the mainsail, and should keep that shape in a constant position, whether hand-held or barberhauled. The crew can keep the upper and lower telltales breaking evenly by slightly raising or lowering the clew to maintain an even sail shape from top to bottom, but do not move the clew forward or back without being told to do so by the skipper or without notifying the skipper you are doing it.**

✔ If your skipper sails by the bridle fly or telltale rather than by the jib, he may want you to play the jib downwind, adjusting it in and out in reaction to changes in the telltales. Be aware of which downwind sailing technique your skipper uses.

✔ As in sailing to weather, the crew can help by watching for boats on other tacks, watching for puffs and wind shifts, keeping an eye on the leeward mark, noting changes in relative positions with other boats and calling the lay line. (Note: If the crew is hand-holding the jib, it may be difficult to watch for puffs, as you are facing forward, and the puffs will come from astern when you are going downwind.)

✔ If you normally hand-hold the jib, you will not be able to do so in very heavy air. Instead, move your jib leads all the way forward and/or out, cleat the jib, and move your weight to windward and aft. Just remember to move your jib leads back again before getting to the leeward mark, so they will be ready for going to weather.

✔ For jibing technique, see "Boat-Handling."

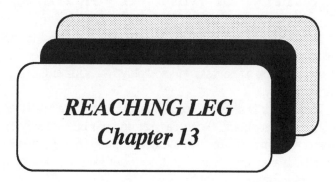

REACHING LEG
Chapter 13

For catamarans, races are won or lost on the weather and downwind legs — the trip to the B mark usually is the "yahoo" leg, the speed contest — a parade with few places changing.

But first let's talk about the elusive and often unpredictable location of the B mark.

The race committee always attempts to situate the A mark directly upwind from the starting line and attempts to situate the C mark directly downwind from the starting line and, therefore, directly downwind from A mark. If the course has been set square to the wind and stays that way, it is relatively easy to orient yourself to the positions of those two marks and find them.

But unless the race committee has already specified the angles between the marks and must adhere to that configuration, the B mark can be located almost anywhere over there on the left side of the course as you face upwind.

This obviously will affect the angle you want to sail when you round the weather mark to head for B. So it is imperative to know the position of the B mark BEFORE you get to A. If you cannot see it and do not know whether it has been set high or low, follow the boats ahead of you or, if you are in the lead, stay slightly above the boats that round behind you but if they are all going deeper, you head deep with them. Stay on approximately the same angle as the pack, but slightly above them — and keep looking for the mark.

SETTING UP THE BOAT FOR THE REACH

If it is a close reach to the B mark, you will need to make very few adjustments. Just ease the sheets a little, keep the traveler centered, move your weight back as necessary, and "play" the sails, adjusting them in and out as necessary.

If the mark is set very deep so that you are on a broad reach, with the apparent wind at about 90 degrees, set up your boat exactly as if you were sailing downwind. If you are laying the mark comfortably, you will play your sails. If you are not laying it, set your sails and sail by them exactly as you would on the downwind leg.

If it is somewhere between a close reach and a beam reach, ease your traveler out just until the lower, backside telltale begins to flow, and cleat the traveler. You will be playing the mainsheet to keep the upper backside telltale from stalling. As described in "Telltales," the traveler setting is dictated by the lower set of telltales on the main, and the mainsheet tension is dictated by the upper set of telltales.

Leave the boards down and the outhaul tight unless it is a broad reach.

The jib will mimic the main. The deeper the reach, and the more the main is eased, the looser the jib will be sheeted so the top can twist off and conform to the shape of the main. Ideally, the deeper the reach, the more forward and outboard the jib leads will be moved.

HELMSMANSHIP

We already know that for sailing both upwind and downwind in catamarans, the straight line is not the fastest way to get between A and C marks. However, for the reach, the straight line is both the shortest and the fastest way to get to the B mark (unless it is set so deep you must tack downwind).

Therefore, the helmsman's job is to steer as straight a course as possible to the mark. Now you will NOT be steering by the sails and the telltales; instead, you will be adjusting the sails in and out to accommodate wind shifts, lulls, puffs, and changes in apparent wind speed and direction.

The jib and main will need to be constantly adjusted, and neither should be cleated at any time on a reach.

Doing this well on a sloop rig involves team coordination and intense concentration. When the telltales stall, let the sails out; when they luff, bring them in. (AS ALWAYS, TRY TO NEVER LET THEM STALL.) Because the wind velocity and angle changes are sometimes too rapid to keep up with, it can help to keep the windward telltales acting up, just on the edge of a luff, to avoid ever getting to the point of a stall.

Weight distribution also is important in maintaining boat attitude with the sudden changes in wind velocity and direction. The crew must be alert and move quickly to keep the boat balanced.

Because the sails develop their greatest speed and power on a reach, this is the point of sail where the boat cannot always go as fast as the sails and is in danger of tripping over its bows (pitchpoling).

When a puff hits and the bows suddenly dive, three things can be done, either separately or in concert:

First, ease the jib as much as necessary to allow the bows to come back up.

Second, ease the main to reduce pressure on the bows even more.

Third, change the course of the boat, and whether you head the boat up or head down depends on the reach's basic angle to the wind. If you are on a fairly close reach, head the boat up to spill air. If you are on a beam reach or deeper, head the boat down in a puff to flatten the boat out so you will have the extra buoyancy of both bows in the water.

A very good rule for reaches is never to cleat the sheets in heavy air. That extra moment of trying to snap the sheet out of the cleat may be just the moment that sends you into the drink.

In addition, by not being cleated, you have a definite "feel" of the power of the wind in the sail, and you can react immediately to that "feel." When a hard puff hits you, you will already have felt its advance thrust and begun easing the sheet.

By not cleating the sheets and by feeling the wind, you have reduced the possibility of capsize; you keep the boat in the proper attitude; and you keep her moving forward at optimum speed.

Often you will find the wind trying actually to trick you. You are reaching along when the wind swings to a header and dies a little. You probably sheet in and head down a bit. It then eases more and swings still more. You harden up still more, head down more, and maybe even start coming in off the trapeze.

And then ... WHAMMO! The wind slaps you hard from its original direction in a tremendous gust, blasting the sail at an angle too far perpendicular to give you thrust — only heeling moment. Hope the mainsheet was not cleated! Hope the jib sheet was not cleated, either!

You want to keep the boat at the proper attitude, as discussed in Chapter 2, "Weight Distribution." Flying a hull or diving a bow destroys forward speed and puts you in a position of possible calamity.

On a screaming reach, maintaining proper boat attitude may require you to have all crew weight as far back on the aft windward corner as possible. On most reaches it is more important for weight to be back than to be outboard, so one way to do it is to have the skipper stay on the boat and the crew trapeze behind him. (If both skipper and crew trapeze side by side, the crew's weight can easily be too far forward — especially if the crew is heavy.) Another advantage to the skipper staying on the boat is that the crew can hold onto the skipper to keep from being thrown forward if the bows dive.

There are going to be times when you cannot react in time to save the hull from going up. If it starts flying, ease both the main and jib sheets until the ascent stops; then as the hull begins to descend, sheet in. This will give the boat a great surge forward, much like squeezing the seed out of a grape.

Your object is to catch the rise of the hull and, by quickly easing the sheets, stop the ascent. Do not let the boat get up on its ear. Getting the boat up high on its side is opening the door for still another puff to knock it completely over; besides that, you will have absolutely no speed.

But you don't want to ease the sheets so quickly or radically that the boat drops hard to the water like a lead balloon and loses all its forward momentum.

Notes for the Crew:
✔ **The reach is your big chance to be a star and work to get the most out of the jib. If your skipper sails by the jib upwind and downwind, all you basically need to do is set it and cleat it. But on a reach you never cleat it — you play it constantly in and out in response to what the telltales are telling you.**

✔ **The jib is the advance man, the scout, the leader. It will catch the changes in direction and velocity a fraction before the main does. When you react to correct the jib, the skipper will be alerted to correct the main.**

✔ Remember that you adjust the sail by moving it toward the telltale that acts up.

✔ You have the additional challenge of being the primary person in control of weight distribution and balancing the boat. Because the skipper must concentrate on steering a straight course and watching other boats and must stay relatively toward the back of the boat as a counterbalance for puffs, you must move forward and back and, if necessary, out on the trapeze. The best way to concentrate on where your weight should be is to watch an imaginary line on the bow where it cuts through the water, and try to keep the water kissing that line. If the water gets above that line, move back; if the water gets below that line, move forward.

✔ On the reach you do not look around, you do not look at other boats. You must have tunnel vision and look constantly up at the telltales and down at the bow — trim the sails and trim the boat attitude. A momentary lapse in concentration can result, at best in lost speed and, at worst, in capsize.

✔ On a close reach, you can usually leave your jib traveler setting the same as for going to weather. But if you are on a beam reach or deeper, move your jib leads forward and/or outboard to open up the slot between jib and main.

✔ When trapezing on a reach, you will be much farther back on the boat than normal, and this can result in a couple of problems. Number one, if you are unable to easily adjust the height of your trapeze ring, you may have trouble getting back far enough. Number two, your trapeze wire is going to be tending to pull you forward, already putting you slightly off balance, and if the bows dive, the sudden deceleration will also try to throw you forward, so brace yourself well with your forward leg. If the skipper stays on the boat, you can use his trapeze wire, if necessary, which will reach better to the back of the boat. And you can trapeze behind the skipper, with one foot on each side of him, and hold onto his life jacket to keep from being thrown forward.

If you play your sails better than the other boats and if you concentrate better than the other teams, you can gain a lot of ground on a reach (although it is difficult to actually pass people, as we will discuss in Chapter 16, "Tactics").

ROUNDING THE REACHING MARK

PREPARE FOR THE MARK ROUNDING.

Your preparations will depend upon two things: The angle you were sailing from A to B, and the angle you will be sailing from B to C. These also will determine whether you make your adjustments before or after you round the B mark.

If A to B is a close reach, it means you will then be sailing very deep from B to C. On the close reach your boat is set up basically the same as for going to weather. Therefore, you will wait until you round the B mark and then proceed with making the adjustments for sailing downwind, as described in "Setting up for Downwind Sailing" in Chapter 12, "Downwind Leg."

On the other hand, if A to B was a very deep reach, the reach from B to C will be a close reach. In this case, you will begin making adjustments BEFORE getting to the mark to set up your boat as though going to weather (described in Chapter 12, "Preparing for the Mark Rounding" in "Downwind Leg.")

Tactical considerations and techniques for this mark rounding are covered in Chapter 16, "Tactics."

THE FINISH
Chapter 14

J ust as you found out all there was to know about the starting line before the start, you should find out everything you can about the finish line long before you cross it. How many times have you heard the story about someone losing seven boats right at the finish line? Chances are he wouldn't have lost any boats had he done his homework.

The finish line is a bit easier than the starting line though. Here, all you need to know is 1) the Favored End and 2) the Favored Tack.

FAVORED END

The favored end of the finish line is the end of the line that is farthest away from the wind, or closest to downwind. *(See Diagram 30.)* (If it will be a beat to the finish line, as it normally is, the favored end has nothing to do with the position of the leeward mark in relation to the finish line.)

You need to know the favored end at the finish for the same reason you need to know it for the start — if you finish there, you will sail a shorter distance than people who finish at the opposite end.

You may ask, "How can I tell which end is favored after I round the leeward pin?"

If you are at the leeward pin, it is very difficult to tell which is the favored end unless it is pretty radically angled.

But, let us say that the Race Committee has not changed the line and is using the starting line for the finish line. Then, if the wind direction has not changed, the end that was favored at the start will be the unfavored end for the finish. For example, if the port end was favored for the start, then the starboard end will be favored for the finish. The end that is farthest upwind is favored at the start, so the end that is farthest downwind is favored at the finish.

Quite often you will find that the RC will shorten and change the finish line. Then what do you do?

An excellent time to check the line is while on your way past the finish line on your downwind leg.

The easiest way to figure out the favored end as you are going by the line is by figuring out what will be the favored tack at the finish.

The favored tack is the one which will cross the line most perpendicular to it. And the favored end will always be the opposite of the favored tack, in terms of port and starboard. *(See Diagram 30.)*

To figure it out by this technique, you must understand that whichever tack you are on downwind, if you come back to weather on that same angle, you will be on the opposite tack. So, for example, if you pass near the starting line going downwind on starboard tack, that same angle (but 180 degrees in the opposite direction), is what you would be sailing back to weather on port tack.

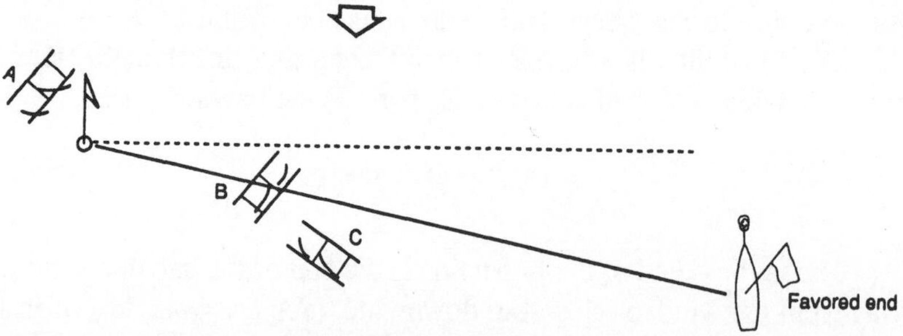

DIAGRAM 30

The dotted line is perpendicular to the wind, indicating that the starboard end is farthest away from the wind and thereby the favored end to finish. Boat A is sailing downwind on starboard tack. As he passes the finish line, it is apparent that his heading is almost perpendicular to the finish line. If starboard tack is most perpendicular downwind, port tack will be most perpendicular upwind, as indicated by Boat B. This means port is the favored tack to finish on and the starboard end of the line is the favored place to finish. Unfortunately, in this example Boat B is finishing at the unfavored end of the line, although he is on the favored tack. Boat C is even worse off—he is finishing on the unfavored (starboard) tack and at the port end of the line.

Therefore, as you are sailing past the line downwind, note which downwind tack is most perpendicular to the line. The opposite tack will be most perpendicular when going to weather, and that will be the favored tack to finish. But the favored end of the finish line will be the opposite of the favored tack.

NOTE: When you are starting, the favored tack (most perpendicular to the line) is the SAME as the favored end, in terms of port and starboard. If, in starting, you cross the line most perpendicularly on starboard, starboard is the favored end to start. However, when you finish, the favored tack is the OPPOSITE of the favored end in terms of port and starboard.

INSIDE AND OUTSIDE LAYLINES

Then there are those Olympic Gold Cup courses where they start you at the leeward pin and finish you at the weather pin. There is absolutely no way to determine ahead of time which end is favored.

In this case you want to tack to the inside laylines, rather than the outside laylines.

Because the finish line has two ends to it, there are actually four laylines involved *(See Diagram 31.)* When we know the favored end of the line, the most common approach is to go to the outside layline for that mark and tack on the layline.

When you do not know the favored end, you can sail the inside layline toward one end of the finish line. When you reach the point where the other end of the line is directly abeam — the "moment of truth" — you are at the point where the two inside laylines cross. Decide at that point which of the two laylines is shortest and take that route to get to the favored end. If the shorter line will require you to tack, consider your tacking time in calculating whether the shorter distance will pay off.

FAVORED TACK

The favored tack, as we have already explained, is simply the tack that crosses the finish line at the most perpendicular angle. *(See Diagram 30.)*

You can figure out the favored tack with the systems we have already talked about in "Favored End."

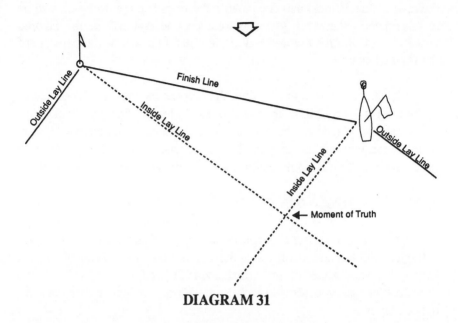

DIAGRAM 31

You may say, "So what? What difference does it make which tack I cross the line on, as long as I go to the favored end?"

But there is a BIG difference. If you are racing one-design and there is not another boat in sight, fine, finish backward if you want to. But in normal racing situations, the concept of the favored tack is extremely important.

For example, and I have seen this happen too many times: The line is heavily port-tack-favored, which automatically means it is starboard-end-favored. The boat in the lead has the race in the bag and tacks just short of the starboard-end layline. Meanwhile the second place boat is coming in on port tack to the same starboard-end layline. The leader hails "starboard" and continues on down the line, knowing he will cross pretty soon. The second place boat replies, "Hold your course," slows down a bit until the leader is clear, and sheets in, accelerating across the line on the favored tack, and for a victory. *(See Diagram 32.)*

Notice that the port boat did not want to turn and bear off behind the starboard boat. Had he done so, he would not have made the finish line. Ah Yes! Ye olde "Slow down to win" slogan again.

Countless times I have seen a boat lose many places, not just one, simply by ignoring the favored tack.

Finish p.6
Favored end taken wins

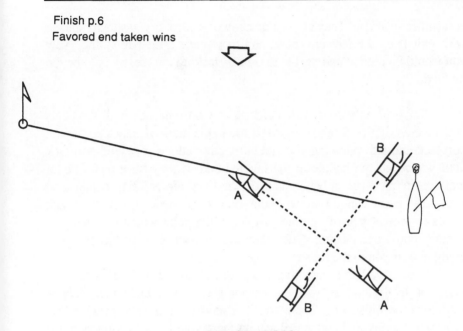

DIAGRAM 32

Boat A exercises his starboard rights and continues to the finish line on the unfavored tack. Boat B crosses behind Boat A, sails a shorter distance to the finish line on the favored tack and wins the race.

Let's say you are not racing one-design, but are racing on Portsmouth handicaps. It is easy to get complacent when you are not racing boat for boat. But whether you owe time to the other boats or whether they owe time to you, every second counts. And if you take 20 extra seconds to get across that finish line, it could mean the difference between a trophy and the cheering section.

So be aware of the Favored Tack.

TACTICS GOING TO THE FINISH

DEFENSE

1) If you are in the lead (or in any position defending against boats behind), it is imperative to make a good mark rounding at the leeward mark by entering wide and exiting close. This gives you a higher line going to weather so boats rounding behind you will not be able to get above

you and control you. They are in a position of control if you should make a wide exit from the leeward mark, and they made a tight rounding. Now you would be pinned and unable to tack — tacking too close would be the problem.

2) If your only concern is defense, stay on port tack until the boats you are covering or defending against round the mark. If they also stay on port tack and are following you and not getting above you, hold port tack until you reach the layline to the favored end. If they have had a better mark rounding or get a better shaft of wind and are pointing higher than you to the point where they will soon be controlling you, you must tack across to protect yourself before you get to the point where they are preventing you from tacking. Once they are in control, they are probably going to beat you to the finish.

If you have had to tack to protect yourself and if the other boat continues on to the layline, you will be doing two more tacks than they in getting to the finish line. Therefore, it is now even more imperative that you go to the favored end and finish on the favored tack, saving as much distance as possible to make up for the two extra tacks.

3) What do you do if the boats you are defending against tack right after they round the mark or at some point before they get to the layline? Tack to cover them. You (or your crew if you have one) should be watching the boats behind you like a hawk. If they tack, you tack immediately. Go across on the other tack until you are laying the favored end of the finish line. Again, watch the other boat(s) like a hawk. If they start to tack first, you tack at the same time. If they have not yet tacked when you are comfortably laying the favored end, tack before they do and go for it.

CAUTION: You had better be sure of the favored end if you are going to tack before the other boat. If you are going for the wrong end and they hold their tack until they are laying the favored end, they could still beat you.

NOTE: If you are only defending against one boat and have no other boats to worry about, you can afford to continue going with that one boat and tack at the same time.

4) If you have a starboard-favored line, with a port-tack-favored finish, you can still come in on the right layline. Just as you get to the starboard end of the line, head up sharply to push the bow across the line, even if you go head to wind. Then immediately bear back off onto star-

board. You are finished if any part of your boat crosses the line. The entire boat need not cross to be finished.

That is one way to beat that port tacker coming in at the starboard pin. You know you cannot tack in front of the port boat because you would be tacking too close. However, you have not tacked until you are past head to wind. That is why you must not go past head to wind and then you must bear off back to starboard. On starboard you have rights. Tacking too close you do not have rights. (Using this technique of stuffing your bows over the line can also shave seconds when you are racing on Portsmouth.)

OFFENSE

1) If you are behind at the leeward mark and your goal is to beat the boats ahead of you, it is just as imperative to have a superlative C-mark rounding by entering wide and exiting close. If you can make a great mark rounding and take a higher line to weather than the boats ahead of you, you may be able to control them all the way to the layline and/or beyond it.

If you rounded the leeward pin in second and you had a good mark rounding, you will find that you are behind, but to windward of the lead boat. *(See Diagram 33.)*

You are in a position of controlling from behind. Of course, you may be getting backwinded and could slip down behind that boat, in which case the tactical picture changes for you.

However, if you hold that position and work up to a point where your air is fairly clear, you can run the leader way out past the layline before you tack. You see, the leader cannot tack in front of you, so he has to wait until you tack.

The secret, in this case, is don't tack right on the layline — you must carry the leader well past the layline so that you will both be reaching back to the finish line.

The other thing that happens here is that since you are in control over when you are going to allow the other boat to tack, you can tack first and get boat speed up while the other boat is still going even farther beyond the layline before they can execute their tack. You are off and going, at an angle that takes you a shorter distance, while they are tacking and then having to make up even more extra distance than you do.

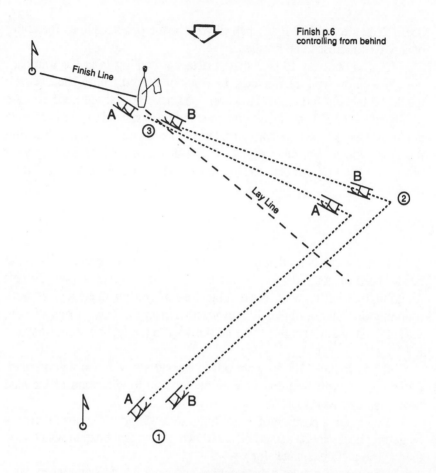

DIAGRAM 33

CAUTION: If you have lots of boats trying to catch you, this tactic of carrying the leader beyond the layline will not work, as you will end up losing the boats behind you. This is an offensive move that must be tempered by using intelligent defense against those behind you.

ANOTHER CAUTION: The leader might try driving off a lot. He is trying to make room to tack. Don't let him. Drive off with him. If you let him get away you are no longer controlling from behind. It would be silly for you to sail close to the wind, letting the leader drive off and tack only to come at you on starboard and be on the layline as well. You would be dead meat!

2) But let's say you don't get a superlative mark rounding. You are either following right behind or slightly to leeward of the boats ahead of you. This is a no-win situation. If possible, and as rapidly as possible, tack out of there. If you get out into clear air and if you know the favored end and the favored tack, you still have a chance of picking off the leaders. If you stay in your follow-the-leader position on port tack, you will probably finish in that position or maybe even lose places to boats behind you that do tack onto starboard. They will have clear air, while you are floundering along in bad air all the way to the finish.

'FOR WHAT IT'S WORTH' DEPARTMENT

1) Never finish in the middle of the line. Always finish at the favored end and on the favored tack, if at all possible. The shorter the line, the less important the favored end may be, but it still is important. However, even if you don't know the favored end, or there is no favored end, or whatever, finish at one end or the other, even if it is the wrong end.

Somewhere along the line, someone told me the psychology of the RC was that in a three-way tie, the first place would go to the boat finishing closest to the RC, the second place would go to the boat finishing right at the port end, and the last boat considered would be the boat in the middle of the line. I have nothing to substantiate this claim, but it certainly makes sense.

2) The distance from the leeward mark to the finish is usually relatively short, so the time it takes you to tack is a major factor in your tactical decisions. If you can avoid throwing in two extra tacks on this short leg, do so. Only do those two extra tacks if necessary to protect your lead against boats behind you or if you have nothing to lose.

As we said at the beginning of the Chapter 11, "The Start," a lot of things can happen between the start and finish of a race — and a lot of positions can change on that home stretch between the last mark and the finish.

WIND SHIFTS
Chapter 15

The best-laid tactical plans can backfire if the wind gods are not on your side. And they don't take bribes — I know because I've tried.

When you go to a chalkboard session on tactics at one of our Rick White's Sailing Seminars, the wind always blows from the top of the board. Unfortunately, it is not usually that cooperative on a real race course. In actuality, the wind never blows from the same direction at all times and on all parts of the race course.

On a given race course the wind can vary tremendously, not only in direction but in velocity as well. You have probably heard frustrated skippers lamenting a day's racing with comments like, "I was out of synch with the wind all day," or "Would you believe Sam and I were going to weather on identical headings, and we were on opposite tacks?" or, "I think I found every hole out there today."

The variable velocities of the wind will often make one side of the course faster than the other. Sometimes the wind will seemingly bestow its favors on one boat while the others sit bobbing in the water.

The two factors that cause sailors all this happiness and grief are WIND SHIFTS and PUFFS.

Wind shifts are variations in direction, while puffs are brief increases in wind velocity usually caused by a gust of wind dipping down to earth from a higher altitude.

This chapter will discuss lifts and headers; the three major types of wind shifts; and the basic dynamics of a puff.

But before we get into the whims of our God-given wind, let us first describe a type of wind shift and wind velocity that is self-induced — apparent wind.

APPARENT WIND

Apparent wind is the wind created by movement through space. You have your boat parked with the wind coming across the boat at 90 degrees, sails out, parked, and you are not moving. Your telltale on the sidestay will show the true wind is blowing at 90 degrees to your hulls.

Now, you pull in the jib and main and off you go, straight ahead and in the exact same direction the boat had been pointing — that is, at an angle of 90 degrees across the true wind.

Look up at the telltale and you will see it flying toward the leeward, aft quarter of the boat. Yet the true wind is still blowing the same direction. You can't see it blowing in the same direction, but you know it still is.

The telltale says the wind appears to be blowing from in front of you now. And it appears to be blowing harder. As you move through the true wind, the apparent wind will always come from more ahead, and with more speed. The apparent wind is the wind that appears to you or is visible to you through your telltales. It is also the wind that you set and trim your sails by.

If you stop the boat again, sails out, parked, you will find that the true wind is where it was before, at 90 degrees angle to the boat. Now the true wind and the apparent wind are the same —because you are not moving.

We all know that most boats sail upwind at approximately 45-degree angles to the wind. A sailor who does not understand the concept of apparent wind might understandably think that he is going the right direction if he just keeps his bridle fly or side telltales pointing back at a 45-degree angle. In actuality, if your telltales are pointing at 45 degrees to the boat, you are more likely sailing at 70 or 80 degrees to the true wind. This could explain why some sailors have difficulty getting to the weather mark — they are reaching back and forth.

The stronger the wind and the faster you are going, the more aft your telltales will flow. It will sometimes appear as if you are sailing almost straight into the wind. But this is the apparent wind. You are still sailing at about a 45-degree angle to the true wind.

The lighter the wind and the slower you are going, the closer your side telltales or bridle fly will come to reflecting the true wind. But as long as there is forward motion of your boat through the air, that motion will produce an apparent wind effect.

HEADERS AND LIFTS

These two terms relate to changes you must make in your boat direction in response to changes in the wind direction. They are the primary means by which we can identify wind shifts and the direction of the shifts.

A lift means the wind has shifted more aft or behind you and will make you sail a course higher than your previous course. A header, on the other hand, means the wind has shifted around more in front of you and will make you steer a course lower than your previous course. When going to weather, this will translate into: A lift lets you sail more directly toward the weather mark; a header will make you sail farther away from the weather mark.

When going downwind, the reverse is true, because a lift will take you farther away from the leeward mark and a header will take you closer.

Some sailors have a difficult time ascertaining whether they are on a lift or a header. The most obvious way to tell that you are on a lift or header is by noticing a change in your steering direction. If you have been steering toward a smokestack on shore and now notice that you are steering well below that stack, then you are on a header. Conversely, if you begin steering higher than the stack, you are on a lift.

One of the best ways is to relate yourself to other boats. When you are sailing a lift, you will appear to have gained on boats below you and fallen behind boats above you. When you are sailing a header, you will appear to be falling behind boats below you and gaining on boats above you. A grid is the easiest way to show this. *(See diagram 34.)*

Another way, which I do not recommend highly, is to sail by compass points. A compass is fine on a long-distance race and when you are out of sight of land or other boats (or in fog), but trying to watch a compass while concentrating on steering your boat is difficult and distracting.

Whatever your method, though, be aware of wind shifts by being aware of your course direction at all times — know at any given time whether you are sailing a lift or a header.

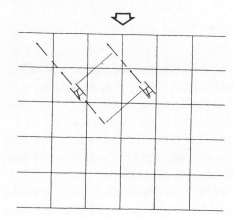

DIAGRAM 34

With the wind straight on to the grid, neither of these boats has an advantage in position over the other.

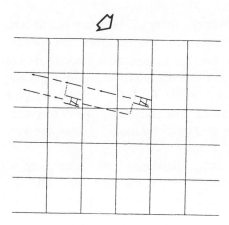

In this diagram the wind has shifted to the left on the grid, a header, giving the boat on the left a decided advantage and a sizeable lead.

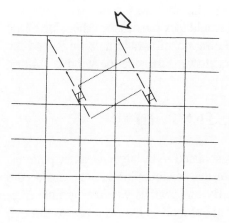

Here the wind has shifted to the right, a lift, giving the boat on the right a decided advantage and lead.

THE OSCILLATING SHIFT

Oscillating shifts swing back and forth across a mean direction. For example, if the mean wind is basically east or 90 degrees, oscillations may swing to 80 degrees and back to 90 degrees and then clock to 100 degrees and back. But the mean direction of the wind is still 90 degrees.

You have probably always heard that you should tack on headers and hold the lifts. That is a great idea in oscillating wind shifts. In that way you will sail a shorter course to the weather mark. *(See diagram 35.)*

Whether to take advantage of tacking the headers in this way depends on two things: The degree of oscillation and the length of time between them.

At any given time on any race course, there will be minor oscillations of a few degrees back and forth, which means you are almost always sailing either a small header or a small lift. The directional variations are not great enough to warrant the time and distance you will lose by tacking. The same thing applies to the timing of the shifts. If the wind is swinging back and forth every minute or so, by the time you tack, you will be on another header and will not have benefited much by the brief time you were on a lift.

In fast boats like catamarans an oscillating shift that takes 5 or 10 minutes to shift back will appear very much like a persistent shift. The slower monohull boats would play the same shift as an oscillater, while the cat might play it as a persistent shift.

In this case, in other words, if the shift was a lift, the monohull would hold on it and the catamaran would tack over to the other side of the course. If the shift was a header, the monohull would tack on it, and the catamaran would maintain his course toward the side the wind is shifting to.

THE PERSISTENT SHIFT

Persistent shifts usually are associated with larger weather patterns. For example, if you were sailing in the Miami, Florida area and a cold front was coming, the normal easterly trade winds would begin clocking toward the south, and keep going right around as the front passes through the area. It would swing to northwest and continue clocking as the front moves out until it settles back into its normal easterly air flow. That phenomenon creates a persistent shift.

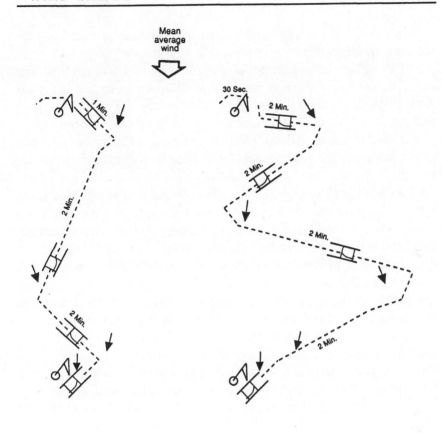

DIAGRAM 35

The boat on the left and the boat on the right start on the same tack at the same time with the same mean wind (the lowest black arrows). Both boats get a header, indicated by the next arrows up. The left boat tacks, while the right boat holds the headed wind shift. Two minutes later the next wind shift, indicated by the third set of arrows, gives the left boat a header, so he tacks back to port, while the right boat tacks and sails the new wind shift as a header. In another two minutes the next set of arrows indicate a shift to the right. The left boat tacks on that header and makes the mark. Meanwhile, the right boat is way behind. The left boat has simply sailed a shorter distance.

Normally, in that circumstance, the weather forecast would call for southeast winds, switching to southwest by a given time.

Out on the race course, this means you want to stay to the right side of the course most of the time, for the wind will continue to shift in that direction, giving boats on the right side of the course the advantage. They will get a header, and when they tack, they will be on a lift to the mark.

However, the wind doesn't just swing steadily to the right. In the real world, it will oscillate while gradually working its way in its persistent direction.

Another good example of a persistent wind shift is a thunderstorm approaching from the left side of the course. Normally a lot of wind will come from the direction of a storm. That is why you will hear sailors say they head toward the storms — more wind and it will be in their favor.

In the case of the storm on the left side of the course, you will get a large counterclockwise veering of the wind, and a huge lift on port tack to get you to the weather mark. The storm will offer a persistent shift to the left. However, perhaps the next time you go up the weather the leg the storm will have gone somewhere else, so don't necessarily head back to the left side of the course unless the storm is still there.

You always want to be on the side from where the wind shift comes. That position puts you on the inside of the wind wheel. *(See Diagram 36.)*

When the shift is persistent, you must forget the law of "tack on headers and hold the lifts." If you started out toward the left side of the course, the persistent shift to the right would allow you to sail on lifts for a long time — almost completely around the weather mark. They call that "The Great Circle Route." If you hold on the lift, you will never get to the mark.

So, when you see the persistent shift happening and you keep getting lifted and the header never comes, you are in deep doo doo. It is time to bite the bullet, take your lumps, do a stitch in time, or any other trite cliche. In other words, get to the side of the course that is getting the persistent wind shift. You will have already lost a lot of boats, but you will beat all the boats that kept holding the persistent lift.

There is a saying, ". . .if the wind goes right, go right, if the wind goes left, go left."

The saying is the same for the downwind leg (as you are facing downwind). "If the wind goes right, go right; if the wind goes left, go left." And normally, whichever side is favored going upwind, usually the opposite side of the course will be favored downwind. *(See Diagram 37.)*

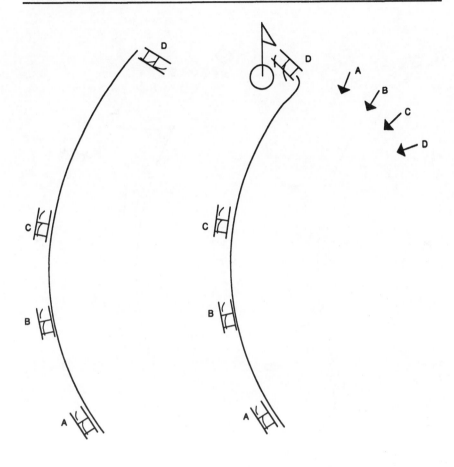

DIAGRAM 36

The boats on the left and on the right start evenly, going to weather on the same tack, while the wind is out of direction A. They move the same distance; then the wind shifts to direction B. Both boats are lifted, but the right boat pulls ahead and higher than the left boat. Again they both move the same speed and distance when wind shift direction C occurs. The right boat again pulls more ahead and higher than the left boat. Finally, wind shift direction D occurs, and the boat on the right gets lifted to the mark, while the left boat must tack and sail back to the mark on a header. The right boat has sailed the inside diameter of a wind wheel, while the left boat has sailed the longer, outside diameter of a wind wheel.

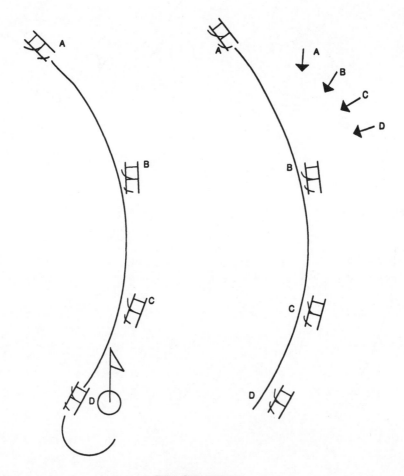

DIAGRAM 37

The boats on the left and on the right start evenly, sailing downwind on the same tack, while the wind is out of direction A. They move the same distance; then the wind shifts to direction B. Both boats are headed, but the left boat pulls ahead and sails deeper than the right boat. Again they both move the same speed and distance, when wind shift direction C occurs. The left boat again pulls more ahead and deeper than the right boat. Finally, wind shift direction D occurs, and the boat on the left gets headed to the mark, while the right boat must jibe and sail back to the mark on a lift. The left boat has sailed the inside diameter of a wind wheel, while the right boat has sailed the longer, outside diameter of a wind wheel.

Another way of looking at it is that if going right paid off going upwind, going right pays off going downwind, because that will be the opposite side. The wind kept shifting right (clockwise).

THE GEOGRAPHICAL SHIFT

The geographical shift is not really a shift, in that it is actually a more or less permanent deviation in the wind pattern on a portion of the race course as a consequence of air being distorted by land masses.

These deviations in wind direction will remain fairly constant and predictable and stay in the same place. Sometimes they will create a nice lift on one side of the course or the other. These type shifts are best discovered by using split pairs — before the race get a buddy to sail one side of the course while you sail the other and then compare notes. *(See Diagram 38.)*

Local knowledge about geographical shifts can give home-pond sailors a tremendous advantage in regattas until the visiting competitors figure the shifts out.

How do you tell the difference in these three types of wind shifts? One way is to wait until after the race, when you can reflect back and say, "Wow! I went to the left and everyone went to the right, I was last — must of been a persistent shift to the right."

A better way is to be on the race course early and check the shifts to see what kind they are, use the split pairs we talked about in Chapter 10, "The Start." While racing, keep your eyes on boats in the corners. The boats on the extreme sides of the fleet will provide your best clues about what the wind is trying to do.

If the fleet seems to keep getting more and more of a lift, and the boats on the inside of the lift are doing even better, that is a good sign it is a persistent shift — it's time to bail out and head toward the shift, even if you have to duck sterns to get there.

Here is a good time to use the theory of "slow down and win." You will probably have boats over you that are keeping you from tacking over to the favored side of the course. Slow down a bit to allow room to tack, then get the heck out of there. Those folks are going to go fast to the wrong side of the course and lose, while you are going to win by slowing down for a second or two and going to the correct side.

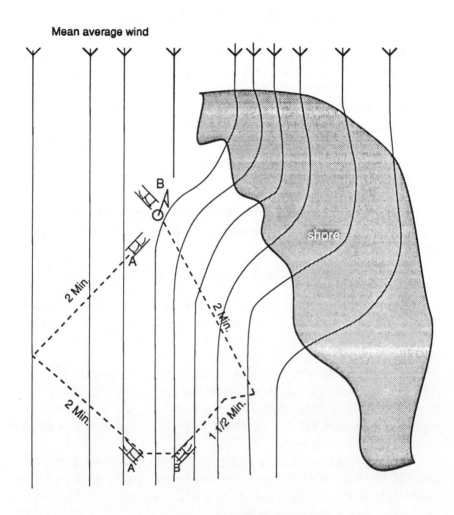

DIAGRAM 38

Wind always tries to cross land at 90-degree angles. Consequently, you get a major wind shift due to geography. Boats A and B start off in opposite directions. Boat B gets a header due to the geographical wind shift off the shore and tacks to get lifted to the weather mark, well ahead of Boat A, who has remained in steady air.

With the oscillating shifts you will notice some of the fleet being headed and some being lifted. Then it's back to the axiom of tack on headers, hold the lifts.

THE PUFFS

As we said, puffs are brief increases in velocity that dip down from aloft, fan out on the water like a cat's paw and quickly dissipate.

When going to weather, you can see puffs coming by the ruffling and darkening of the water, and by watching other boats to windward of you. If they suddenly go up on their ears, get ready. By being prepared for the arrival of a puff, you can convert the extra wind into power and forward motion instead of flying a hull and spilling air.

A puff can put you on either a lift or a header, depending upon what part of the puff you are in. *(See Diagram 39.)* On the weather leg puffs are important primarily because they briefly give you a little more wind. But it is virtually impossible to dictate what part of the puff you are going to be in — whether you will get a lift or a header out of it. And as soon as it swoops across your boat, it is gone, romping on down the lake. Just try to be ready for it and use the extra power it brings with it.

While sailing downwind, however, puffs can be played to some advantage, as you are going basically the same direction the puff is. When you see a puff coming from behind (or actually 45 degrees over your aft shoulder), pay attention to whether it is giving you a header or a lift. Remember, going downwind, you want headers, because they will take you closer to the mark. The basic rule is the opposite of upwind sailing: You want to tack on the lifts and hold the headers.

When the puff hits, if you are on port tack and get lifted, you are on the left side of the puff. Jibe now, and you will be on a header and also staying in the puff for an additional boost of speed. If the puff stays with you long enough for you to get to the right side of it, you will be lifted again. So jibe again and get back on a header and back into the center of the puff. A puff is sort of like a wave — you want to ride it as long as you can.

Having an understanding of lifts, headers and puffs can be an enormous help tactically. Unfortunately, it is an inexact science which nobody has truly mastered; but the more we can learn, the better sailors we will be. This chapter is just a basic starting point for acquiring that knowledge.

For further information on this subject, see the guest chapter contributed by world champion sailor and meteorologist Bob Curry.

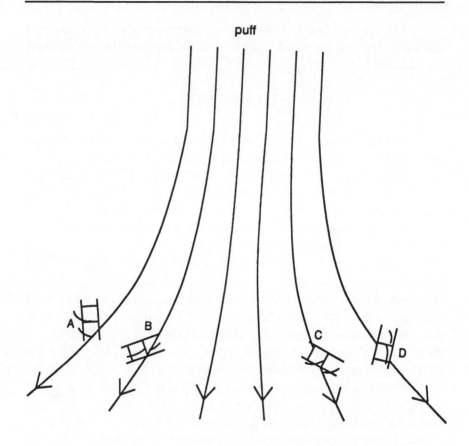

DIAGRAM 39

A typical cat's paw hits the water and spreads. Boat A is sailing downwind and gets a lot more wind and a header, which really helps in getting to the leeward mark quickly. He is on the ideal side of this puff. Boat B is beating to weather on port and has entered the puff from the wrong side. He is being headed and will then sail back into the mean wind direction, but will probably not get much of a lift going out the other side, as the puff will have passed by and dissipated. Boat C, like Boat A, is headed downwind and gets more wind, but he is getting lifted away from the leeward mark. He should jibe to stay in the puff and get a header down to the next mark. Boat D is close-hauled and has gotten an increase in wind velocity, as well as a lift to the weather mark.

A book to cover all tactics for every situation would fill a whole library. However, there are certain basics that can get you winning in your local pond and can serve you well at the national and world level.

I will never forget the time my mother crewed for me on my Shark catamaran back in the 1960s. She had never sailed before, and prior to the race I had her wash the hulls, because that is what the faster sailors, like my wife's father, did before every race.

After we had been beating to the weather mark for quite a while, and apparently weren't doing very well, she observed, "I don't think it has anything to do with washing the boat — it's when you zig and when you zag."

As usual, my mother was right. When to zig and when to zag, both upwind and downwind, are what tactics are all about. (But it really does help to wash your boat.)

This chapter contains the basic tactics to consider at all times as well as specific tactics for use on the weather leg, the downwind leg and the reaching leg. Under separate subheadings toward the end of the chapter you will find additional useful information to help you in making your tactical decisions, including "Leverage," "Using Ranges" and "The Numbers Game."

The special tactics and strategies to use at the start and at the finish are contained within those chapters.

THE MESS YOU LEAVE BEHIND

You should realize that your boat does not simply go through the water without leaving a devastating "debris" of mixed-up air and water behind it.

As you can see by *Diagram 40,* when going to weather the wind to the leeward and aft of your boat leaves a mess of eddies and areas of simply no air.

To the windward side it leaves behind an area of backwinding. Because your mainsail has a curve to it, the wind that comes off the back end

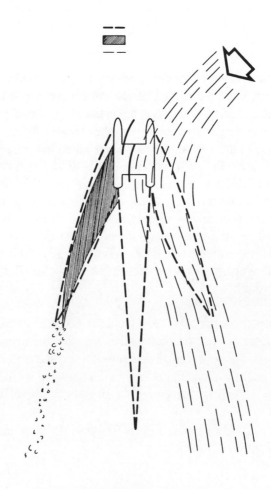

DIAGRAM 40

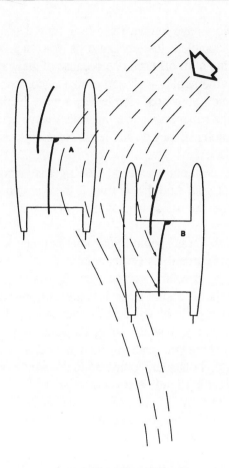

DIAGRAM 41

Boat B is being backwinded and consequently impeded by Boat A.

of it is going a different direction than the wind that started out at the front of the sail. *(See Diagram 41.)*

In addition, your sail is an obstruction to the wind. The effect on the oncoming wind is much akin to a traffic jam — it changes the speed and direction of the wind.

That new wind direction will affect any boats immediately to windward and aft of you. Their sails will see the air from a different direction than what your sails are seeing. They will in effect be getting a header. They will no longer be able to point and will eventually drop back or fall down behind you.

Monohull sailors have known for a long time that a port tack start that fails is not a complete loss, because as you duck those countless sterns, you are getting a lift off each one because of the way the air is bent off the back of their mainsails — it's sort of like a geographical windshift.

As for the water, your boat also leaves a wake behind it. Although the sleek hulls of the catamaran leave much less wave action than do the broader, deeper monohulls, they do still leave some.

It sounds like the moral to this is: Don't get anywhere near another boat that is ahead of you. And that is true, if there are no other factors to consider. It falls under the basic tactic of "Stay in clear air."

Downwind, the "mess" behind your boat is much less damaging to boats around you and particularly behind you.

Off the wind, boats behind you can actually draft you, like a van behind a semi, getting a lift on the air as it comes off your mainsail and, in effect, gaining a faster point of sail. Just as your sail was backwinding the boat above and behind you while going to weather, so does the main backwind the boat behind you going off the wind. This means the boat behind is sailing in a slight header, compared to the wind you are sailing in. Therefore he can sheet in slightly and get more speed.

That is why occasionally, you will have a closely-following boat ride right up on you and even into you. In addition, they may be getting a little extra boost by riding your wake.

BASIC TACTICS

There are seven basic, tactical, racing rules that you should always keep in mind regardless of whether you are sparring with opponents or are pretty much alone on the race course.

1. Sail toward the side of the course having the best air and sea conditions.

2. In oscillating wind shifts, tack on headers, hold on lifts when going to weather; tack on lifts, hold on headers when going downwind.

3. In a persistent shift go to the side the wind is shifting toward when going to weather; go to the opposite side downwind.

4. Tack as little as possible; but tack when you should.

5. Always take the tack that brings your heading nearer the mark.

6. Stay in clear air.

7. Don't overstand the lay line, but never, NEVER overstand the left layline on a marks-to-port course going to weather or the right layline on a marks-to-port course going downwind..

When you are dealing with an offensive or defensive tactical situation, it is often necessary to take action that is contrary to these basic sailing rules. But use them whenever possible, and always take them into consideration when making decisions.

If you are all by yourself on the course, either in the lead, in the back, or even mid-pack, use the basic sailing rules and sail consistently until you are in a position where you begin confronting other boats.

DEFENSIVE/OFFENSIVE TACTICS

There are basically only four situations requiring defense or offense; however, they make up all of racing.

1. You are being overtaken from behind for reasons you do not yet know. (Use Defense.)
2. You are leading and being challenged by one competitor. (Use Defense.)
3. You are leading and being challenged by several competitors. (Use Defense.)
4. You are behind. (Use Offense.)

TACTICS ON THE WEATHER LEG

Overall, your ability to be first to the weather mark depends on a combination of correct sail shape (based on wind, water, and crew weight conditions), and well-coordinated steering and sheeting to go as high and as fast as you can.

But ability alone will not suffice. On the mental side of the game are certain strategic maneuvers that can ensure victory or dictate certain defeat. So let's look at weather leg tactics, broken down under the four basic defense/offense situations.

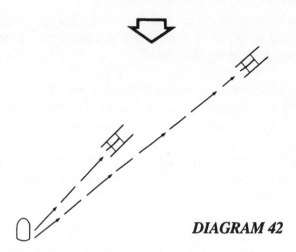

DIAGRAM 42

PROBLEM: *You are being overtaken from behind for reasons you do not yet know.*

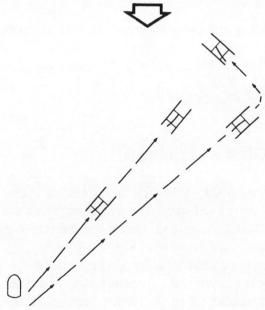

SOLUTION 1: *Tack immediately, losing some ground, yet still remaining ahead.*

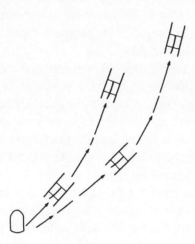

SOLUTION 2: Hold port tack and possibly get into the same wind pattern as the overtaking boat.

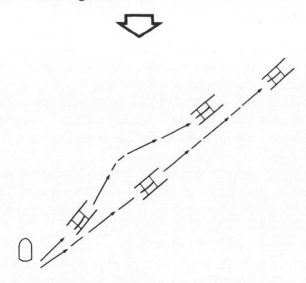

SOLUTION 3: Hold port tack and possibly the overtaking boat will get into your wind pattern.

1. YOU ARE BEING OVERTAKEN FROM BEHIND. *(See Diagram 42.)*

Let us say you have just rounded the leeward pin and start off close-hauled for the weather mark. The next boat around hardens up as well, but points 5 or 10 degrees higher. He seemingly has a lift that you did not get in rounding. It is not unusual for a boat to appear to be pointing higher after first rounding the mark. However, if the competitor continues on a lift, you must make a decision, and quickly.

If you hold on to see whether his lift will continue and it does, then you will soon be in a situation where, if you tack, you will cross his stern. Since that would serve no purpose, you probably should hold onto the tack with the expectation that you both will soon be in the same wind pattern.

Had you tacked upon first seeing that the competitor had a lift, you would have lost a lot of ground to him, but you would still be ahead. This probably would have been a good decision.

Sometimes, when you have a good-sized lead, you can tack at the leeward pin, then tack back just before the competitor rounds. This assures you that you will get the same air as the competitor, and you will be to windward as well, allowing you to get any shifts before the competitor.

The golden rule in covering is to stay between the next mark and the competition. Tacking to the inside of the course does just that.

2. YOU ARE LEADING BUT BEING CHALLENGED BY ONLY ONE COMPETITOR.

Whether you are sailing near the back of the pack or mid-fleet or in the top, you will notice that somehow you are always racing someone. There almost always will be a boat near you, and you usually choose your course and tacks with reference to that boat.

Suppose in this situation that you are on port tack and ahead; approaching is a competitor on starboard tack, but behind. *(See Diagram 43.)* You may simply clear his bow; or you may instead tack to a safe leeward position.

In the safe leeward position, the wind bouncing off your sails is backwinding the boat that is windward and aft. The wind he is getting is a few degrees more of a header and it is somewhat disturbed air. Also, he must contend with your wake.

So the safe leeward position will allow you to pull out ahead faster and to point higher, while he will go slower and head down until soon you will be blanketing him with your eddying air shadow on the leeward side.

If you have enough room to go above the starboard boat, tack and blanket him — that would be even better. But beware! Inherent in the cata-

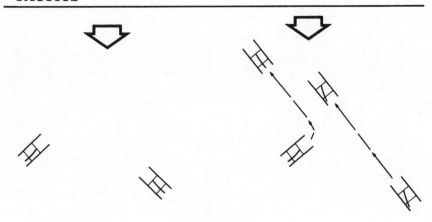

DIAGRAM 43

PROBLEM: You are on port tack and ahead.
SOLUTION 1: Tack to safe leeward position.

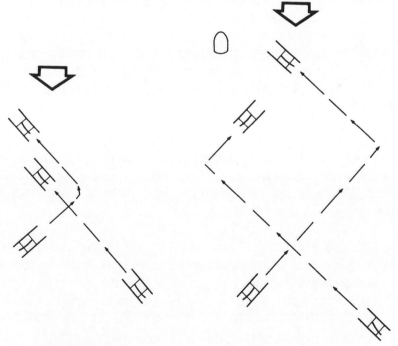

SOLUTION 2: Tack to cover if there is time and room to
complete the tack.
SOLUTION 3: Hold port tack until reaching the lay line
and then tack to starboard.

maran is an inability to tack very fast. If your tack is not completed and you are not off and moving on starboard tack in time, the competitor will have broken through your lee, and he then will establish a safe leeward position on you.

Now let us assume you are on starboard and ahead, while the other boat is on port, not far behind. *(See Diagram 44.)* You can obviously use your starboard rights to remain ahead, but what of the next meeting with the same boat?

If you know that the next encounter will be at the windward pin, or even on the starboard layline to it, you will be wise to tack to port, below and ahead of the port-tack competitor, thereby establishing a safe leeward position. He will not have the drive or the pointing ability that you do, and you should soon be able to lift up from under that position and on up to a position of blanketing him.

Had you tried to tack on top of the port tacker, you would still have been in the process of regaining speed, allowing him to break through your lee and into the safe leeward position.

If you are a bit more in the lead and have enough room, the best thing to do would be to go slightly above the port tack boat and tack. But in doing so, remember that you must be able to get through your tack and get moving before he is able to get through your lee-blanketing effect to establish a safe leeward position.

In this circumstance, a good time to throw over the helm is when you get to your competitor's weather hull. By the time you make the turning arc to port, you will be above him by a boat length or two, and in getting your boat under way again, you will be throwing that competitor a lot of bad air. (Your wind shadow, by the way, goes in the direction that your telltale or bridle fly is pointing.)

Your one other decision could be to exercise the starboard rights and not tack to port until you reach the layline to the mark. However, then on your next encounter with that boat, speeds being equal, he will be on starboard, with you on port, and it could be marginal as to whether or not you can clear his bows. You will have to be prudent and dive behind his stern and then tack, a maneuver that will lose you a great deal of distance, and certainly that particular competitor.

Still another situation has you in the lead and to windward of your competitor on the same tack.

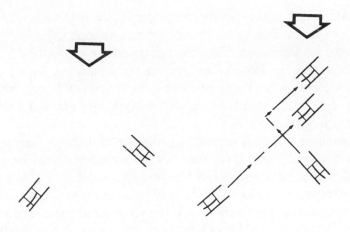

DIAGRAM 44

PROBLEM: You are on starboard and ahead.
SOLUTION 1: Tack and cover the port boat if you can complete the tack in time to remain windward and ahead.

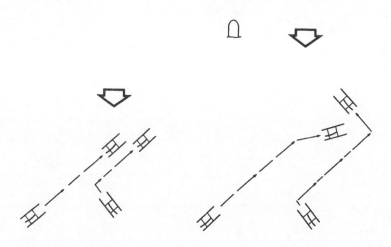

SOLUTION 2: Tack to safe leeward.
SOLUTION 3: When the weather mark is near, tack to port and then on the lay line you will have starboard rights.

You should stay between the competitor and the next mark. *(See Diagram 45.)* That is, if he tacks, you should tack as soon as he is directly behind your sterns, or sooner. You are then covering his every tack.

You may not be feeding him "gas" the entire time, but you are in the ideal position of getting the same air he does. If you don't cover him, he may get some unexpected big wind shift that you may not, and suddenly the roles will be reversed.

Sometimes it is NOT a good idea to cover too tightly — giving the boat below you all your bad air. For example, you want to head for the favored left side of the course and so does your competitor.

If you blanket him too closely and all he is getting is dirty air, he will tack. However, you don't want to tack, but you must to cover him. In this case, keep him happy and allow him decent air, yet cover him loosely — stay between the competitor and the next mark.

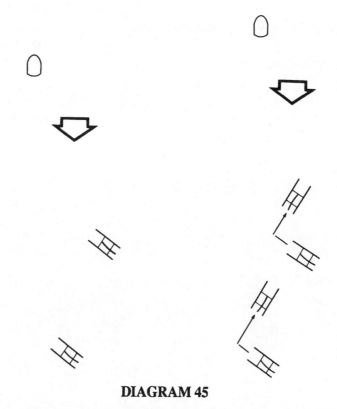

DIAGRAM 45

PROBLEM: You are ahead on the same tack.
SOLUTION: When he tacks, you should tack to cover.

3. YOU'RE LEADING BUT BEING CHALLENGED BY SEVERAL COMPETITORS.

Your defense in this situation is quite tricky. Visualize yourself rounding the leeward pin and heading out on port tack. As you continue to sail on that tack, you notice that all your competitors are staying on the same tack as well. That is just great, for if they continue to parade along behind you, you have it made.

However, watch for those who take the other tack. Once they have split tacks, see who they are. In many races your job is simply to beat a few key boats to preserve your place in the standings. If it is the first race of a regatta, you have no idea who you are going to have to beat, so you must judge who you think will give you the most competition before the regatta is over. At any rate, if the tough competition has split tacks with you, you should tack to starboard and cover them.

In a variation of the above situation, half the fleet is on the right side of the course, while the other half is on the left. *(See Diagram 46.)* You should be working a bit closer to the middle, watching to see who appears to be gaining an advantage. If the left side looks as though they have gotten a particularly nice shift, it is in your best interest to head for that side of the course to cover.

That decision could easily be wrong, however, and you might lose all the boats to the right side.

In making that decision, you should definitely weigh the competition in each group as well. If your most formidable foe is on the right, you might be wise to head for the right side of the course.

☛A good way to tell which side is doing well and which side isn't — look at the boats on the left side and see if they are going faster than the background. Then check the right side. The side that is going faster than the background is doing better at that time.

4. YOU ARE BEHIND.

The best rule in this case is to do something different than the boats ahead of you are doing. *(See Diagram 47.)* You must take the offensive. If you simply do the same thing as the boat or boats ahead of you, you will just be joining their parade. Then you are being very cooperative by allowing yourself to be covered.

However, don't go off into never-never land. Sure! You could make out like a champ, but usually you will simply be the chump, losing more and more ground.

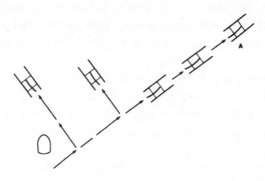

DIAGRAM 46

PROBLEM: You are leading and being challenged by several competitors. Half the fleet splits tacks.

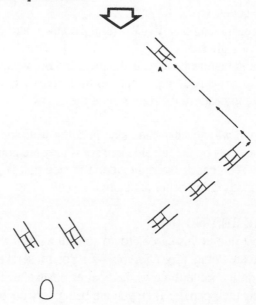

SOLUTION: Tack to middle of course and cover the most threatening side, dependent upon which particular competitors are the most formidable.

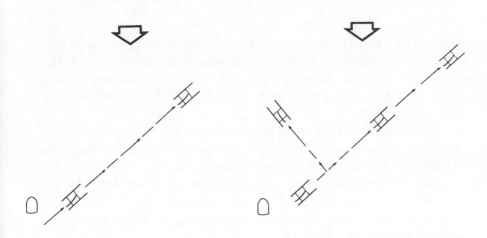

DIAGRAM 47

PROBLEM: *You are behind.*
SOLUTION 1: *Split tacks; try to get into different wind patterns.*

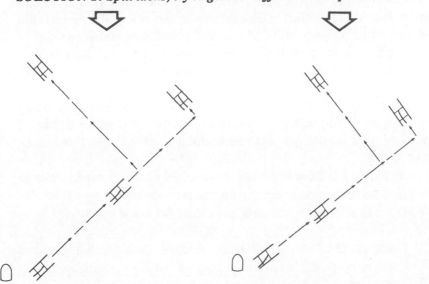

SOLUTION 2: *If lead boat tacks, sail at least 100 yards above him and tack.*
SOLUTION 3: *When lead boat tacks on lay line, sail somewhat above him before tacking.*

A good example is where you round the leeward pin and everyone is going to the right. The right side is favored, but you are in bad air and behind. Should you tack off to the unfavored, left side of the course? No! Tack off to starboard and sail a reasonable distance into clear air, and tack back to port and again head for the favored side. You have done something different but not drastic.

If you split tacks after rounding the leeward pin, the lead boat should, according to our previously laid-out defenses, tack to cover you. You should then tack again to get out from under cover.

Keep in mind that if there are a number of other boats in the race and two of you have a tacking battle, you both will be in the tubes with reference to the other boats. So decide carefully: Are you trying to duck the cover of just one boat or many?

But let us assume the boat ahead has covered you but is not affecting your air. You have clear air and are moving well.

You may elect to hold onto that port tack and sail as efficiently as possible. And he may be so worried and anticipatory of your next move to get out from under cover that he will not be sailing quite as efficiently. Consequently, you may be able to move out ahead and maybe up toward him more to weather. Then in the case of a header of any kind, you should tack immediately — you will find you have gained substantially on him.

When you are approaching the lay line (usually the right layline, since you never want to overstand the left layline), there is another especially good maneuver. After the boat ahead of you has tacked, sail somewhat above where he tacked, and come about. This allows you to stay in similar air. If you both get a lift, you will close the distance on him. If you both get a header, you are still behind but have not lost that much ground.

In addition, if there is a header, you might make the mark, while he must tack two more times. Again, you will gain. On a lift you will be able to drive the boat harder to the mark and should not lose much ground.

Going on to still another situation, the boat leading is starboard and ahead; you are port and behind. (See Diagram 48.) If he does not tack to safe leeward on you or tack to blanket you and simply sails on by, exercising his starboard rights, you have nothing to worry about, particularly if you are nearing the "A" mark. Simply keep sailing efficiently; and, with a good clean tack to starboard at the lay line, you may either have him on starboard or least be worrying him sick. It may even be a good idea to hail

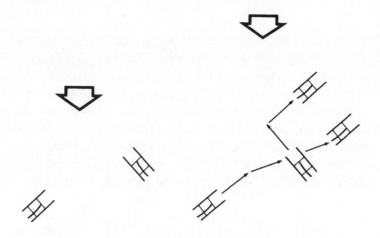

DIAGRAM 48

PROBLEM: The lead boat is starboard and ahead;
you are port and behind.
SOLUTION 1: If the lead boat tacks to cover, drive
off and through his wind shadow into clear air.

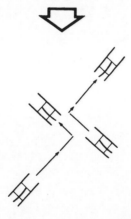

SOLUTION 2: If the lead boat tacks to cover, tack
to starboard and into clear air.

him to "hold course" before he hails you — to keep his mind at rest and to entice him into sailing on past you, and the layline.

Had that starboard boat tacked to either a blanket position or a safe leeward, then you would most likely have had to tack back out to starboard to get into clear air.

Suppose in another situation that you are on starboard and behind; and here comes the competitor on port and ahead. *(See Diagram 49.)* If you are fairly far behind, you may sail on beyond him and under his sterns for a short way — perhaps 50 to 100 yards — tack, and be in clear air.

Or you could tack below him at a distance where you will not be blanketed by his sails, and concentrate on driving forward and as high as possible, with the hope of working into a safe leeward position.

If your distance behind is not too great, your best bet would be to tack under and work toward a safe leeward position.

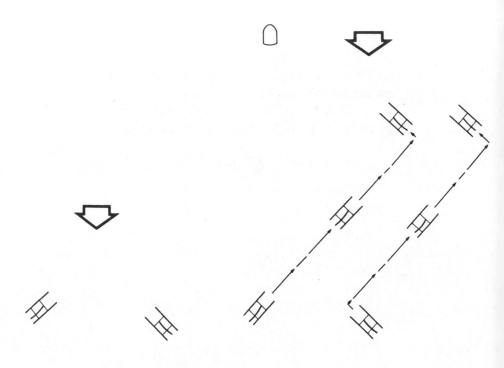

DIAGRAM 49

PROBLEM: The lead boat is port and ahead; you are starboard and behind.
SOLUTION 1: Tack to port and at the lay line you will again have starboard rights.

TACTICS AT THE WEATHER MARK

Understand that there are no mark rounding rules in effect at the weather mark for boats on opposite tacks. Those rules are designated for reaching and running marks, or jibing and rounding marks.

So, the rules that do apply are port/starboard (as if the mark were not even there), and the inside overlap rules for boats on the same tack.

Obviously, if you come crashing into the weather pin on port tack, do not call for room at the mark. You may not call for room, you may not cross in front of a starboard boat and cause him to steer away to miss you, and you may not tack in front of a starboard boat, either.

LAYLINES

The left side layline:

But let us back up a bit here. You should never be coming in to the weather mark that close on port anyway, unless you are a genius at judging the layline. Earlier I had mentioned to never, NEVER overstand the left layline on a port-mark-rounding course — that is simply extra mileage being sailed at your expense.

You want to tack early before you get to the layline for a number of reasons:
1. You will probably be sailing less distance. *(See Diagram 50-A.)*
2. If you get a lift on port tack you will be right at the mark, while the boats that overstood, will gain no advantage by the lift. *(See Diagram 50-B.)*
3. If you get a header, you will gain even more on the boats that went further, and you will reach the starboard layline sooner and have the starboard tactical advantage going to the pin. *(See Diagram 50-C.)*
4. The parade of boats heading for the pin on starboard tack will be more thinned out, allowing you more room to squeeze in and tack to the mark, than had you been right at the pin. *(See Diagram 50-D.)*

NOTE: When you are on port, approaching the starboard parade to the mark, you see a tight bunch of boats and back a ways is a hole to get through. Here is another place to slow down and win! Instead of heading away from the mark toward the oncoming hole, hardening up and tacking, slow your boat down, wait for the hole to approach you, then speed up,

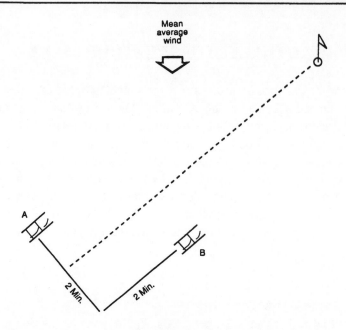

DIAGRAM 50-A

To begin with, Boat A has sailed one minute extra distance past the lay line.

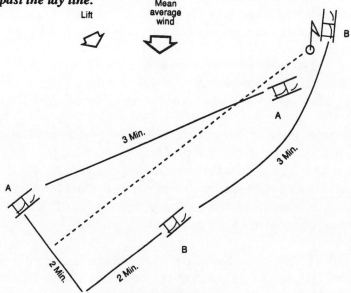

DIAGRAM 50-B

Boat B is lifted to the mark; Boat A reaches to the mark, but is behind due to extra distance sailed.

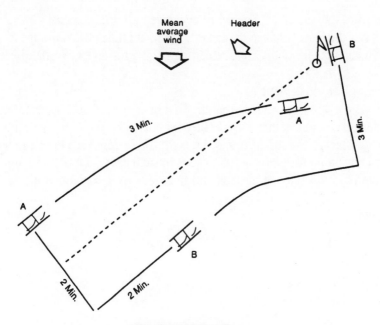

DIAGRAM 50-C
In this example, Boat B takes the header and tacks to easily beat Boat A.

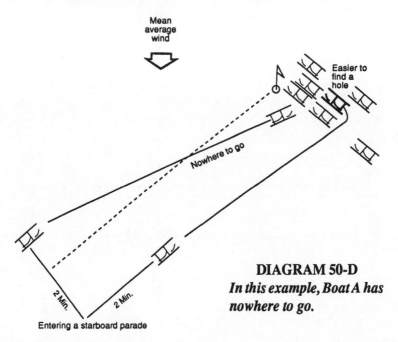

DIAGRAM 50-D
In this example, Boat A has nowhere to go.

blast through and tack. You will have saved a lot of distance — the winners sail the least distance the fastest. There are times when it pays to slow down and take the short route rather than going fast in the wrong direction.

The right side layline

Have you ever noticed that the first boat goes a little over the layline for added insurance, then tacks. The next boat goes just past the first boat's line and tacks, and the next and the next. *(See Diagram 51.)* And there is good reasoning for going a little higher in such cases, but before long most of the herd will be sailing tens and hundreds of yards above the layline.

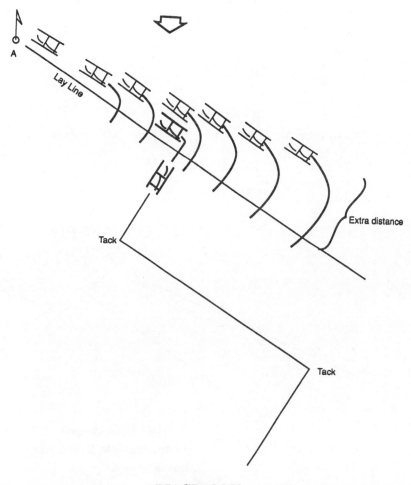

DIAGRAM 51

Again, this is simply extra mileage. And your job is to sail the shortest distance around the race course, the fastest.

When you see this building up, you might try tacking before the layline, and then tacking back well before reaching the left layline, then find a hole, or tack under. You should have picked up a fair amount of distance and some boats.

Start thinking about the weather mark before you get there.

You don't want to be in a position of having to just pinch your way around the weather mark, for a few good reasons:

1) Boats that approached higher on the mark will quickly drive over you and kill your air — you will lose your ability to drive and go to weather and probably will hit the mark.

2) The wind could head you at the last moment, and again you would hit the mark.

3) Even if you do eke your way around the mark, your board may pick up the mark's anchor rode and pull the mark into you.

4) If you cannot make the mark, you will probably be in heavy traffic and unable to tack to port. Then you must jibe away from the mark and try to sneak through the starboard parade to get to the starboard layline.

In other words, try to give the weather mark a little room in your approach.

TACTICS ON THE DOWNWIND LEG

You will have fewer tactical decisions with respect to other boats downwind than going to weather. The fleet tends to be more spread out on this point of sail. In general, on the downwind leg you will be best benefited by observing the seven basic sailing rules listed near the beginning of this chapter.

Before getting into specific defensive and offensive tactics for the downwind leg, I want to issue a couple of cautions regarding lifts and headers downwind.

How to tell if you are on a lift or header is explained in Chapter 15, "Wind Shifts." However, it is important to remember that when you are going downwind, a lift takes you farther away from the mark and a header takes you closer to the mark — the opposite of the rule you followed on the weather leg.

In addition, on the downwind leg, because there are so many variations in sailing styles and sailing angles, it may be more difficult to ascertain lifts and headers by your relationship to other boats. The important thing is to watch for boats that are going both deeper and faster than you. If you can see no difference in boat or sail trim, try to get in the same air.

The four tactical situations presented for the weather leg also apply for the downwind leg, but the tactics you can use are far more limited. Defensively, there is relatively little you can do.

You can't get a safe leeward on another boat, because you have no backwinding position on the downwind leg. And residual wave action from your boat causes little, if any, problem for boats near you.

The main tool with which you have to work downwind is the wind shadow thrown off to leeward and slightly aft. If you choose to use this weapon, keep in mind that the eddies and lack of air off to your leeward will fall at a point opposite of the direction of your apparent wind. If your bridle fly or sidestay telltale point at a 90-degree angle from your hulls, then your shadow will be off to your leeward side at about that degree. *(See Diagram 52.)*

You may use this wind shadow effect in deciding when to tack to cover a competitor. However, blanketing as a tactical tool downwind does not really come into play too much until you get into closer quarters — near a mark, for example.

Remember, also, that on the downwind leg, blanketing is an offensive tactic, whereas it is a defensive tactic going to weather. Off the wind, you must be behind the other boat (in relation to the mark) in order to blanket that boat.

Tacking to blanket a competitor can be disadvantageous, however, because you may then be blocked and hindered from tacking again yourself.

1. YOU ARE BEING OVERTAKEN FROM BEHIND.

Suppose you have rounded the weather mark and are off on a starboard tack, sailing as deep as you normally do while tacking downwind.

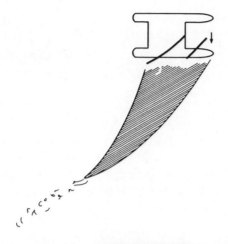

DIAGRAM 52
An important downwind tactical tool is the wind shadow
that extends to the leeward of your boat, approximately as
shown here.

The next boat around the mark sets up for his off-the-wind sailing and is
heading 5 degrees deeper and going just as fast. *(See Diagram 53.)*

If that competitor continues to sail deeper and as fast, then you must
immediately make a decision.

One solution is to tack immediately, cross his bows and, if he remains on starboard tack, jibe back to starboard and stay between him and
the next mark. Do not jibe into his bad air, however.

You also could elect to hold the present tack with the hope that the
wind he is getting will soon reach your boat and you both will be heading
as deep, which will allow the competitor to gain but not overtake you.

If you wait too long to make a decision and, by tacking, would cross
the other boat's stern, then you should hold the present tack and await a
different wind shift.

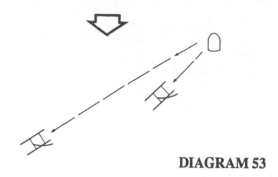

DIAGRAM 53

PROBLEM: The following boat rounds the mark and sails deeper and as fast.

2 AND 3. YOU ARE LEADING AND BEING CHALLENGED.

Your only defense is to keep your boat between the competitors and the mark and attempt to stay in the same wind patterns and on the same side of the course as the competitors.

4. YOU ARE BEHIND.

As in going to weather, the best tactic is to do the opposite of the boats ahead of you. If the lead boat jibes to cover your splitting, you may then opt to hold the tack (since you are in clear air) or jibe.

Remember that the lead boat's covering on the downwind leg is not a blanket cover and is not hurting you, as the lead boat is downwind of you. Still, the lead boat should try to remain between you and the next mark — he should not allow you to get in different wind patterns than those he has.

By holding the tack that you and the leading boat are on, and sailing efficiently, you may be able to drive deep and fast to get nearer to the lead boat. Your big hope will be to work down in to a position where you may blanket him with your wind shadow.

Luffing up a windward boat is a defensive tool you might use to prevent a boat from passing to windward. Most commonly employed on reaches, it is occasionally used downwind. My advice on luffing matches is to avoid them. Both boats involved will lose too much ground to the rest of the fleet.

Generally, you are best advised to concentrate on sailing deep, fast, and efficiently on the downwind leg rather than worrying too much about tactics . . . UNTIL you get to the leeward mark, where tactics can get interesting.

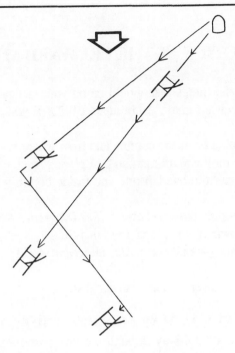

SOLUTION 1: *Jibe across his bows and then jibe again to stay between the following competitor and the mark.*

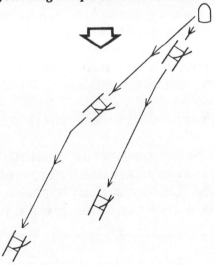

SOLUTION 2: *Hold the tack and hope the wind your competitor has reaches you before he does.*

TACTICS AT THE LEEWARD MARK

There are six things that should be on your tactical checklist before you get to the leeward mark. And I mean BEFORE you get to the leeward mark:

1) Know what boats are coming and from where.

2) Prepare for the mark rounding.

3) Remember the overlap rule and inside boat rights. *(See Diagram 54-A.)*

4) Watch for the pinwheel effect. *(See Diagram 54-B.)*

5) Slow down to win. *(See Diagram 54-C.)*

6) Enter wide — Exit close. *(See Diagram 54-C.)*

Let's take a closer look at this checklist:

1. KNOW WHAT BOATS ARE COMING AND FROM WHERE.

Before you are halfway through the downwind leg, you should already have a good idea of what boats you will be confronting at the leeward pin. You can set up a range or transit on your boat that will give you an idea of what boats are going to be near you.

For example, if you are steering from the main beam and look across a point that is approximately a 45-degree angle — the leeward end of the rear beam, perhaps — and see how many boats are ahead of that line, they are probably ahead of you. The boats aft of that line could be behind you. And if you see changes in those positions you will see who is doing better and who is doing worse.

If a boat that was ahead of the transit moves aft, you are doing better.

Another possible way to measure the relationship of other boats is to compare that boat with their background. If the other boat is moving faster than the background, then they are doing better than you. On the other hand, if they are going slower than the background, it means you are doing better than they.

The point here is to sail your boat as fast as possible, but be aware of the other boats. Will you or will you not meet them at the leeward pin? If you meet them at the pin, from which direction are they going to be coming?

These are the things you must know as you approach the leeward pin. You must know how many boats you are going to be dealing with and from what direction they are coming.

You don't want any surprises!

2. PREPARE FOR THE MARK ROUNDING.

This actually comes under physical preparation for the mark rounding, and is covered thoroughly in "The Downwind Leg" Chapter. However, we mention it again here, because an important reason for taking care of adjustments early is that it frees you to think about the other boats and the tactics and plan ahead for confrontations at the mark and concentrate on controlling your boat. You definitely want your "head out of the boat" for a crowded mark rounding.

You may have the best of intentions for avoiding the pinwheel and slowing down to win; but you will not be able to execute your plan if you are dashing around the boat doing your "housekeeping" chores.

3. REMEMBER THE OVERLAP RULE AND INSIDE BOAT RIGHTS.

This might be a good time to review the rules. And they are not very difficult.

Put simply, if any part of a boat is overlapped on the inside of another boat before they enter an imaginary circle two boat-lengths from the mark, then the inside boat has to be given room to round that mark.

Let's take the outside boat. *(See Diagram 54-A.)* If you draw a perpendicular line across the stern of that boat and to windward, any portion of any boat inside of that line is overlapped — whether the overlapping boat is a mile away, or right next to him.

As for the rules, then, you have an advantage coming into the mark on starboard tack and near the left downwind layline, thereby giving you an overlap on boats coming in on port tack and on the right downwind layline.

How much room must the outside boat give? Enough for the inside boat to make a rounding as if you weren't there. And, if the inside boat was coming in on starboard tack and must jibe, sheet in and head up — all in one move — chances are that maneuver will take up quite a bit of room. So there is not a lot of point in yelling at him that you are not going to give him more room. He must be given all the room he needs. Suppose he accidentally drops his mainsheet and lets go of the tiller for a second to grab it.

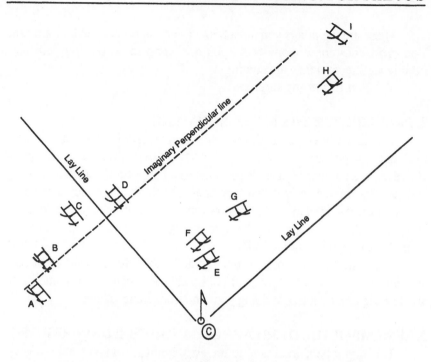

DIAGRAM 54-A

In this case all the boats have inside overlap on Boat A. If Boat B was not there, Boat C would not have inside rights. However, in this case Boat C has an overlap on Boat B and Boat B has an overlap on Boat A; therefore, C has an overlap on A.

The boat will make a wider turn than if he did a great job. But you had better not hit him or you're out.

The rules do not require that inside jibing boat to be the best sailor in the world, making the cleanest jibe and mark rounding in the world. They simply say that you must give him room for a seamanship-like rounding. And his seamanship-like rounding could be pretty sloppy.

4. WATCH FOR THE PINWHEEL EFFECT. *(See Diagram 54-B.)*

The boats that must give way to inside boats usually get stuck on the outside of the "pinwheel." Not only do you sail a greater distance when you go around the outside of the wheel, you also are being blanketed by all the boats closer to the inside of the wheel and are, therefore, going slower. When the rounding is completed and you start going to weather, you will be trapped below all those boats, in terribly disturbed air and probably un-

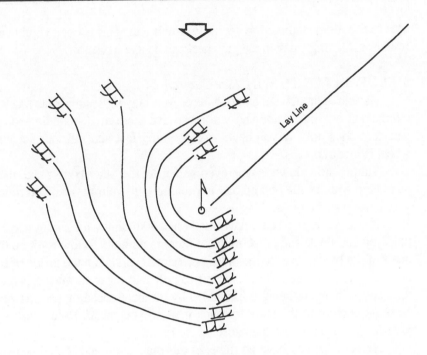

DIAGRAM 54-B

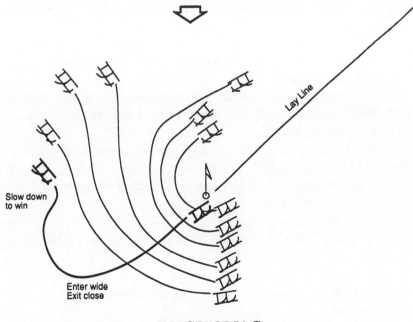

DIAGRAM 54-C

able to tack onto starboard to get away from them. This is not a good mark rounding. Getting stuck in the pinwheel can be a real disaster.

5. SLOW DOWN TO WIN. *(See Diagram 54-C.)*

As you approach the leeward mark, you may see many boats that are overlapped on your inside and you must give them mark-rounding room. But, that does not say you have to keep going fast and fall into the Pinwheel Effect trap.

Simply slow down, swing even wider, let the other boats make their turns, and wait for the opportunity to proceed with your turn, so you round very closely to the mark.

If the preceding boats have made bad roundings, they may leave a hole you can duck into at the mark. If there is no hole, follow right on the heels of the boat closest to the mark — you will still be on the inside of the pinwheel and will be able to tack off to port into clear air after rounding the mark, if you are being backwinded by the boat ahead of you. Always be close enough to the mark to touch it when you round. Rule 6 still applies here — Enter wide, exit close.

Remember, you have no rights in this maneuver, and sometimes you really have to camp out and wait for a hole to clear. But it will soon be there and you must be patient. You will be far better off to bide your time and exit close to the mark than to hurry and get caught on the outside of the pinwheel.

With this maneuver, I have seen boats enter the area in 15th place, and come out 3rd. It doesn't pay off to go fast all the time. Sometimes you must sail slow and smart.

But, wait a minute. How do you slow down? Here is where Chapter 1 on boat handling can pay off. You now have total control of your boat and can do anything with it.

When sailing downwind we have been creating a flow across the backside of the sails, right? We have been operating at 180%, right? Well then, bring the sails in tight and reduce the sailing efficiency. Smack the jib in tight to the main, closing off the slot.

You can go sit on the back of the boat — that really slows a cat down quickly. You can also jam the rudders back and forth. They make excellent brakes.

CAUTION: Do not drag your feet or hands in the water. That is against the rules.

6. ENTER WIDE — EXIT CLOSE. *(See Diagram 54-C.)*

There is the classic, textbook mark rounding where you maintain high speed and narrowly miss the mark at the very apex of the turning arc. While this rounding is fast, it is very seldom used unless you have a huge lead or you are way back.

The tactical rounding, on the other hand, calls for approaching the mark wide and coming very close to the mark after you have become close-hauled, at the end of the turning arc. *(See Diagram 55.)*

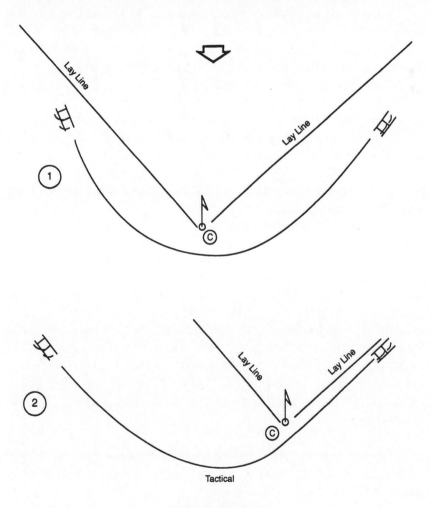

DIAGRAM 55

Example 1 shows a textbook mark rounding; Example 2 illustrates a tactical mark rounding.

Instead of heading directly at the mark, try heading for a point 20 feet to the right of the mark and start your turn there, so that when you pass the mark, you are already hard on the wind. This tactical rounding gets you closer upwind and puts you in a better position tactically on the boats ahead of you and behind you.

TACTICS FOR THE REACHING LEG

If the mark is a close or beam reach you do not need to ease the sheets much as you first round the mark. Most skippers want to go high on the reaching mark. That is not the best way to get there; however, for the most part it can be the safest course to keep from being passed.

If the boat(s) ahead of you go straight at the mark, you are better off to follow them and do the same. Boats behind may try to go up higher to drive over you, however. And if they are showing signs of being able to do so, you must sail higher as well. Once the first boat goes over you and takes your air, an entire parade will continue to go over you.

Defensively you must stay between the next mark and the competition. If they go high and look as if they might drive over you, you must come up and cover yourself.

If they stay behind, then all is fine.

If you are behind and are trying to be on the offense, you may try to drive over another boat. But do not take a course that is very close to the boat you are trying to drive over. That is very insulting, but worse, you are asking for a luffing match — a game where you both lose.

By the way, the leeward boat being passed does not have to hail, nor does he have to give the windward boat ample room and opportunity to respond to the luff. In other words, the leeward boat can jam his rudders over and head up directly in front of you. If there is a collision, you will be doing a 720. So if you are driving over someone, stay a safe distance to windward.

Suppose you are behind and the boats ahead of you all go very high, fending one another off — as they quite often do. Here is a good place to pick off a few boats, and a bit of distance.

Head straight for the mark. There is an old saying, "What goes up, must come down!" Sure, they will go faster, but they will be going higher. When those boats come back down they will be going very slowly. Meanwhile, you will have been going fast the entire time, and will continue to go fast right up to the reaching mark. Another added advantage — you have the inside room at the mark.

ROUNDING THE REACHING MARK

The same tactical checklist that applies for rounding the leeward mark, applies here, with one addition. However, there are differences in the execution of the checklist, as we will explain.

1) Know what boats are coming and from where.

2) Prepare for the mark rounding.

3) Remember the overlap rule and inside boat rights. *(See Diagram 54-A.)*

4) Watch for the pinwheel effect. *(See Diagram 54-B.)*

5) Slow down to win. *(See Diagram 54-C.)*

6) Enter wide — Exit close. *(See Diagram 54-C.)*

7) Know where the layline is to the leeward mark.

1) KNOW WHAT BOATS ARE COMING AND FROM WHERE.

On most reaching legs all the boats will be approaching the mark on the same tack but coming in at slightly different angles, depending on the course they sailed in relation to the rhumb line. An exception to this may be if the B mark is set very deep and it is necessary to tack downwind to get to it. In that case boats may be coming in on both tacks, just as at the C mark.

2) PREPARE FOR THE MARK ROUNDING.

This is covered in depth in Chapter 13, "Reaching Leg." However, it is mentioned again in this checklist because of its importance in making it possible to execute tactical decisions.

3) REMEMBER THE OVERLAP RULE AND INSIDE BOAT RIGHTS.

Both are the same as for the leeward mark rounding.

4) WATCH FOR THE PINWHEEL EFFECT.

Again, the position of the reaching mark affects this. If the B mark is set high, you want to attempt to be on the inside of the pinwheel. However, if you are behind, you now have two options: You can slow down and wait to get on the inside of the pinwheel, OR you can simply not jibe at the mark. Keep going on past the pinwheel and when you are far enough below the pack to be in clear air, jibe and proceed to the C mark. Caution: Do not do this if it is going to cause you to overstand the layline to C.

On the other hand, if the B mark is set low, the pinwheel effect becomes extremely important — DO NOT allow yourself to get on the outside of the pinwheel in this case, or you will be in bad air all the way to the C mark.

5) SLOW DOWN TO WIN.
Use this technique to stay out of the pinwheel, just as in going downwind. See Chapter 1, "Boat Handling," for techniques to slow down.

6) ENTER WIDE — EXIT CLOSE.
This is of lesser importance when the B mark is set high, but it can still be used to some tactical advantage, especially in defending against boats behind you. But when the B mark is set very deep, it is imperative to enter wide and exit close, for the same reasons that apply when rounding the C mark to go to weather.

7) KNOW WHERE THE LAYLINE IS TO THE LEEWARD MARK.
This knowledge affects the execution of the entire checklist in preparing for and rounding the B mark. In addition, if you do not know where C mark is before you round B mark, you can lose your tactical advantage over boats behind you by sailing the wrong angle.

Another important tactical reason for being aware of the layline to C comes into play when the B mark is set high and you will be sailing downwind to C. The B mark (reaching mark) is also commonly referred to as the "jibe mark." For monohulls that sail straight downwind, this is invariably true. However, for both monohulls and catamarans that tack downwind, it is not always necessary to jibe at the "jibe mark."

If the B mark is not on the layline to C mark and it is going to be necessary to tack downwind to get there, you can, instead of jibing, simply bear off and head downwind on the same tack until you reach the layline to C and then jibe.

This is an especially good tactic if you are behind and on offense and all the boats ahead of you jibed right at the mark. By continuing on to the layline, you will be doing something different.

Remember, this only works if you are certain that the layline to C is beyond the B mark. If it is not, you will have overstood C mark.

LEVERAGE

One of the basic rules of offensive tactics is to do the opposite of what the boats ahead of you are doing. But this is not always true.

Unfortunately, people have a tendency to think this means that you should go out on flyers — if the leaders are going that way, I should go the opposite way — heck, what have I got to lose?

A LOT! Let's talk about leverage. The farther away you go to the opposite side of the course from another boat, the more leverage there is in relation to that other boat. In other words, you are going to come out smelling like a rose or you are going to come out smelling like rotten milk.

Say the whole fleet goes out to the right layline and you are dead last. You decide you are going to go over to the left layline. Do something different; right? In this case you are doing the correct thing, because you had absolutely nothing to lose and everything to gain. And if the wind shifts to the left side of the course, you may be first to the weather mark. If it doesn't you will still be no worse than last place. You may be more last than before, but the score is the same for last and more last.

However, the farther up you are in the fleet, the less leverage you want to take a chance on. You have to play the percentages.

Say you have a 20-boat fleet and you are running in 10th place. You want to move up, but you don't want to move back. You want to go to the side where the wind is and where the leaders are, but you don't want to just follow along and hold your position. What can you do different without jeopardizing the position you already have?

In this case, you should tack out of the parade, go to the middle of the course and tack back. If you get a lift, you will gain; if you get a header, you will probably not be in much worse shape than if you had not tacked to the middle.

Let's say in that same fleet you are running second or third. Unless you are compulsive gambler, in this case you don't want to take a chance on much leverage at all. You want to stay with the one or two boats that are ahead of you and go where they go, so you can stay in the same wind patterns and try to outsail them and make less mistakes.

Or, as a small leverage option, you might tack away for a hundred yards or so and tack back to the same side of the course as the lead boats. Meanwhile, you want to be sure you will not lose to any boats behind you in accomplishing this small gambit.

That little hitch upwind could possibly help you gain some on the leaders. Or it could allow you to lose a little bit. Notice that we are talking about losing a "little bit" by taking this small hitch. We don't want to go off the opposite way and possibly lose a lot.

USING RANGES

When you line up the two ends of the starting line with an object on shore to get a transit, you are using a "range."

You also are using ranges when you line up a mark with something on shore so you can find it easily the next time around the course.

The above examples have involved using objects outside the boat. However, you also can use ranges consisting of parts of your boat to find out whether boats on other parts of the race course are going faster or slower than you and also to tell you well in advance whether you are going to have a port-starboard confrontation with another boat. This knowledge can be helpful in making tactical decisions.

For example, if you are sailing to weather on the right side of the course and you want to know how a boat is doing over on the left side of the course, find two points on your boat that you can sight across and line up with that other boat. Do this from your normal position on your boat. Now, as you sight down the range on your boat, if the other boat begins moving ahead of your range, he is going faster than you are; if he begins falling behind your range, he is going slower than you are.

(Caution: The same indications can also mean one or both of you has gotten a header or a lift, but this can be verified by other indicators, such as a reference point on shore for which you are heading or changes in relationships with other boats.)

Let's say you are on port and approaching another boat on starboard. Line him up with a range on your boat. If he starts moving ahead of the range, you know two things: 1) he is going faster than you and 2) he is going to cross in front of you.

If he starts moving behind the range, you know he is going slower than you and that you will be able to cross his bows. However, if the boat stays right in your sights, directly on the range, it means you are on a collision course and should start thinking now about what you are going to do about it.

There is another range of sorts that also can tell you if another boat is going faster or slower than you. That is by using the background beyond the other boat. Here you are creating a range of the boat and whatever is beyond it. If the background is moving faster than the other boat (moving forward of it), it means you are going faster. If the background moves slower than the other boat (moving backward from it), it means you are going slower than he is.

THE NUMBERS GAME

Your tactical decisions will change during the course of a regatta as things narrow down and you know what boats you have to catch and/or what boats you have to cover.

On the first day of a regatta you don't know who is good, who is bad, or who is ugly — or where you fit into the picture. In this case you get your big picture and sail by the basic tactical rules above.

In other words, sail your own race.

By the second day (which in most cases is the last day) you know where you stand and what you have to do. When everybody runs over to look at the standings when they are posted on the bulletin board, it is not so much to see where they finished as to figure out the point spread — who do we have to catch and who do we have to cover? Or how many boats do we have to put between us and the other guy, regardless of where we finish? Or, how can I make sure this guy gets a really bad throwout so he has to keep that 7th place finish?

Now we're into the numbers game, which really makes things interesting and adds to your tactical variables. But at the same time, it helps you to give more structure to your game plan, because you now know exactly what has to be done.

On the last day of a regatta, or maybe the last race, if first place is up for grabs between two boats and you're in a solid third place with nobody else close and you have a chance at second, you can afford to use more leverage. The first and second-place boats are going to be worried about each other and not paying much attention to you. You can afford a bad finish because you will still get third even with a bad throwout, so you can go out on a long limb if you want to. It's not going to hurt you, and it may help you.

If you can keep track of the numbers better than the other guy, it can sometimes give you a critical tactical edge when you get down to the last couple races. And people do sometimes err in their calculations. I'll never forget the time I sat out the last race of a regatta because I thought I had it in the bag, only to find out I had figured wrong.

That's a very sad way to lose a regatta.

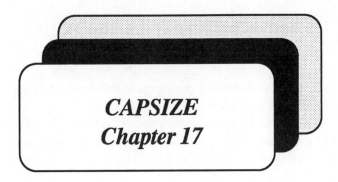

CAPSIZE
Chapter 17

Among monohull sailors, catamarans have a much-undeserved reputation for being tippy and flippy. This seems strange in light of the fact that there are great numbers of round-bottomed monohulls that will virtually roll over at the dock by themselves, and most certainly if you step onto their gunwales, while a catamaran will barely move.

Because of the inherent stability of a boat that is approximately half as wide as it is long, it is difficult to capsize most catamarans in light to moderate air. Wind alone usually will not do it — it takes a lot of weight in the wrong place to make it roll over.

Conversely, if you do manage to capsize it in lighter air, it will be difficult to right it again without enough wind to help it back on its feet.

On the other hand, although it is easier to capsize in heavy air, it also will be quite easy to right the boat, using the technique we will describe in this chapter.

But why capsize in the first place? Almost all catamaran capsizes are preventable.

In heavy air the forces that act on any boat are the same —wind, friction and gravity. When properly controlled, they are not in themselves a reason for capsize; and a catamaran is less inclined to capsize than most light, high-performance, unballasted monohulls of similar size. Regardless of the type of boat, the ultimate cause of capsize almost invariably is some foul-up in the control by the skipper and/or crew.

To understand how to prevent capsize, it first is important to understand the physics that make it possible and the foul-ups that make it happen. And since the situation almost invariably occurs in heavy air and seas, this chapter will relate exclusively to those conditions.

PHYSICAL FACTORS

The three physical factors responsible for capsize are the boat's friction with the water, heeling pressures of the wind on the sails, and the final, deciding factor, gravity.

Boat friction in the water becomes a factor because the sails are capable of going through the air much faster than the boat can go through the water. This can cause the boat to want to trip over its own nose and cause a pitchpole (capsize forward.)

This is counteracted by easing the sails a little to reduce speed and power or by moving the crew weight as far aft as necessary to keep the bows from tripping — or by a combination of the two.

The other factor is the wind pushing against the sails, trying to make the boat heel and fly a hull. When the hulls cannot go forward fast enough for the power generated by the sails, the boat will instead tend to be pushed over sideways. Again, this can be controlled by first getting the weight as far outboard as possible on the windward side; next in order would be to apply lots of downhaul; and then, after the downhaul is as tight as it can be, ease the traveler. Easing the jib sheet would be the next thing to try, and the last thing to do would be to ease the main sheet.

If you begin flying a hull, once the hull gets up to a certain point, the wind pressure is no longer hitting just the sails, it is also hitting the underside of the trampoline, trying to push you over even more.

When the boat reaches its balance point, gravity comes into play, and the weight of the mast and sails will be working together with the wind to help take the boat the rest of the way over.

As on any high-performance boat, reactions on a catamaran in heavy air must be quick and instinctive. The boat can easily get out of control in the hands of a novice going for the thrills before he learns the basics.

Experimenting to see how high you can fly a hull is a fun thing to do, and it is good to know the limits of your boat, but it is important to remember that at a certain point you will have gravity working against you in the weight of the mast and sails; and the wind will be working against you by pushing on the bottom of the trampoline.

This same effect of the wind can work to flip you over backward if you are in irons in heavy air and the wind gets under the front of your trampoline.

FOUL-UP ON BOARD

Capsizes are more likely to occur during racing than daysailing, because the skipper is not free to pick an easier or less precarious point of sail; and he is pushing the boat to its limit, walking a fine line between preventing capsize and keeping the boat moving with the greatest possible speed and power.

The specific reasons and "excuses" for capsize are almost endless; but generally, they boil down to three basic things that go wrong in a myriad of different ways: A sheet that is not released; improper weight distribution; and/or steering errors.

SHEET FOULUPS

■ Sheets can get jammed in the cleats, or the jaws may be at the wrong angle to release easily.

■ The jib sheet may get caught on something on the mast and backwind the boat into a capsize.

■ The mainsheet may have washed out the back of the boat so the skipper cannot release it in a puff.

■ A sheet may tie itself into a knot that jams in the block.

■ The ratchet may be off on the jib block, putting so much pressure on the sheet that the crew cannot get it out of the cleat.

WEIGHT FOULUPS

■ Either skipper or crew cannot unhook from their trapeze rings in time to get across the boat during a tack.

■ The skipper loses his footing when a puff hits and slides down the trampoline to the leeward side, taking the boat over with him.

■ The crew is on the trapeze and aft when the bows dive, throwing him off-balance so he flies forward, pulling the boat over with him.

■ Crew weight is not moved aft fast enough or far enough on reaches and downwind legs and during jibes.

STEERING FOULUPS

■ The helmsman reacts incorrectly to a puff and turns the boat the wrong way.

■ The tiller is pushed or pulled, but the tiller extension is not locked, so the rudders do not respond.

■ A rudder kicks up, reducing steerage.

■ The rudders cavitate on a reach or downwind, reducing steerage.

■ The skipper falls overboard but continues to hold onto the mainsheet.

■ The skipper gets thrown forward from the trapeze on a reach — still holding onto the tiller, he pulls on the rudders, forcing them to turn the wrong way and capsize the boat.

CLEAN UP YOUR ACT

☞ If a boat is well organized, it tends to get into problems much less than one that operates in a constant state of Chinese fire drills.

For example, you should have a clean deck, free from any clutter that may grab and foul a sheet at the wrong time.

☞ Sheets should be tended constantly to ensure they are not washed overboard. An overboard sheet will prevent you from easing the sail. You see, the sheet comes directly from the ratchet block to your hand. If it is then trailing from your hand into the water, when you try to ease the sheet, the resistance of the sheet dragging in the water is as great as the tension on the block. As a result, the sheet does not go out; the sail is not eased; and the boat is in jeopardy of capsize.

☞ The mainsheet, because so much of its length is loose on the deck going to weather, is easily washed overboard. A good way to keep the mainsheet on the boat is tie a bungee cord across the trampoline about halfway between the fore and aft beams and through the loop of the mainsheet. (This is assuming your traveler line and mainsheet are continuous.)

☞ Clear, crisp commands by the one in charge help define what is to be done aboard. Often, in heavy weather, the sounds of the sea and the wind can overwhelm soft-spoken orders; and mistakes are then easily made.

Notes to the crew:

✔ Keeping the deck "neat" and the lines organized is your responsibility. You should tend the mainsheet for the skipper going to weather so it does not wash overboard — and rescue it if it does. Heavy air tends to keep making chaos of the lines, and they will constantly catch on things and tangle themselves in new and creative ways. Try to keep the jib sheet separated from the main and keep a close eye on your jib blocks to make sure they are not going to jam, twist or tangle right before a tack.

THE DANGER SPOTS

Capsizes are most likely to occur in three major situations. In their order of probability, they are: 1) the reach; 2) the jibe; and 3) the tack. If you review the chapters on Boat-Handling, The Reach, The Weather Leg and the Downwind Leg, you have most of the knowledge you need to prevent capsizes, so we will not reiterate that information here.

Whatever you do, try never to let a boat capsize during a race. It's not a good time to get in your righting practice. You probably have read that if you don't capsize once in a while, you are not trying hard enough. But I would suggest that you learn just how much you can get away with at some other time, not while you are racing.

Certainly, you should learn the characteristics of your craft and then push it to the hilt. But first learn where the hilt is.

If you are going to experiment with finding your boat's limitations, do it, number one, when there is an onshore wind and, number two, when there are other boats around to help, if needed.

RIGHTING LINES

Before even going out sailing, you should have installed some form of righting lines on your catamaran. There are many sophisticated rigging setups for righting lines, usually strung beneath the trampoline, and you can easily check out various systems by looking at other boats or by asking catamaran dealers.

But since simple is often best, all you really need is a line that is easily held and tied to the center of the main beam. It must be long enough to be thrown over the hull and reach to the water.

THE CURE: Power-Righting

After you make that pilot error which has put your boat in this extremely inefficient position on its side, you are probably wondering what to do next. Let's go through the capsize from the beginning.

As the boat is beginning to heel and fly a hull, you and your crew should be on the windward (rising) hull. Once the boat, for whatever excuse or reason, reaches a point-of-no-return angle on her side, she probably will go over due to the wind forces on the bottom of the boat and the weight of the mast, sails, and rigging. You might still stop the capsize at this point by getting your weight out to windward to counteract those forces.

But assume you couldn't stop the flow of capsize direction and the boat goes over. She will go over reasonably slowly. When a capsize occurs, it usually seems like a slow-motion replay on TV. Instead of just sitting there watching the show, you should be clambering to what is now the bottom hull, bringing the righting line over the upper hull, and while standing on the bottom hull lean out and away from the boat, holding the line.

The sooner you get the righting line ready and start leaning out, the less likely it is the mast will sink and the boat will "turtle," that is, go totally upside down, with the hulls up and the mast pointing toward the bottom. From the turtled position the boat takes much longer to right. In addition, if you are sailing in shallow waters, the mast could get stuck in the bottom, adding to righting difficulties and possibly damaging the mast.

Your object in going over the upper hull and leaning out immediately on the lower hull is still to attempt to equalize the pressures on each side of the lower hull's gunwale; the gunwale now is the fulcrum point for a teeter-totter.

Keep the boat balanced on that fulcrum by use of your righting lines and your weight.

If you can keep the boat on its side, the wind will blow the boat around to the ideal righting position. The truly ideal righting position would be with the bows pointing straight into the wind, but this is difficult to achieve. So our goal is to get the boat swung until there is at least a 45-degree angle between the leading edge of the mast and the wind and a 45-degree angle between the bows and the wind. *(See Diagram 56.)* Again,

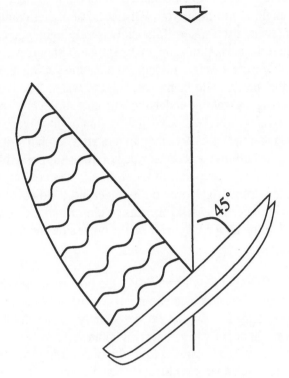

DIAGRAM 56

With the boat on its side, let it swing around until it has reached the
power-righting position in relation to the wind as illustrated above.

the closer you can get the bows into the wind, the easier the boat will be to right.

Weight distribution will help you line the boat up in this ideal righting position. While hiking out on the righting line, get your weight toward the bow of the boat. When you submerge the bow, the wind will blow the stern end of the boat around. Soon you will see the wind coming at the boat in a 45-degree angle to the leading edge of the mast.

It is recommended that the sheets be uncleated before beginning the maneuver, although in some cases it can be righted from the ideal righting position without doing so.

Once in the ideal righting position, all the crew weight should be hiked out as far as possible, with skipper and crew hanging side by side on the righting line. Try to stand straight out from the hull with your bodies at about a 45-degree angle to the water. If your hiking angle is too low, you will be in the water before the mast has come up far enough to right the boat. If your hiking angle is too high, you will not be applying enough pressure to get the mast out of the water. If the crew is very light, you can get additional leverage if the crew climbs up on the skipper's shoulders.

At this point, with the crew weight hiking and the wind getting under the front of the sail, the mast should begin clearing the water. The wind should already be helping by getting under the sail and supplying even more lift.

Once it is obvious that the boat is coming up, grab the dolphin striker or main beam close to the hull that was on its side before the airborne hull hits the water. Otherwise, the momentum of the mast and sail coming up could cause the boat to capsize right over on its other side. However, if you righted the boat with bows at least 45 degrees or closer into the wind, the chances of the boat going all the way over on the other side are significantly lower.

HERE IS A BIG DON'T: Don't try to right the boat with the wind coming from aft, because when it does come up, it will probably capsize again, even though you may be hanging on desperately to the dolphin striker or beam. Or worse, it may try to sail away without you.

If a crew member becomes separated from the boat during the capsize, the remaining crew member should stand on the bow, partially submerging it so the bows will swing around toward the wind, and the boat will not be blown too rapidly away from the crew member attempting to swim back to it.

TURNING TURTLE

Suppose you made two pilot errors; first, not preventing the capsize; but worse, not preventing the boat from turning turtle.

You and your crew should place your weight at the stern of the boat on the upside-down hull that is the most leeward to the wind. Then start pulling on the righting line steadily. This should get the windward bow to come up out of the water quite a way; as the wind gets under it, the bow will gradually start to come up more and more.

The higher the bow gets, the more the force of the wind and waves will help to start the boat up on its side. Once the boat gets close to being on its side, you should walk forward on the same hull and continue righting action as described above for when the boat was merely on its side.

One common reason for a boat turtling is that the mast fills with water, making it considerably heavier. This additional weight also makes it much more difficult to right the boat even when it is on its side.

To compound the problem if the water cannot drain out again, your boat is more susceptible to future capsize because of the weight aloft. It is sort of like sailing with a concrete block tied to the top of your mast.

If you are aware that your mast leaks, make every attempt to seal it so it is watertight. Some people fill their masts with foam flotation, which is very good insurance against turtling. (If it cannot be sealed, at least make sure there is a way for water to drain out again.)

These righting techniques are workable only for the smaller, beach-type catamaran designs, although they can be deployed to a certain extent by larger, wider and/or heavier boats. However, some boats, once turtled, cannot be righted without outside assistance.

The best way to right one of these boats is to tie a line from the mast base and bring it aft down the bottom of the deck or trampoline (which is facing upward) to the helping boat. Use a fairly short line; too long a tow line makes righting very difficult.

When the towing boat begins pulling, the crew should stand at the aft end of the overturned boat, at or near the rear beam, forcing it down and forming a water shovel out of the stern. A crew member also should hold the tow rope centered in the middle of the deck, steadying it precisely between and parallel to the hulls. The pulling boat, by applying steady yet increasing power, will pull the boat up end over end. The sails and rigging will have no pressure on them, making it easier to right and saving a great deal of damage. She will come up out of the water like a Sailfish.

Larger or wider boats have two other options available to them to help right themselves, provided they do not turtle.

One is a quick-release extension on the sidestay that will lengthen the stay on one side, so the weight of the mast and sails are not as heavily counteracting the leverage of the crew.

The other is a water bag that can be filled and lifted clear of the water to give enough leverage to right the boat.

One advantage to capsizing a catamaran, compared to many monohulls, is that, once righted, it shakes the water off its sails and you are on your way again — not still sitting there with a boat full of water.

REVIVAL
Chapter 18

BY MARY WELLS

This is audience participation time — a brainstorming session of sorts — to address a troubling problem that affects the entire sailing community and attempt to come up with some solutions.

Small-boat sailing and racing have been on the decline for the past 30 years. Fleets have been dying out at clubs all over the country. Even catamarans, which gave the sport a shot in the arm in the late '60's, '70's, and early '80's, are feeling the effects now of this decline.

There are a myriad of possible reasons people give for this downswing in general and for catamarans in particular. Among them:

● The economy is bad

● Small-boat racers are going to larger racing boats

● Fleet members leave when they start having children

● Older members stop sailing because they feel they are too old

● No younger people are joining the ranks

● There are too many other activities that compete with sailing for people's leisure time

● Even small one-designs are becoming too expensive for many to afford

● People with families want a boat they can all day-sail on comfortably or sleep on for short weekend trips

● There is not enough class loyalty; and, therefore, fleets are being diluted by the proliferation of catamaran designs

● People seem to be more interested in owning the latest, fastest design than in racing in an established, one-design fleet

●Young people just out of school are too busy trying to start a career and too poor to afford a boat

●The young people who do sail often take the path of least expense by crewing on a big boat

●People sell their two-man boats and get a unirig because they can never find crew

●People today are lazier than they used to be and they want sports that don't require as much effort as sailing does.

●"I'm just too busy."

Discussions of the problem usually go in an endless circle of possible reasons and always come back to the same question: But what can we do about it?

I submit that most of the above-mentioned "reasons" for the decline of one-design sailing are things that were just as true 40 years ago when the sport was rising to a peak of popularity.

Too old? Bunk. Sailing is one of the few sports you can do until the day you die. Some types of sailboats, including some types of catamarans, are more athletic than others — you just have to pick the right boat.

Too young? Kids can start crewing as soon as they can help pull in a sheet.

Too poor? Sailing is one of the cheapest sports there is. Good, used sailboats are everywhere for bargain basement prices. And if you can't afford a boat, you can easily find a crewing job on one for nothing. Just hang around any fleet, and you'll be able to sail.

You have a wife and small children and your wife doesn't want to sit on the beach all day while you are sailing? Get a babysitter to come with you to the beach, so your wife can sail with you. Most teenage girls would love to spend a day at the beach, and cheap. Or take turns with another sailing mother. Or find another crew until your children are old enough or until your wife can start crewing again.

My happiest childhood memories are of the weekends I spent at the beach playing in the water and having picnic lunches while my father was out racing. While my sister and I were young, my mother was on the beach with us, along with the wife and children of my father's crew.

Sailing was always a part of my life. And when I was old enough, I began racing with my father. When my sister was old enough, she began racing with my father. Because of this early exposure, we are sailing to this day, at ages 50 and 46, in different parts of the country.

Your spouse doesn't want to be involved at all? That is one of the most important problems and one we hope this chapter will help address.

Too busy? This is not bunk. If you are too busy to find time for yourself and for recreation, it means you would rather work and don't really want to have fun. It means your work IS your recreation, so you don't need a boat, or golf clubs, or a tennis racquet or anything. If you're happy with your life, so be it.

In the final analysis, if people really WANT to do something badly enough, they will usually find a way to do it. They will surmount any or all of the above obstacles.

So if people are dropping out of sailing, the important thing to realize is that it is not because they CAN'T do it — it's because they don't really want to do it. And the question we really have to be asking is, "WHY don't they want to do it?"

The answer to this is very simple: They're not having fun. So the solution is also simple: We need to put the FUN back into sailing, and we have to provide something for everyone, based upon their reasons for sailing in the first place. Let's think about what those reasons are.

WHY PEOPLE SAIL:

People get into sailing in general for a variety of reasons:

• They have always been attracted to the water and have read books about the romance and appeal of sailing.

• They have watched other people sailing and think, "If they can do it, I can, too."

• They sailed when they were younger and are returning to the sport.

• It's something the whole family can do together, as opposed to say, golf or hang-gliding or tennis or racquetball.

• They want a boat so they can get out on the water, but they don't like the noise and smell and fuel expense of motorboats.

• They are fascinated by the idea of sailing — using the wind to go where you want to.

• They have been involved competitively in other sports, such as motocross or car racing, and want to get involved in competition that will be less damaging to their bodies. These people get into sailing specifically with the idea of racing.

This last group is an exception, because most people do not begin sailing with the idea of racing. They begin with the idea of relaxation and fun.

People specifically get into catamarans for additional reasons:

● Their past experience has been on catamarans and that is all they are familiar with.

● They have sailed monohulls, but they want to go faster.

● They figure, "If I am going to buy my first sailboat, I might as well buy a fast sailboat, because faster means more fun."

● Most catamarans can be launched off a beach, so you don't have the additional expense of launching fees at a ramp or of belonging to a yacht club or sailing club.

● Many couples get into cats because they are two-person boats that are ideally suited to male-female teams.

● They are interested in physics and technology and want a type of boat that is on the leading edge of those things. They are the engineers and the 'tinkerers.' Because of the speed of catamarans, the effect of small changes is much more dramatic and noticeable — an appeal to the designer/innovator types.

WHY PEOPLE JOIN A FLEET:

Now that we have thought about the reasons why people buy sailboats in general and catamarans in particular, let's talk about why they would think about joining a fleet or club, as opposed to just sailing by themselves.

The reasons for joining a fleet include:

● Being able to have fun with a bunch of other boats instead of by yourself.

● Wanting to be socially a member of a group of people who have similar interests.

● Giving a structure to their recreational plans involving sailing.

● Having a healthy, outdoor activity that their whole family can participate in.

● Wanting to be able to race.

Note that I have put "racing" at the bottom of the list here, and I will get into that right now.

PROS AND CONS OF RACING:

Racing has been both the catalyst that has helped build catamaran fleets and the nemesis that is helping to destroy them.

What happens is that it starts out with racing being fun, and you get more and more people involved, and soon almost everyone in the fleet starts participating. But then it begins to become less and less fun, because people start getting TOO serious about the racing and racing is the ONLY thing they are doing and the only thing they are interested in.

Skippers become so concerned about winning the season series or becoming "Skipper of the Year" that they lose sight of the reason they got into sailing in the first place, and they forget that not everyone feels the way they do.

You would think every Sunday series of races is a world championship. New members of the group will get disqualified because of minor infractions of fleet rules they don't yet know. Skippers start yelling at their crews (often their spouses) and the spouses rebel. Soon that couple drops out of sailing. And it's no wonder. When it gets down to a choice between sailing or holding your marriage together, there aren't any options.

And just as unfortunate, when people think only in terms of racing, if they aren't doing very well and don't seem to be getting better, they eventually get discouraged and just drop out of sailing altogether.

And that's my point. It doesn't have to be that way. We have to get a perspective on this racing thing before it dies completely.

Certainly, no sport is complete without competition. And it is almost instinctive. If you're sailing a cruising boat to Bimini and you see another boat overtaking you, you're probably going to roust your crew out of the hammock and put up more sail. But when it gets to the point where you or your crew is no longer able to enjoy the adventure of sailing, you're going too far.

Too many people think that racing is the only real purpose for a fleet's existence — and too often that is true. And this attitude can ultimately result in the fleet's downfall. A well-balanced, well-rounded fleet with activities that appeal to everyone will inevitably be a healthier, stronger fleet. And it will inevitably grow, because of the fundamental fact that people can overcome any obstacles when they really enjoy doing something.

Almost every catamaran fleet sails off beaches where there are other catamarans just "playing." If you ask these people why they don't belong to such-and-such fleet, they will probably say, "Nah, I'm not into racing."

Let's get rid of this "For Racers Only" label.

HOW TO PUT MORE FUN INTO SAILING:

☞ Have a light-air capsize-and-right contest, close to the beach. It isn't easy to capsize a catamaran in light air; it also isn't easy to right it. This could make for great photo opportunities.

☞ When there is wind, have a capsize clinic in shallow water to demonstrate how to right the boat.

NOTE: Things you do close to the beach are fun spectator events for the people who are not sailing.

☞ Choose up sides and have a paintball war — reconstruct the Battle of Lake Erie (or a pirate battle or any other kind of battle) on catamarans.

☞ Have an annual fleet regatta, open to all catamarans in the area (or state, or country), with races and games and contests and a barbecue/picnic and maybe a parade with the boats decorated as floats. Have activities for everyone, including the children. This can be a one-day or two-day event.

☞ On a weekend right before Halloween, have everyone come in costume and have a "pumpkin hunt" on the water. Everybody has to bring two or three small, plastic play balls (about 10 inches in diameter), preferably orange. A boat — preferably a powerboat —takes them out and disperses them on the water. At an audible signal, everybody leaves the beach and starts hunting down the "pumpkins." The person who brings back the most wins a prize — maybe a pumpkin pie. Also, of course, have prizes for the costumes. (The most difficult part of the pumpkin hunt is keeping them on your boat until you get back to the beach.)

☞ Play ball tag. Using marks, lay out a large circle or box on the water that all the boats have to stay inside. One boat is "it" and has the ball, and they have to try to hit another boat. If the other boat is hit by the ball, they are now "it," and the other boats have to try to avoid them, while staying in the confines of the "box." If you go outside the box to avoid the ball, you are automatically "it."

I've been told one of the strategies of this game is to throw the ball so that it will bounce off the other boat and they have to retrieve it. If it hits the sail and falls onto their deck, they can pick it up and throw it right back at you.

☛ Have a treasure hunt. Give a clue to the first point. When sailors find that point, they will find a clue to the next point, and so on, until they find the "treasure." The person who brings back the treasure is the winner.

☛ Scavenger hunts - The list of things to be brought back will depend on the area you are sailing in. If you are on an inland lake surrounded by houses, your scavenge list can be extensive. If you are on an undeveloped bay, the list will include various types of organic and inorganic things that can be found in that area, like clamshells, seaweed, sand, coral, leaves, driftwood, bird feathers, beach glass, mosquitoes, mangrove roots, discarded tires — whatever people should be able to find. Put a time limit on the search.

☛ Picnic trips — take the whole family and a couple of coolers and sail to an island or another beach across the lake —someplace different — have a picnic and sail back. This can also be an informal race each way, if it makes it more fun. But if racing means someone is going to "cheat" by leaving behind any of their beer or food, forget the racing.

☛ "Cruises," maybe even overnighters, camping on the boats or on the beach.

☛ Have a hull-flying contest — who can keep it the highest the longest. (More great photo opportunities.)

☛ Waterski behind the boats. It definitely can be done, but you need the old-style, wide waterskis.

☛ Have a "drag" race — Every boat has to pull someone behind on an innertube.

☛ You don't always have to sail your sailboat. Get an outboard bracket and a little motor so you can be more versatile — go places difficult to navigate under sail. Get some clamp-on, battery-operated lights and go places at night. Go up a river or through a swamp. I know this is a really revolutionary idea, but you can even leave your mast at home and just take a power cruise if you want to explore a canal or river that has a lot of bridges. There are lots of adventures out there waiting for people to make them happen. There are places you can go with a sailboat that you can't with a powerboat. Take advantage of that.

HOW TO PUT MORE FUN INTO RACING:

Racing does not always have to be serious. There are many things you can do to make races more interesting and fun — even for the people who don't want anything to do with serious racing.

☛ Backward race — This is sort of like a backward drag race. You set up a normal starting line and set a finish line down at the leeward mark. Before the start everybody gets upwind of the starting line, starts the race going backward and backs down to and across the finish line. (Of course, before you do this race, you have a clinic to explain how to go backward and how to go backward faster.) And you don't want to do this race in heavy air.

☛ Anchor start — crews have to swim to the boat from the beach. This can be designed either that your sails are already up or that you have to raise sails after you get out to the boat.

☛ LeMans start off beach and finish back on the beach.

☛ Surprise race — the race starts normally, with a normal triangle, but you have secret instructions inside a balloon that is to be broken open when an audible or visual signal is given at some unknown point during the race. The instructions will tell you where you are to go from wherever you are at that point. They may tell you to turn around and go back the way you came. Or they may tell you to head for the floating bar across the lake. You never know.

☛ Relay race. Divide the fleet into teams of three boats each. One boat from each team will start and race to the weather mark, where the second boats from each team will be waiting. The first team boat hands off or tosses a "baton" (or ball or whatever) to the second boat on his team, which will race to the B mark. The third boats of the teams will be waiting there to take the batons and race to the C mark. Meanwhile, the boats that started the race will have sailed down to the C mark and will be waiting to take the batons and race to the finish.

☛ A Columbus race. This is a windward-leeward race (or maybe even just a leeward race), where people are not allowed to tack downwind — they have to go wing and wing, just like in the old days of catamarans and just like most monohulls still do, and certainly like Columbus did to get here.

☛ Based upon the above, just as a learning experience, have a race where half of the boats get to tack downwind and the other half have to go straight downwind, and see what the difference is when you get to the lee-ward mark. It could be very interesting.

Then do it again, with the two groups switching roles.

☛ Reaching race. Set up a two-way course across the wind that will be a LONG beam reach both directions. This will be fun for both the daysailors and the serious racers. On most race courses the reaching leg is very short, and catamaran courses often don't include a reach at all, so this will be a chance to have a really fun speed race.

☛ 720 race — the first boat around each mark has to do a 720. Make sure it is a race with lots of mark roundings, to make it more difficult to figure out the strategy so you can still finish first. (No sandbagging al-lowed. A good way to prevent sandbagging is to threaten the possibility of shortening course.)

☛ Crew race — your crew must be on the helm throughout the race and will give the orders and make the decisions (although they may con-sult with their former-skipper-now-crew).

☛ Women-only race. Women team up on the boats and race. This is absolutely sex-discrimination — no men allowed. It doesn't matter whether a woman is normally a skipper or a crew — for this race she is qualified. When women race with women and against women, a very in-teresting thing happens: Those who did not like it may find out they can actually enjoy racing. Because women don't take everything as a life-or-death-crisis situation, there is less pressure. And when there is less pressure, you tend to sail better. If you have enough women in your fleet, I think this is a great way to get them more excited about sailing.

☛ Long-distance races. Lots of people who are not interested at all in racing around the buoys are crazy about long-distance races. And I think the concept appeals to all of us: Get from point A to point B as fast as you can, the fastest way you can. It's sort of like playing Rugby — hardly any rules. Just go fast and know what reefs or shoals you can get over and which you have to go around.

☛ Have a tacking contest — Starting two boats at a time, see who can do the most tacks in five minutes.

☛ Have 720 contests — see who can do a 720 the fastest.

All of the above, whether fun or informative events or non-serious races, will still be fun for the hard-core racers, but at the same time they are fun for the nonracers and the non-serious racers.

OTHER THINGS YOU CAN DO — AND NOT DO:

☞ When you have social events or non-sailing events, whether it is at a bar or restaurant or at a member's home, make sure everyone feels like part of the group. Fleets are not that big to begin with, and it is destructive when people segregate into cliques — the social group, the racers, the cruising sailors...

Remember that everyone is in this group because they love sailing, regardless of how they do it (or, in some cases, whether they do it at all anymore). So try to structure your events around themes of water or sailing, so everyone feels a common bond. (Remember, a lot of people who belong to NOW are not women, and you don't have to be black to belong to the NAACP.)

If anyone starts thinking, "This is just a social club" or "This is just a racing club" or "This is just a cruising club," you are going to lose members.

☞Above all, don't try to push racing on confirmed nonracers. It's hard for some people to understand why everyone doesn't want to race, but pushing people into it will only result in pushing them away.

☞ Show videos of sailing-related things — like the America's Cup or the Worrell 1000 or maybe a charter cruise in the Bahamas. Have a member who has a camcorder take videos of your own group racing or just having fun on the water, and show them at a party.

☞ Speaking of charter cruises, why not get your whole fleet together to take a charter cruise to the Bahamas — either on one big boat or a group of smaller ones. There are bareboats in south Florida that can sleep anywhere from 12-24 people for a week.

☞ Have speakers come in to talk. There is an endless variety of subjects. When we were in Tucson one time, the fleet had speakers come in and give a slide-show presentation on their research on whales in Alaska.

☞ Have someone take videos of all the fun events you have during the year and then show them at your end-of-season party.

☞ Make sure someone takes photographs, as well, and try to get every fleet member on film at one time or another. Keep fleet albums for each year.

☞ Finally, one important thing we can do is eliminate segregation among catamaran fleets. The proliferation of catamaran designs has resulted in diluting fleets. A fleet with two or three boats is no fun for anyone. Perhaps at this point it is time to consolidate fleets and form "catamaran clubs," open to all classes, and with portsmouth races available to those who do not have enough boats for a start.

THE IMPORTANCE OF A NEWSLETTER

One of the most important forms of glue for any fleet (or any class association, for that matter) is an interesting and informative newsletter that comes out often and that isn't just about racing. Get social and fun stuff in there, things about equipment and tuning and safety, places to go for short daysails or overnight cruises, etc. A lot of people don't bother to learn much about what there is to do in their own area. They reach out and back within a few miles of a beach for a couple years, get bored and take up another sport.

Put in informative tidbits about the waterlife and the birdlife seen in your area when you are at the beach or sailing. For example: Where do the seagulls in Michigan go in the wintertime? Where do Florida's pelicans sleep at night? What is all that seaweed or grass that sometimes floats on the water and where does it come from? How does algae in lakes affect people with allergies? All you have to do to get ideas is think of questions.

Read sailing magazines, and when you see something interesting about your class of boat, send it to the newsletter chairman so they can put a paragraph about it in the newsletter.

Put in notes about political things happening that affect sailing in general or your class in particular.

A newsletter should not be the job of one person — and it should not be a job that is dreaded because "it is too much work." It should be a fleet effort. Everyone should contribute items to it. And questions that would make interesting little articles should be assigned to various people to research.

At the beginning of the year, send all the fleet members a long list of questions and possible mini-topics and ask people to pick out things that interest them and or that they already know about and send you two or three paragraphs.

Have a "Tips" column that everybody can contribute to. Like how to jury-rig a repair for some part that breaks; an easier way to raise a mast; how to make your own cat tracks — cheap; how to build a cabin on a Hobie 18 and turn it into a houseboat....well, you get the idea.

The well of information you can draw from is bottomless, and there should never be a reason to have trouble filling up a newsletter. In fact, the problem should be the reverse.

NOTE: If your fleet is doing interesting things, it is a lot easier to have an interesting newsletter, so adding more fun stuff to your schedule gives you more to talk about and, in turn, generates more interest and makes more fun events possible.

WHAT YOU CAN DO TO BUILD UP THE RACING

☛Open up your fleet races to all catamarans and provide a Portsmouth fleet.

☛Put on clinics prior to the skipper's meeting on each race day for the novice sailors. Discuss rules, boat tuning for the conditions that day, how to find the marks, etc.

☛Have races occasionally where the veteran sailors crew for the novice sailors or the mid-fleeters and help them out. Or have the veteran skippers and novice skippers switch crews. A novice crew can learn a great deal by sailing with a skilled skipper; and by the same token, a novice skipper can learn a lot from a good, well-trained crew.

☛Be nice to and tolerant of new racers or new members to your fleet. Don't be a hardnose and say, "You're disqualified" for some minor infraction they don't even know about. It's a sure way to turn people off.

☛Don't yell at novices when they make mistakes on the race course — talk to them after the race and explain what they did wrong and how to do it right.

☛Always be positive and encouraging and helpful.

☛Don't wait for them to ask — tell them everything you know (not all at once, of course). One of the common complaints of newer racers is that the hotshots in their fleet don't want to share their "secrets."

I think part of that problem is that people don't know what or how to ask. Not too long ago someone sailing their first race with our fleet was sailing his Hobie 18 wing-and-wing downwind. He must have wondered where everybody else was going, but he didn't ask later on the beach. In this situation, it is up to the more experienced fleet members to explain the concept of tacking downwind.

And if someone is always reaching off into never-never-land upwind, explain to them how to trim their sails and use their telltales to point up to a normal, 45-degree angle to the wind.

If you do not help people get better, they are going to get discouraged, and you are going to lose a fleet member.

☛ If you don't have fleets divided by ability level, you may attract more racers by having a "fun racer" class. A lot of people are intimidated by the aggressiveness of the "serious" racers and would enjoy racing if they could do it for "fun," without feeling like everyone is out for blood. This kind of class might get more of the women and children off the beach and onto the water, too — and that's the whole key: getting people on the water. You might be surprised — the "fun" class might get bigger than the "serious" class.

☛ Have free clinics for your fleet on a REGULAR basis. These can be put on by members or you can get an expert to come in once in a while, if possible. Each clinic should be fairly short (like an hour or two at most) and devoted to a specific topic, such as:

Boat tuning
Sail shape
Boat handling
Tactics
Rules
Safety
Heavy air sailing
Light air sailing
Downwind sailing
Capsize and righting
Crewing
Mark roundings
Starts

The idea is to make the clinics an ongoing series that will keep people interested and keep them learning, without taking too much out of their day when they want to be out sailing. Most of these clinics would be of equal value and interest to the nonracer as to the racer.

☛ Have a "drill" day. Instead of serious races, have seminar-type drills to practice boat-handling, starts and mark-roundings. We are soon publishing a booklet with drills you can do alone or as a fleet to improve sailing skills.

SEMINARS

To go a step further, professionally run seminars are a great way to revive your fleet or club's enthusiasm as well as improving skills.

Find out about seminars that are available to people learning how to sail or for race training and let your members know about them through your newsletter.

The Ontario Sailing Centre in Canada has a series of five-day seminars every year, featuring a different type of boat each week. They have one week dedicated to catamarans.

In this country the only permanently established race-training program I know of for catamarans is Rick White's Sailing Seminars, based on the Ontario program. He recently branched out into monohulls beginning in the spring of 1991, with seminars for Sunfish and Lasers.

Rick White's seminars are held in the Florida Keys in the spring and fall, but the seminars are on the road the rest of the year, and they will go just about anywhere, so if you would like him to bring a seminar to your area, just give us a call.

What is really important to stress is that the hard-core racers, if they don't want to have fewer and fewer people to race against, have got to stop being so concerned about being number one and start thinking about the other guy a little more.

We have to be willing to give a little bit of our time to getting more people involved and keeping everyone happy, instead of just thinking about ourselves and our own goals and trophies. You can't win a trophy unless there is a race. And you can't have a race without other boats and people.

It doesn't mean much to be number one in your local pond if you're the only one.

TO GET NEW PEOPLE INTERESTED IN SAILING.

☛ Send your newsletter to everyone you know who has that type of boat — or any class of boat if you're an open club — so they'll get interested in joining your group because it sounds like so much fun.

☛ Get the local dealer involved and interested, if he isn't already. Get him to join the fleet or club and get him to participate in races and social functions, so he is a friend as well as a supplier. An active, supportive dealer can make a tremendous difference in the health of a fleet.

☛ Have a learn-to-sail day. If you schedule, say, four of these a year and bill them as open sailing clinics for anyone to learn to sail, and advertise them by getting articles in the local news media, you will accomplish a number of things:

1. You will help people learn to sail who would not otherwise take the initiative to go out and do it.

2. You will be introducing them to catamarans.

3. You may get a new fleet member out of it.

4. You will be making big points with the community as a service-minded organization.

☞ Have a take-a-ride day. On a smaller scale, you can just take people out for rides to give them a taste of what sailing is like or introduce people to catamarans.

☞ Take a friend out sailing with you. You never know who is going to get hooked on it. One of our best friends in South Florida is Henry Rodriguez. He used to have a fast powerboat with a tuna tower, and his big thing was water skiing and going fast.

He went for a sail on a cat on a windy day and was immediately hooked. Since then he has sold his powerboat and has become one of the most enthusiastic and hottest sailors around.

☞ Almost everyone belongs to other clubs and organizations or church groups. Groups like that are always looking for guest speakers and programs. Give a talk and slide show about sailing. Invite that whole club out for a day on the water with your fleet. Get them interested. You may get a new member or two.

☞ Get a youth sailing program going. I know the kids don't want to do it. They'd rather watch TV or go to the mall. But MAKE them do it. Get them involved in sailing as a family activity. If it's your own kids, get them excited about it and make them feel like an important part of the team. With me and with my sister, my father accomplished that by putting us on the helm. Once you've been the driver, sailing is hard to get out of your system.

☞ It's always harder to teach members of your own family, whether it's your wife or your kids. So try having kids and/or spouses go out on a boat with one of the other sailors when they're in the early learning stages.

☞ If you have school-age children (or even if you don't), start a sailing club in the local schools.

☞ Get your local community college to have a course, either credited or noncredit, teaching people to sail, and get your fleet involved, either helping personally or loaning boats.

☞ Go to a local high school and give a talk to the gym class about catamaran racing as a sport — and as an Olympic sport. Maybe at the same time you can find some potential crew members.

WHEN YOU TAKE SOMEONE FOR A FIRST RIDE:

Everyone had a FIRST TIME at sailing. If they had a great experience, perhaps they decided to get a sailboat themselves. If they had a bad experience, they may have said, "Never again."

If you take someone sailing for the first time, always make it a FUN experience. Don't take someone out on a day that's going to scare them to death. They'll think, "Gee, this is sort of fun, but I could never do it." On the other hand, don't take them out on a day that's going to bore them to death, either.

If you take someone with you in a race, get them excited about the competition and try to make some sense out of it for them, explain what's happening as you go along; but don't take them out in a race you really need to win. Whatever you do, don't turn them off by yelling at them.

A HOME OF YOUR OWN

Lastly, I want to address one valid problem that small cats have that is not usually shared by monohull one-design fleets. Most catamaran fleets have no "home," while most monohull racers belong to a yacht club or sailing club, store their boats there and race out of there. Some catamaran fleets are fortunate enough to have a "home beach"; others do not even have that.

It is unquestionably an advantage to have a clubhouse to call home — a place to get out of the sun or out of the rain. A place to store the beer and set up a barbecue and have picnics. A roof to draw the group together. A place to display trophies and pictures and to show videos and have meetings. A place where you can work on your boat and sand your battens. A place where you can comfortably spend the day with your family even if you aren't sailing. A place with restrooms and maybe even a shower.

On the other hand, beaches are what the beach cat was designed for — to give people the freedom to sail wherever there is a beach and not be confined to places that have launching ramps or hoists, as monohulls are. It opened up sailing to a lot of people who could not afford or did not want to belong to an established sailing club.

Therefore, catamaran sailors have become nomads, traveling from beach to beach for regattas. Sand, porta-johns, hot dogs and beer are fun for a few years — but eventually, for some, the romance wears off and people start wanting commitment, security, a home to call their own.

If you think your fleet may be suffering from beach burnout, there are three possibilities — and probably more.

1. All of you can join an existing sailing club. This has many advantages. The club probably already has all the facilities you need, both for comfort ashore and racing on the water, including crash boats, marks, flags, etc. Because you are already a fleet, you can join right in with their regular racing program. And when your fleet hosts regattas, you will have the whole club to help you out, instead of just your own fleet members. If there is room in the drysail area, you may also be able to store your boats there — or at least get on the waiting list for spaces. It will cost more to belong to a club, but your existing fleet expenses also will be greatly reduced.

2. Find an existing commercial operation or facility that you can sort of blend in with. For instance, a beach-boat rental concession might want to lease or sublease space to you for your club, as long as you do not interfere with the operation. If there is no building you can use or share, find out if you can put up an inexpensive storage shed or pole building. Even a travel trailer with an awning would do the job. The more activity that is going on around a rental concession, and the more boats on the water, the better it will be for his business, too.

A beachfront bar is another possibility — you lease some beach, and he gets a guaranteed batch of customers — not to mention the customers who will come just to watch the sailboats.

One club we know of rented the first-floor storage area of a small, beachfront apartment building.

3. Start a whole new club. And this is not an impossible dream. Most small sailing clubs — and some large ones — started out with a loose-knit group of sailors meeting at members' homes. With creative thinking and hard work, they made their dream of a real club come true.

It can be at waterfront property owned by a fleet member or just a sailing enthusiast. You might obtain a nominal-fee lease for a section of government-owned property if your club provides learn-to-sail programs and other water-related activities that are open to the community. A sailing club in Massachusetts has the use of an old, abandoned house on a former military installation. Sandusky Sailing Club in Ohio, Miami Yacht Club, the Jericho Sailing Center in Vancouver, B.C., and the Stuart (Florida) Sailing Club are only a few of the clubs that exist on government-owned property.

Do not dismiss this idea as being too expensive until you research the possibilities.

On the other hand, this project needs enough boats and people to make it feasible — one fleet probably will not cut it. This is a case where sailing loyalty must supersede fleet loyalty. So talk to all catamaran fleets in the area and all catamaran owners you know to find out if there is interest. If there is not enough interest to form a "catamaran-only" club, spread out into monohulls — open your arms to anything that sails.

Not only is there strength in numbers, if many different classes are included in your club, you don't have to lose touch with someone just because they decide to buy a different type of boat or go to a different fleet — they will still be part of the club "family."

NOTE: It is difficult for the modern beachcat sailor to imagine sailing without a wide, sandy beach. But catamarans can be launched on ramps and by hoists just as monohulls are — so if you find a site that is ideal in every way except that it does not have a beach, do not discount it automatically. There are even creative ways to deal with launching across rocks and over walls. We have been at clubs that do both.

In the days before the term "beach cat" was coined, it never even occurred to most of us to launch our P-Cats, Sharks and Tornadoes on a beach — we used hoists, right along with the Thistles and Lightnings and Snipes, et al.

THE BORING BUT IMPORTANT BASICS:

☞ Join and support your local fleet and your national class association.

☞ Join United States Sailing (formerly USYRU) and lobby for changes and improvements when necessary.

It may not seem like we need USS, but the reason it seems like we don't need them is because of all the work they have done over the years to refine the sport and the rules so everything will run smoother for all classes, from sailboards and cats to IOR's.

In truth, catamarans need USS far more than the monohulls do. We are only now, after years of discrimination, beginning to get equal recognition in clubs and starts in races that formerly prohibited multihulls.

USS now has a multihull council and area representatives around the country. Our multihull council has a vote in every decision made by the organization. USS has an ongoing program to standardize and improve handicap ratings for multihulls. They need our support so they can continue to support the cause of multihulls as well as all sailboat racing in the country.

And finally: It seems like every fleet or club needs a catalyst — someone who makes things happen and keeps the vitality and enthusiasm level high. Unfortunately, too often such a person also ends up doing all the work and eventually gets burned out. If your catalyst gives up, the whole thing falls apart.

The way I look at it is that a fleet or club is like a marriage — it takes a lot more than hull-flying and love to hold it together. It takes a lot of work and dedication, too. And if the existing members are not willing to do that work, the fleet will die of attrition, and members will eventually go their separate ways.

So it is very important for everyone — everyone who cares — to help out and get involved. If you have a stake in the success of this group 'marriage,' you are more likely to work at it. And the more people who are involved, the more likely you are to make it work.

This book is entitled "Catamaran Racing." It has told you how to make your boats go faster and how to win races, but that information is only important to the group of existing racers. And going fast and winning races is only important when there are other people to race against.

What we really need to address is how to get more people into the sport and how to keep the people we have, how to revive enthusiasm and get more boats on the water in all of our local ponds, lakes, sounds, bays, rivers and oceans.

Once you get people sailing, racing is a natural evolutionary development for some people — others will never care, and that's fine, too. The important thing is to keep sailing fun for everyone, whatever they want to do with their sailboat — just so long as it doesn't rot in their back yard.

As we said at the beginning of this chapter, this is audience participation time. We have thrown out a bunch of ideas. You probably have more, and you probably don't like some of ours. But it's time to stop scratching our heads and **DO SOMETHING.**

GUEST CHAPTERS

When it comes to sailing, nothing is written in stone and there is not one totally RIGHT way to do things, as will become very apparent when you read the following guest chapters.

There are differences in the way things are done from boat to boat, from sailor to sailor, from country to country, and from year to year.

Listening to the varieties of approaches people take to solving the same problems and the varieties of basic sailing styles can be informative, but it can also be confusing. Who is right? Who should I listen to?

The answer is that no one is right and no one is wrong and that you should listen to everyone. The more you learn about different techniques, the more things you can try until you find the combination that will become your personal sailing style. It's sort of like mini-skirts -- they don't look good on everyone. You have to find out what works best for you and for your boat.

All of those who have contributed to this book by helping with the following chapters are very successful sailors, and no one can argue with success. But what works for them may not necessarily work for you, and vice versa.

We do not always agree with everything they say, and they probably don't agree with everything in this book. But that is part of the endless fascination sailing holds for all of us who have made it a part of our lives.

The same question will bring slightly different answers from everyone. The same theory will be explained in slightly different ways. Some theories seem to contradict each other. One sailor takes the high road and one takes the low; each thinks his road is the right one; and often they arrive at the same destination at the same time.

Sailing is rampant with theories. Some have been proven, some disproven, some are still up in the air, and the rest of them reside in the minds of sailors everywhere -- just as every true sailor has in his mind an idea for a great boat design.

Do not pass up any of these chapters just because they are not about your particular type of boat. There are many new insights and valuable pieces of information in each chapter that can benefit you regardless of the kind of boat you sail.

A Q&A INTERVIEW WITH RANDY SMYTH

Randy Smyth, U.S. Olympic silver medalist in the Tornado in 1984, has won 26 national multihull championship titles and three world championships since 1980. He has won major titles on the Prindle 16, Prindle 18, Prindle 18.2, Prindle 19, Nacra 6.0, Stiletto 23, Stiletto 27, Formula 40 and Hobie 21.

Twice ProSail Formula 40 Champion, he successfully defended that title against all challengers. He has won the Pacific 1000 and has twice won the World (formerly Worrell) 1000, and has set course records in both of those races. In 1990 he won the Tahiti Mondiale Cat Challenge.

He has won the Tornado Worlds seven times, the North Americans twice and the Europeans once. He won the Prindle 19 Nationals in 1986, 1987 and 1990. His 1985 victory in the World 1000 was on a Prindle 19.

He was a sailing and design consultant to Dennis Conner's America's Cup campaign in 1988, and he is the only multihull sailor ever to be voted Rolex Yachtsman of the Year.

From his home port in Ft. Walton Beach, Florida he operates a sailmaking business, The Smyth Team Sails.

As this book went to press, he was in the midst of his campaign to win the Olympic berth on Tornadoes for the 1992 Olympics.

This chapter concentrates on the Prindle 19, but at the end we have included a section spelling out some specific differences that need to be applied to sailing a Tornado. Otherwise, most of the information in this chapter is applicable to both boats.

TELL US ABOUT THE SAILS ON THE PRINDLE 19.

The jib on the Prindle 19 is fairly full. This is essentially a footing boat. Everything is set up to go fast. This is partly because the centerboards are not extremely efficient upwind. The draft on the jib is back at about 50 percent.

The main needs to carry its draft fairly far back — close to 50 percent. This allows you to carry your jib pretty far inboard in light air.

A big mistake a lot of new Prindle 19 sailors make is trying to set up the main with a fairly round entry at the front. If you take a batten out of the middle of the sail and look at its camber, you want the back end and the front end of the batten to look about the same.

The Prindle 19 has the option of mylar or dacron sails, and the mylar have proven to be quite a bit quicker. The tri-radial panel layout for the main is very versatile as far as making it flatter or fuller. The mylar jib is a bi-radial cut, which seems to work better than the vertical-seam jibs.

WHERE DO YOU PUT YOUR TELLTALES ON THE SAILS?

I put two sets of telltales on the main and two sets on the jib. The upper set on the main is up by the Prindle "P" on the sail, about 9-12 inches back from the mast. The lower set are about a third of the way up from the bottom, the same distance back. On the jib they are spaced about the same, one set a third of the way up and another two-thirds of the way up, 9-12 inches back from the forestay.

The reason I put my telltales that far forward, as opposed to, say, on the fullest part of the draft, is that a sail will tend to stall from the leech forward. In other words, the power is maintained the longest in the forward part of the sail. For maximum power, I want my sail on the critical edge of stalling.

If you put a telltale back by the leech, it will be stalled all the time — you cannot get your sail out far enough to prevent it. If you put it on the maximum point of draft, that is a conservative setting — you'll be in the ball park, but you won't get maximum power.

DO YOU RAKE THE MAST ON THE PRINDLE 19?

I keep my mast fairly straight up and down for all conditions. It is probably raked aft at most 1 1/2 feet, but I don't really know how to determine that for sure. I just have a sort of relative measuring system I use so I can compare my mast rake to the rake on other boats.

I take my trapeze wire forward and adjust the hook or ring so it just touches the inside of the hull right where the bridle attaches. Then I take it back to the stern, and on my boat the ring will touch the centerline of the hull 8 inches forward of the rear beam. This doesn't tell me specifically how much my mast is raked. But I can go to another boat and do the same routine, and if the trapeze ring touches his deck, say, 6 inches forward of the rear beam, I think of it in terms of, "he's got 2 inches more mast rake than I do." As I said, this is strictly a way determining relative mast rake between boats. If boats with "2 inches" more mast rake consistently go faster, then I can think about changing my own mast rake.

This is a more accurate way than looking at what holes people have their sidestay or forestay adjusters in. Stays are not all the same length.

DON'T YOU NEED TO RAKE BACK MORE TO LOAD UP THE RUDDERS TO HELP YOUR BOARDS, SINCE THEY ARE NOT AS EFFICIENT AS THEY COULD BE?

Believe it or not, even with my mast almost perpendicular, the rudders are already loaded up. This boat has a long boom and a very large mainsail, so the boards and rudders are loaded equally.

HOW DO YOU SET YOUR RUDDER RAKE?

We put a batten or straight-edge vertically against the transom and down along the rudder, and the front edge of the rudder should be about 3/8"-1/2" forward of that line. This amount of rake still gives you a nice weather helm feel.

One thing I would like to note about the Prindle 19 rudders. When you first get your boat, you should wet-sand to eliminate the mold line or bead on the leading edge of the rudders, or you will get cavitation.

DO YOU PUT MARKS ON YOUR LINES AT SETTING POINTS?

Yes, I try to put marks on all my sheets and adjustment lines — the mast rotation line, jib lead adjuster, barber haulers, downhaul, jib luff tension and sheets — so we know the basic places to set them immediately for different conditions and points of sail. Then we can fine tune, if necessary, from that base point.

UPWIND

WHAT IS THE PRINDLE 19'S MOST EFFICIENT UPWIND ANGLE?

Upwind is not the 19's best point of sail in general, because its boards are not as efficient as they could be. You can't feather it up much — it needs to sail fast.

However, it does handle chop better upwind than many boats because of the sharp entry of the bows — they knife through it well.

HOW DO YOU SET UP THE BOAT FOR SAILING UPWIND?

JIB LEADS

The jib leads will be set all the way forward if you have one of the new bi-radial sails like I am building right now. If you have the older, conventional, vertical-seam sails, you will have the leads about halfway back on the track. These settings seem to work for all conditions.

In light air I carry the lead 9 inches inboard from the leeward hull, which keeps the jib about 2 1/2 inches off the spreader, but in heavy air I pull them all the way out. This opens the slot and allows the boat to accelerate in the puffs.

Moving the jib clew farther outboard allows you to sheet tighter, and that flattens the jib, giving you less heeling force, and, therefore, you can go faster. It is similar to what you are doing when you move the main traveler out in heavy air so you can sheet harder.

JIB LUFF ADJUSTMENT

I do not have a luff adjuster that is controlled from the tramp, because mylar sails do not need as much adjustment on the luff. If wind velocity changes a lot, we adjust the luff between races. But if you have a dacron jib, which tends to stretch more, it could be beneficial to have the luff adjustable from the trampoline.

DOWNHAUL

Because I sail with prebend in my mast, the downhaul is the primary tool for flattening the sail. I have 12-1 purchase on my downhaul, and the crew can control it from the trapeze.

For just sailing along normally, when you downhaul more, you also sheet the main harder, and if you ease the downhaul, you also ease the sheet a little. But when you get a puff and you have the option of easing the mainsheet or tightening the downhaul, it often works better to tighten the downhaul. If you see a dark spot of water coming, and if you can tighten the downhaul just before the puff hits, then you don't have to sheet out the main. That really pays big dividends.

MAST ROTATION

The mast should be pointed to the shroud upwind. If you have prebend in your mast, this will be the setting for all wind conditions.

If you are not using prebend and are sailing with loose diamonds, the mast will be pointed at the shroud up to about 12 knots of wind. Above that you will start to rotate gradually more. By the time it gets up to about 20 knots, the mast should be rotated to 10-12 inches in front of the shroud.

Most Prindle 19 sailors are using prebend, unless they have the old, crosscut dacron sails that weren't designed for prebend.

WEIGHT DISTRIBUTION

The Prindle 19 is a transom-dragger, so in light air upwind you need to move crew weight forward as far as possible without creating too much weather helm. The crew may actually be lying on the hull ahead of the beam, and the skipper will be right behind the beam.

In heavy air my crew will have his aft foot at the shroud, and I will have my forward foot at the shroud.

This boat does not have a lot of rocker in the hull, so weight distribution has to be more extreme than it would be in a boat with a lot of rocker — you will move farther forward in light air and farther back in heavy air.

HOW ARE THE SKIPPER/CREW JOBS DIVIDED UPWIND?

The crew handles the mainsheet. The jib sheet is wrapped around one ankle, and the downhaul is at his other foot.

I have the tiller and the traveler; and the jib lead adjuster line is by my forward foot on the deck. Actually, either of us can reach the jib lead adjustment.

WHAT IS YOUR UPWIND SAILING TECHNIQUE?

First I get my jib and main set so both sets of telltales on the jib and the upper set on the main are all breaking the same, with the windward side telltales acting up a little and the back ones flowing. Then I just sail by the lower set of telltales on the jib.

HOW DO YOU DEPOWER THE BOAT AS THE WIND PICKS UP?

In heavy air, the depowering procedure is to first trapeze to hold the boat down, then go to more downhaul. The third step on this boat is running the jib leads out.

If the boat is still flying a hull, it is very important on the Prindle to immediately ease the traveler out so you can keep the boat driving and going fast. The boat likes a lot of mainsheet tension, so it is important to travel out to the point where you can keep the sheet tight.

HOW DO YOU DO A ROLL TACK?

Before going into the tack, my crew hands the mainsheet to me. If we are on the trapeze, he will come in first, and he will cross the boat just after it goes through the eye of the wind. He tries to keep the jib telltales flowing all the way through the tack until the jib is in on the other side.

When the boat comes head to wind I ease out 2 1/2 feet of mainsheet — this is a big sail, and you have to let out a little more than you would on many boats.

I stay on the trapeze until my butt gets wet, and then I come in and cross to the other side. The bows are probably 20 degrees past the eye of the wind when I start across.

I go forward immediately as I am bearing off on a slight reach. The jib is in already, but not too tight. And so I can start bringing in my main and heading back up to a close-hauled course. I hand the mainsheet back to the crew.

DO YOU TACK YOUR RUDDERS?

I don't sail with my weather rudder up. The boat has little enough in the water as it is, so you need all four flippers going.

DOWNWIND

WHAT IS YOUR NORMAL DOWNWIND SAILING ANGLE?

The Prindle 19 is really fast downwind — it has a lot of sail area. It also has a low rocker and a long, flat run — a high speed shape. It sails fairly high, because it has the ability to generate a lot of boat speed. I keep the apparent wind (the bridle fly or sidestay telltales) pointing slightly aft

— at least at an 85-degree angle. I'm probably jibing through a 95-degree angle.

HOW DO YOU SET THE BOAT UP FOR SAILING DOWNWIND?

CENTERBOARDS

You have to keep both boards halfway down so that they fill the centerboard slot. Otherwise, you will get a lot of gurgling, which means drag.

MAST ROTATION

The mast must be rotated as far as it will go, which is about 110 degrees. The boat has positive rotation, so the crew is responsible for controlling mast rotation.

JIB SETTING

Barber haulers work very well on the Prindle 19 for holding the jib in the correct position downwind, so it is not necessary for the crew to hand-hold it. The barber haulers will, of course, be pulled all the way out.

WEIGHT DISTRIBUTION

As I mentioned, the Prindle 19 is a transom-dragger. You have to get ridiculously far forward when you are sailing downwind in light air. You determine your position on the boat based on your ears. Adjust your position until you can no longer hear any noise from the back of the boat. Since the crew does not have to hand-hold the jib, he can go wherever he has to in order to eliminate drag from the transoms.

WHAT IS YOUR DOWNWIND SAILING TECHNIQUE?

My normal downwind sailing technique is to set the sails and then sail by the lower telltales on the jib, just as I do going to weather.

When I first round the weather mark and start downwind, I try to head right down to my downwind heading and maybe even deeper. If my crew and I are right on top of it, we can take advantage of the speed we generate going from a beat to a reach and then heading down. If we're coming around the mark on starboard, my crew will be easing out the jib with his left hand and sheeting in the barber hauler with his right hand as we are turning, trying to keep the telltales flowing and the jib pulling. If everything works, we can head extra deep and carry it for maybe a boat length or two before coming back up to our normal downwind course.

When I'm on course, with my bridle telltale at about an 85 degree angle to the boat, my traveler is about 3 inches farther out than the inside of the hull. For fine-tuning, I will bring in the traveler just until the lower backside telltale stalls, then I let it out until the telltale flows and cleat the traveler. Then I pull in the mainsheet until the top telltale stalls on the back side and I let it out until it flows and cleat the sheet.

The jib is pulled all the way out with the barber hauler, and that works for most conditions.

An exception is when you are surfing waves and, although you are going deep, you are building up a lot of apparent wind because of your speed. Then you can pull the main traveler in as far as the hiking strap. In these conditions, we will ease the jib barber hauler only 3 to 4 inches, sheet the jib fairly firmly, and play the main traveler.

As I said, that is an exception to the normal downwind technique, but now there is also a bigger exception. We call it "Wild Thing." This is a whole different downwind technique that was developed in the Tornado class and is now filtering down to the other catamarans.

WHAT IS "WILD THING"?

For Wild Thing I send the crew to the leeward hull and I sit in the middle of the tramp to heel the boat and get the windward hull out of the water.

This reduces wetted surface by 40 percent, and the boat starts developing more speed and apparent wind.

I put my leeward board all the way down, and I will have the main traveler out only 9 inches to a foot from center. The jib will be sheeted quite tight, with the barber hauler eased off 4-5 inches. It's hard to be too specific because, for one thing, we're still perfecting this technique; and, for another thing, the reason it's called the "Wild Thing" is because it is unconventional and it's non-stop adjustments.

Of course, another reason it's called "Wild Thing" is because it can be a pretty wild ride, and the crew is going to be getting real wet sitting on the leeward side.

Once you get going fast, your side telltales or bridle fly will be at about a 70-degree angle, but you actually will only be heading maybe 5 degrees higher than the boats that are sailing with the normal downwind techniques.

In Wild Thing you will steer up and down more, but your average course will still only be about five degrees higher than normal, and you will be going a lot faster.

Another big difference is that instead of setting the sails and sailing by them, the jib and main are played all the time, just as they would be on a reach.

Your goal is to sail the boat balanced on one hull, just as you would going to weather.

HOW DO YOU STEER FOR WILD THING?

It's pretty freeform, as far as the steering. Although your bridle fly will be pointed at approximately 70 degrees to the boat, you don't sail by that and you don't sail by the telltales on the sails. You are steering more based on waves and boat speed, with your goal being to sail the boat balanced on one hull, just as you would going to weather — you have to keep the windward hull just clear of the water.

If the hull starts lifting higher than that, you steer the boat deeper. But before the windward hull can touch down and get wet, you steer back up again to maintain your speed and apparent wind.

HOW DO YOU GET WILD THING GOING TO BEGIN WITH?

First we put down the centerboard, head up and bring in our sails to the settings I mentioned, to accelerate, but in the wrong direction. Then my crew goes to the leeward side, and I move to the center of the tramp — however far to leeward we have to move weight to get the windward hull out of the water.

This reduces the wetted surface by 40 percent, which allows the boat to go even faster, and we are now able to head the boat down to almost a normal downwind angle while still maintaining the same speed and apparent wind.

DO YOU CONTINUE TO KEEP YOUR WEIGHT TO LEEWARD FOR THE DURATION OF WILD THING?

Yes, because your goal is to both keep the windward hull out of the water AND sail deep. If you move weight to windward, you will have to sail a much higher course in order to keep the hull out of the water, which would defeat the purpose.

WHEN YOU ARE STEERING UP AND DOWN TO BALANCE THE HULL, HOW DO YOU KNOW WHAT ANGLE YOU ARE REALLY SAILING IN RELATION TO THE OTHER BOATS OR HOW DO YOU KNOW IF YOU HAVE GOTTEN A WIND SHIFT?

Well, you don't. You don't have any way of telling that until you jibe and see how far ahead you are. Unlike "mild thing," you don't get any immediate feedback from your telltales or from watching other boats.

IN WHAT WIND CONDITIONS DO YOU USE WILD THING?

Wild Thing only works in moderate to heavy air. It does not work in light air, so if the air lightens up, you have to go back to the normal technique, which we are now calling "Mild Thing." Or you can go back and forth from wild thing to mild thing.

By the way, I don't recommend trying this for the first time in a big race where you don't want to risk a capsize. It takes a while to perfect — we're still working on it ourselves.

The limiting factor is the possibility of pitchpoling. But this is usually only a danger when you have short, steep waves that can catch your leeward bow. It is not a problem in ocean waves or small chop.

HOW DO YOU EXECUTE A JIBE?

My jibing technique is as described in this book (Chapter 1, Boat Handling). The difference with the Prindle 19 is that the jib is relatively small and the main is the dominant force, so the crew needs to rotate the mast immediately. Until the mast is fully rotated, the sail cannot develop full power.

THE REACH

HOW DO YOU SAIL A REACH?

On a beam reach in the Prindle 19 I will put my leeward centerboard all the way down. If I know I can fly a hull the whole way, I will pull the windard centerboard all the way up; otherwise, I leave it halfway down so the board will fill the trunk and not cause drag if the hull comes down on the water.

We play our sails and try to keep the windward hull just off the water.

TORNADOES

ARE THERE ANY SIGNIFICANT DIFFERENCES IN SAILING TECHNIQUES BETWEEN THE PRINDLE 19 AND THE TORNADO?

The boats are very similar as far as the way they sail and the sail adjustments available to you on the boat. I use the same general sailing techniques for both boats. But there are some differences:

* The Tornado centerboards are more efficient than those on the Prindle 19; and, therefore, the Tornado can sail a little higher upwind, and you are able to feather more.

* The Tornado has more of a rocker than the Prindle 19, and your weight distribution will not need to be as extreme. In heavy air upwind the skipper will sit right behind the shroud and the crew will trapeze right ahead of the shroud. In light air you will both move forward another 2-3 feet.

In general, your weight adjustment is less radical on the Tornado than on the Prindle 19. You will not move forward as far in light air or back as far in heavy air.

* It is a little more difficult to "roll tack" the Tornado. Being 10 feet wide, it is a much more stable boat and it is harder to get much "roll" out of it, so you have to really accentuate your weight distribution. This can be tricky, because you have to stay on the leeward side longer, but you have 20 percent farther to go to get to the other side, so you have to allow yourself enough time. But it's definitely worth the effort to get the boat around faster.

* Sailing downwind, the Tornado's centerboards can be pulled all the way up. It does not have a problem with creating suction and drag in the centerboard trunks because it has gaskets which cover the openings when the boards are all the way up.

In the wild thing and on reaches, the Tornado's leeward centerboard will be halfway down (as opposed to all the way down on the Prindle 19).

✳ The jib luff on the Tornado must be played upwind, and the crew controls it from the trapeze. Because it is tensioned by a halyard that comes down inside the mast, whenever the mast bends, it loosens the jib luff. When the mast straightens up, it tightens the luff.

If you prepare for a puff by downhauling harder, thereby bending the mast, you also have to tighten the jib luff. When the puff has passed and you ease off the downhaul, you also have to ease the luff back off to where it was before.

✳ Obviously, because it is a wider boat, my upwind jib lead settings on the Tornado will be different in terms of actual inches. In light air the jib leads will be inboard 16 1/2 inches from the inside of the leeeward hull. In heavy air they will be out to 9-10 inches in from the hull. Very rarely, maybe in 25 knots or more, we will pull them all the way out to the hull.

✳ Tornado sailors don't sail with their windward rudders up anymore, as many were doing for a few years. We have done a lot of speed tests, and they have proven that it definitely doesn't work for the Tornado. The boats with their windward rudders up were slower than those with both rudders down.

SPINNAKERS
Chapter 20

By RANDY SMYTH

Spinnakers are becoming more and more popular on small cats, but most people do not know how to get maximum performance out of these big sails.

Asymmetrical catamaran spinnakers are designed for speed. They are capable of generating a lot more apparent wind than a jib can ever do, and you have to sail the boat fast to get full benefit out of the sail.

STEERING

Just like on a boat with a jib, where you have a steering telltale that you sail by on the jib, with a spinnaker, you steer by the luff.

I put my telltales 12 inches back from the luff, 6 to 8 feet up from the bottom, where they're easy to see. Just as I do on my jib, I keep them down fairly low on the spinnaker so I don't have to look way up.

Your focus as skipper is to watch the luff of the spinnaker, keeping it on the edge.

For your steering, you're really concentrating on speed — that's everything that's important downwind. You want to keep it in a nice speed window, whatever you want to call it. If you head down too low, your boat will just slow way down, and the leeward telltales will hang. It'll feel like, "Gee, all that sail area and we're just not going anywhere."

Well, the spinnaker is stalled. It'll look great, but it's not doing anything. So you've got to keep it hot. You've got to keep it going fast, and you've got to sense that speed. And once you get going real fast by reaching up, you'll be able to come back down to a normal downwind sailing angle. People tell me, "Oh, with my spinnaker I can point a lot lower than the guys with jibs." When people tell me that, I know they're going too slow.

Since your focus is on the spinnaker luff telltales, you can fine-tune your speed with the spinnaker sheet. Trim in tighter for speed, and ease to go lower and slower. Usually, your best speed/angle combination will result in a 90-degree jibe angle.

That technique works until it starts getting pretty windy. When the hull starts coming up, you can just steer by flying the hull, just like you do upwind, except that your reactions must be the opposite of what you would do upwind. When going to weather, if your hull lifts, you pinch up higher to the wind, and when the hull drops, you fall off again. But when you are going downwind, your steering response is the opposite. If you start lifting a hull in a puff, you MUST head down. When the hull settles down again, head up. If you head up in a big puff with a spinnaker, you will probably capsize.

When the wind builds above about 10 knots while flying a spinnaker, try to get the same feeling that you have going to weather. Try to keep that windward hull just kissing the water — just don't forget: **IF IT RISES UP, DRIVE OFF.**

Now, it's windy, wild and a bit scary — how do you get it to drive off? The secret is to never rely completely on your rudders. Let your sails help you steer the boat. Okay, we've got a huge sail in the front of the boat like a gigantic jib already trying to make the boat drive off. Just to help it, in those puffs ease the mainsheet, not the spinnaker sheet. You don't want to collapse the spinnaker. In a big puff, leave the spinnaker full. That's helping you turn downwind and that's what's going to save you from a capsize in a major puff. **EASE THE MAINSHEET.**

For the traveler, all you really need in a windy situation is to ease it off about a foot. A lot of wind is blowing through there on the leeward side. If you ease off the traveler more, the battens in your main will probably invert from the backwinding of the spinnaker.

So in the puffs it's all mainsheet. Ease the mainsheet, and the spinnaker will just pull the bows downwind (even if the rudders for some reason stall), and the hull should come back down.

That's the easy part. The other part is you have to recognize that after you head down and the hull comes down and you start feeling comfortable, you're probably not going fast. If you wait too long, everything will start stalling and really slow you down. Like I said, you're steering by the boat speed. If you start going too slow, head up; if it starts getting too hot or scary, head it back down. But that's the way to think about steering.

TUNING FOR MAXIMUM SPEED

LUFF TENSION

Whether to pull the halyard all the way to the top and/or the tack all the way to the end of the pole depends on the individual spinnaker and on your point of sail. It is a fine-tuning adjustment.

You need some slack in the luff of the sail so the sail can fill the way it was designed to fill. If you have the luff tight, the sail will not fill right; the luff will be forced into a permanent curl. For each boat and spinnaker you have to find the right amount of curve needed in the front of the sail so that it will stay right on the edge of a curl but not curling too much. If it always has a curl in it, it will be hard to sail your boat fast, because it will keep wanting to collapse. Adjust this by easing the luff off a little.

Tightening the luff a little (by pulling it up with the halyard or pulling the tack to the end of the pole) will cause the front edge of the sail to get rounder and fuller. Loosening the luff, by slacking it off with the halyard or from the end of the pole, will cause the sail to get flatter.

If you need to reach up higher to the wind — when you've overstood "C" mark, for instance — you can slack off the tack at the pole.

WHAT TO DO WITH THE JIB

The other big question is what to do with your jib — whether to leave it up or take it down or furl it. The answer to that usually is determined by how long your pole is. If you've got a long pole, you can leave your jib up all the time. But some boats have a bridle system between the bows instead of a pole, leaving only a small gap between the jib and the spinnaker. In this case, the jib needs to be rolled up. So if you've got a long pole, go ahead and leave the extra 60 or 80 square feet of jib up. In fact, even with relatively short poles, such as the one on the Hobie 18SX, I think you'll probably find that in winds over 7 knots it's better to leave the jib up.

There are three advantages to leaving your jib up:

Number one, obviously you are trying to add square footage downwind, not take it away.

Number two, when you do jibe, you'll find the spinnaker slides by an unrolled jib better than a rolled-up jib, so you'll have a slightly easier task of jibing the boat.

And, number three, it's obviously one less thing to do at each mark, when you should be concentrating on the spinnaker sheet and getting the spinnaker flying properly or dropping and stuffing it.

Now, leaving the jib unrolled only works for that technique I described of sailing the boat hot. If you sail fairly slow or lower than the sloop-rig boats, then the apparent wind will swing aft and the jib will blanket the spinnaker. But if you sail it the way I'm trying to recommend — hot and fast — then the apparent wind is far enough forward that there is plenty of slot and the jib will work along with the spinnaker.

The jib will be sheeted in pretty much like a close reach —it will be in fairly tight; but again, just go by the telltales. In general, I leave my jib a little bit loose. If the jib stalls, it leaves a big, swirling turbulence that can collapse the spinnaker. So I let the jib luff the first 8 or 10 inches back — I leave it a little bit loose, but not flapping, so that it never does stall.

THE MAINSAIL

I set my mainsail to the telltales just like I do without the spinnaker. The bottom telltale is the traveler telltale, and the top telltale is the mainsheet telltale. When I am sailing the angle I want, I bring in the traveler until the bottom telltale stalls on the back side. I let it out until that telltale flows, and I cleat the traveler. Then I sheet in the main until the top telltale stalls, let it out until it flows, and cleat it. My main is set. Normally, this will leave the traveler at about 9-12 inches out from center.

If you are used to sailing downwind with a jib, it will seem strange to have the traveler in so far and the mainsheet so tight. If you don't use the telltale technique of overtrimming until it stalls, you won't know that they need to be that tight. In fact, the first time you sail with your spinnaker, you'll probably sail with it like you normally would, and think everything's fine. It may look fine. Your telltales will flow, but you'll be missing miles of power.

Plus, if you don't sheet the main in, with that huge sail in the front of the boat trying to make you turn left all the time, you're going to be having the rudders hard over trying to turn right and you'll have huge drag on your rudders. So you really heal two things at once by sheeting in properly — you get full power out of your main and you'll find you can straighten your rudders out and the boat will be balanced better. So it's very critical to get your main tuned for maximum power — fly that top telltale to the mainsheet and the bottom telltale to the traveler. Don't ignore your main.

OUTHAUL

When you sail only with a jib downwind, you normally ease off your mainsail outhaul to give 7-8 inches of camber in the bottom of the main. But with the spinnaker, because there is so much air blowing through there that can cause backwinding, you want your outhaul tight and the bottom of your main flat.

Another contrast to sailing with a jib is that you do not need to rotate your mast as much. If you have a rotation preventer, you can just release it and let the mast rotate to 80 or 90 degrees, but you don't normally need to use positive rotation to rotate it farther. The apparent wind is pretty far forward, so if you rotate to 110 as you would do with a jib, the mast will create too much drag.

THE BOARDS

The spinnaker is a sail that develops quite a bit of side load. Contrary to what most people do, you have to keep the daggerboards or centerboards down. The Prindles, Tornadoes and Hobie 21's all need both boards fully down. Boats with large boards, like the Nacras, are fast with the boards three-fourths of the way down.

JIBING

From the skipper's point of view, jibing might seem simple. You don't have to touch the traveler, you don't have to touch the mainsheet. All you have to do is steer a nice smooth arc. But the skipper really is in charge of the timing of this whole operation.

What I do is before the jibe I'll take the spinnaker sheet away from the crew. I've got the tiller in one hand and the spinnaker sheet in the other. I slowly start my turn while easing out on the spinnaker sheet. I am trying to get the spinnaker to fly out away from the boat and forward.

If I just hold the spinnaker in tight while the boat is turning, it will collapse against the jib, mast and spreaders. So the object here is to float the spinnaker out in front of the boat at the same rate as I'm turning, so I like to do that myself.

The spinnaker continues to float out and forward as I continue to turn until I reach the point where I am headed dead downwind. At that point the spinnaker will hang down because there is no wind — it is behind the mainsail.

When I see the spinnaker hang, I tell the crew to sheet it, and he starts pulling on the new sheet hand over hand to pull it through to the new side.

So I've helped the crew a lot because by the time he pulls it around, I have already eased the spinnaker out as far as it will possibly float. By the time he starts to pull on it, it will come across pretty easily. If I had not floated it, it probably would have caught on the spreaders or who knows what.

There is still a major finesse job to do here at the finish in the steering as the spinnaker is coming through.

When he starts sheeting on the new side, if I just jam the helm over, I can still ruin the jibe by having the spinnaker still get caught on the wrong side of the forestay and pile up against the jib.

So I continue a nice, smooth turn until the clew comes past the jib. Then I swing the helm pretty hard, which swings the apparent wind forward and blows the spinnaker right through to the new side. So the last part of my turn I steer fast to help the wind fill the spinnaker.

Some people like to jibe the spinnaker all the way around the outside of the pole. I personally like to bring the spinnaker through between the end of the pole and the forestay. Both ways work, but I feel that in taking it around the outside, there is always a chance of the spinnaker sheet catching around the pole, which can be a bad situation. You don't want to have to go out on the bow to clear it in windy conditions.

When you complete the jibe, obviously, you are sailing by the spinnaker, just as you would by a jib, so it is important to get it set in the right place when the jibe is completed.

The best way to do this, because you have miles of sheet to deal with, is to put a little black mark on the sheet at the point where it goes through the block at the setting that seems to work best. Then you can immediately get it set pretty close and then do any fine-tuning from that black mark. This will help make your jibes more consistent.

When you're jibing, you can ignore the jib until you get the spinnaker around. Just uncleat it and let it do its own thing. Whether the jib is flapping or whatever, it's not going to affect your speed during the jibe. It's sort of an afterthought: "Okay, now I'll pull the jib in after we're going."

So don't let the jib dominate any of your thinking during a jibe — let your full attention be on the spinnaker. Keep the BIG PICTURE in focus — the jib is about 60 square feet, while the spinnaker is about 400 square feet.

SETTING THE SPINNAKER

As I come around the A mark to head downwind, I ease the mainsheet about 3 feet, followed by the traveler, which is usually eased about a foot. (Final tuning of the mainsail can wait until the spinnaker is set.) I will make a smooth turn, but I will head down to a little deeper than a "normal" 90-degree turn.

Meanwhile, the crew eases the jib about 2 feet and cleats it. As with the main, final trimming of the jib can wait until after the spinnaker is set.

On my boat I handle the spinnaker halyard, so as I am making my turn downwind, the halyard is across my lap. I sit on the tiller and pull up the spinnaker as fast as I can, hand over hand. Meanwhile, the crew pulls the tack to the end of the pole. Then he grabs the sheet. When he sees the halyard reach the top, he quickly sheets in.

(NOTE: If your boat is rigged with a combination spinnaker halyard/ tack-line system, you will not have the step of pulling the tack out.)

As soon as the spinnaker is up and sheeted, I head up until it fills. Once I have speed, I head back down slightly and start steering by the spinnaker and by the speed.

DROPPING THE SPINNAKER

When you are approaching the leeward mark, get everything ready for going upwind, as usual. Set your downhaul. Put your boards all the way down, if you had them up a little bit. Center your traveler and pre-set your mast rotation. Finally, sheet your jib for going to weather BEFORE you drop the spinnaker.

The spinnaker halyard can get knotted up, and if one little kink gets caught in the cleat when you're dropping the spinnaker, it can ruin your whole day. So before we are ready to drop it, I just throw the halyard over the back of the boat and let it drag in the water. That way there are no kinks in it. There is no way it can get tangled up. If it gets tangled, we're going to overrun C mark and give up way more than we ever gained on that whole last leg.

I also want to make sure there are no kinks in the tack line, so I throw that overboard, too.

There are several different ways people divide up the skipper-crew jobs for dropping the spinnaker.

On my boat I take care of the halyard. I'll be sitting on the wing, hooked into the trapeze.

I've got the mainsheet and the tiller clamped together in one hand and the spinnaker halyard in the other hand.

When it's time to drop, the key thing is you have to steer downwind. If you are going along on the hot angle of sail we talked about, with a hull flying a little, you'll never get the spinnaker down. If the crew goes down to the leeward side, the boat will capsize. So the key to make it easy and quick for your crew is proper steering. Of course, you have to plan ahead tactically and make sure nobody is to leeward of you.

My crew will go to the leeward side up near the main beam, and he grabs the foot of the spinnaker. When he tells me he has it, I start easing off the halyard as he is gathering in the sail. I watch what is happening, and if the sail is going in the water or falling down between the hulls, I'll stop easing it. When he has it under control, I'll keep easing it off. Then it's his job to uncleat the tack line when he wants to and pull the tack of the sail in to the trampoline. As he is pulling the sail in, he is also stuffing the sail into its bag. So he's pretty busy.

But the jib is already taken care of, so I can literally round the mark without needing him, as far as the jib. I can sheet my main and hop out on the trapeze and be already sailing, while he's stuffing the last little bit. Then he can come up and get out on the trapeze. That way if things get tangled up or whatever, you don't have to stop the boat to take care of it.

If you have a bag on each side or a bag sewn to the tramp that goes all the way across, you can drop the spinnaker on either side, depending on which tack you are on. However, you must keep in mind that the next time you raise it, you will have to raise it from the same side you dropped it on. To raise it on the other side would require you to somehow get the halyard, the tack line and the sheet attachment point around to the other side, which would be a very difficult feat on a small catamaran.

Therefore, tactically, you have to think about what tack you want to be on when you raise it again before you drop it on this leg.

THE HOBIE 18
Chapter 21

BY HOBIE ALTER, JR.

National Champion Hobie 14, 1978
National Champion Hobie 16, 1979, 1980, 1981, 1982
Champion of Champions winner, sailing a Prindle 16, 1979
National Champion Hobie 18, 1978, 1981
World Champion Hobie 16, 1982
Winner, Worrell 1000, 1982
National Champion Hobie 17, 1990

Sailing ability must come with the name. Hobie Alter, Sr., and his three children — Hobie, Jr., Jeff and Paula — all have had remarkable racing success.

Hobie, Jr. started his career when his mom signed him up for a summer sailing course at the age of eight. "We had class for a week and then a race. My boat cleaned everybody in the race, and I got my first taste of sailboat racing. I said, 'Hey this fun.'"

At about the same time his father bought a P-Cat, which they played around with in the Laguna Beach area of California. His dad designed the Hobie 14 when Junior was ten, "so it was kind of a natural for me to start sailing that."

He said the key to success is getting to know your own boat and acquiring a feel for what makes it go faster, rather than worrying about what other people are doing.

TUNING

MAST RAKE

Although my mast is not as far aft as many, I do rake my mast aft on the Hobie 18. It seems to be a bit easier to sail that way than with it perpendicular, and I want to put the lateral resistance load on the rudders as well as the boards.

Overall, I like the steerage much better with the aft-raked mast, as I feel the boat more acutely through the helm. There is more helm, but it is not excessive.

As to how far back I rake the mast, there is no sure measurement that I use. I judge by the distance between the blocks when the mainsail is in and fully sheeted. Then I look for about a foot or a little less between the blocks. If that distance is about 6 inches, then I feel that the mast is back too far.

There are times when I will rake it a bit farther forward: in flatter water and lighter winds. In these cases there is no worry about the bow diving, and a bit more power does not hurt, either.

Some sailors think that off the wind you sacrifice some power with the mast raked aft, but I do not think so. If you drive the boat well and do not sail too deep or too high, then it will sail just about as fast as a boat with forward raking.

The rake I have downwind may change from the weather leg, however, as I do not use a tight rig. It isn't really sloppy, but it isn't tight. That way the leeward shroud will give some off the wind and allow the mainsail to twist off nicely and fill out, rather than have an inverted crease running down its length caused by the shroud pushing back on the mainsail.

Also, the slackened rigging allows the mast to stand up straight for off-the-wind sailing. So maybe that is why I am not getting hurt on the downwind legs.

MAST ROTATION

The mast controls the fullness and flatness of the sail by degrees of rotation. The less rotation you use, the fuller the sail and the more power. The more you rotate the mast, the flatter the sail will become and the less power you will have, although the sail will be capable of faster speeds.

If I want the sail full, I will set the mast rotator at about 70 degrees. If I want the sail flatter, I set the rotator at about 90 degrees. Should a required sail shape be somewhere in between, then I would set the rotator between 70 and 90 degrees, wherever I thought the sail looked right for the condition.

MAINSAIL

The sail should vary in draft as you go up. For example, the bottom part of the sail should have a moderate draft located about 45 percent back in the sail, the draft working gradually forward until, at the top, it will be located farther forward, at around 33 percent, and it will be a little fuller.

I like the leech to flatten out somewhat, and that is why at the top the draft must be farther forward. The distance fore to aft at the top of the sail is so short that the draft must be forward in order for the leech to develop any flatness. I want it flat so there is no chance of the leech hooking to windward, causing flow detachment and increased drag.

I run the diamond tension fairly tight, compared to everyone else. The measurement to the point where I can press them against the mast is about a foot. That way I get a fairly uniform mast bend. Some people run them up to two feet, but I think that is too loose.

As for the battens, I really don't put much work into them. In the Hobie they all come the same way, so there isn't much you can do with them, except taper them.

The bottom six battens should be left untapered, as they are already flexible enough and the untapered battens allow the draft to be located at about 40 to 45 percent in the sail, which is what you want.

The higher up the battens, the shorter, and there you should taper them so the draft will be up 33 percent in the sail.

Overall, I just look for a good sail shape, and if the battens need to be tapered to accomplish that, then I do it. So the shape I want is moderate at the bottom, with the draft at about 45 percent, and progressively fuller and farther forward —up to 33 percent — as you go up the sail.

As for batten tension, I simply snug them into the pocket just enough to take the wrinkles out of the sail. The sail material should be taut, but the battens should not be jammed in. You see, actually the batten, loose or tight, does not have that much to do with the curve of the sail.

The really important sail-setting devices are the downhaul and outhaul.

In light air, or when I want a full sail, I do not downhaul that much — just enough to get the wrinkles out. The outhaul I ease off a bit to get a little shape in the lower batten.

If the air becomes moderate, then I harden down the downhaul and take the outhaul out farther.

In heavy air I really honk down pretty hard on the downhaul and take the outhaul car all the way out.

THE JIB

The one thing I do that other people do not do is set my luff tension on the beach. Since I carry a looser rig than most, I do not know how tight to set the jib luff control without sheeting the main. So I sheet in the main and then go up and set the luff tension. I do not like a tight luff control on the jib; I set it just enough to take out the wrinkles. There is not a great deal of tension on it. In fact, I have accidentally set it so that there were wrinkles, and it sailed just as well, if not better.

By setting the luff tension in this way, you know exactly what it is going to look like going to weather. If you set the jib luff too tight, the sail will tend to cup up front, causing a distorted sail that breaks funny and whose telltales do not read right. Overall, that is hard to sail by.

With the moderate setting of the jib, you have a flatter entry into the wind, a better profile.

The draft is something I do not worry about with the Hobie 18 jib, because they all come the same way. If I had my choice, I would prefer the draft a bit farther forward; but since that cannot be done, I sail with what I have.

My jib settings are set in the middle of the track at almost all times. I do not deviate much from that, since I don't think the jib lead tracks do much good, anyway — they don't give much variation to the lead angles.

Some people, I have noticed, run their jib leads aft in heavy air; I, on the other hand, tend to run mine forward. Moving the slide forward is similar to running the traveler outboard on the Hobie 16; it opens the slot a bit more. If it is heavy air, you are not sheeted hard, anyway and by sliding it forward and slacking the sheet, you open the slot.

WEIGHT DISTRIBUTION

Upwind, I like the bow down into the water, with the average water line running about halfway up the bow. If the air is pretty light and the seas smooth, then you can dig in the bow more.

In trapeze weather you want the bow still taking the average water line at about halfway up the bow. In lighter air you want the crew on the leeward side and forward to get the bow down deep.

Off the wind I do not like to get the bows too deep, particularly in heavy weather. But in lighter air I want to balance right over the rocker of the boat, so that the sterns are out of the water.

In light air, on all points of sail, you must be sure that you do not get too much weight on the windward hull. The weight must be dispersed so that the boat is well balanced.

HELMSMANSHIP

TO WEATHER

The traveler is always set right in the middle. The only exception to that is when it is really blowing hard; then I would let it out 4 to 6 inches. I do all my sail trimming pretty much with the sheet tensions.

In heavy air I carry my jib sheet tension really soft and work the main extensively. I figure the thing that makes you go faster than the next guy is to work harder: dumping your main more and pulling it in more often. really working the mainsheet.

The farther out you put the traveler, the less you have to work. With the traveler in the middle, you have to work that much harder. The twist off the top is far better, the power low in the sail is better, and the boat definitely goes faster and higher. But, again, you do have to pay for it in labor.

Pointing high or driving off really do not enter my mind while sailing in trapeze weather. I just try to hold the boat down. If I fall off too much, I cannot hold the boat down without easing off the sheets or traveler.

On the other hand, if I am holding the boat down with no problems, then I will pull the main in good and tight until the boat begins to come up again. The technique is sort a combination of how hard you sheet in and how high you fly the hull. You want to balance the boat and the sheet to get the maximum forward and windward effort.

You do not want to lift the hull up, but you must be sure you have enough power to do so whenever you want.

In heavier air I simply use the hulls and the feel of the boat and its speed to determine my point of sail. I do not really use a telltale or anything. I just keep the hull kissing the water, assuming that the sails are all set properly.

When the air lightens up and it is no longer trapeze weather, then I begin sailing by the telltales on the jib and the main. First I set the sails where I want them; and then instead of changing settings, I steer by the telltales on the sails.

TACKING

In the Hobie 18 I turn pretty fast, using the speed of the boat to get through the wind quickly. You must not exaggerate the quickness of the turn to the point where you stall the rudder in the process, but you do want a quick turn. Some sailors seem to pinch up for a while or start up so slowly that they bleed off all their speed before getting into the turn itself; then they do not go through the turn fast enough.

Backwinding the sail should only be done in choppy seas. I normally have the jib cut loose right away. Holding the rudders over at the turn angle all the way through the turn is a must. If you let go of the rudders and they straighten out during the turn, you have blown the tack. They must be held in the proper arc all the way though the tack.

Sometimes, in the heat of the race, your mind is so involved on the race and tactics that when you get ready to tack, your mind is still on something else. You cannot do that. I just tell myself to forget the race and make this particular tack a good one; and then, after the tack is completed, I get my mind back into the race. That way you concentrate on the tack itself, and chances are you will not blow it. A blown tack can cost you a lot of ground.

As for weight distribution in a tack, I get right back on the after bean and stay there, while the crew is located right around where the jib sheet blocks are. This gets the weight pretty far aft, allowing the bows to get out of the water, and you develop really good relative steerage between the rudder and the board.

DOWNWIND

When sailing downwind on the Hobie 18, I let the main traveler out to a point just inside the hull. The traveler does not easily go all the way out, anyway. Then I cleat the sheet with the sail twisting off at the top. That means the mainsheet is pretty slack.

Generally, the main does not flow that well when sailing downwind. The telltales never seem to make much sense, which really makes it difficult to know exactly where to sheet the main. It seems as though if you ease off the sheet until the backside flows, then the windward side would be luffing. So according to the telltales, it appears that the main is oversheeted a bit, but that allows the jib to set properly and flow the air through the slot.

For my course downwind I sail at about 90 degrees apparent wind. I will sail a bit higher to get the boat speed and then fall off to somewhere below 90 degrees, but not into a stall. If I start to get too deep, I head it up quickly to get the speed back again.

My primary telltale is my jib. I use it as a guide for sheeting; and then once it is set, I sail by the jib, keeping the jib telltales flowing. It seems to be very important to keep a good slot between the main and jib as well. So I set the jib, then adjust my main to complement the jib.

Another good telltale is my bridle fly. I will keep the feather running at about 90 degrees to the boat. That will change a little bit, depending on conditions.

If I catch a wave, I will just run deeper downwind. If it's choppy and I get a better speed by going a little higher, well, then I go a little higher.

It still all relates to feeling the boat and getting the most speed. You might take a few seconds and ease the main and see if you can feel any difference. If it is slower, then put it back to where it was. If you harden up the sheet and if feels faster, leave it there. You have to keep experimenting to get the most boat speed at all times.

JIBING

There is no really hot technique for jibing. The big secret to a good jibe is timing; that is, mastering WHEN to jibe. Unless you are forced to jibe quickly, you should wait until you are driving off and heading deeper than 90 degrees. That way all you have to do is to drive off a little deeper yet and round it to the other tack. You keep a fast line that way.

If you jibe from a high position on the wind, you have farther to go around than if you tack when driving off. And, of course, if you catch a wave and are going very deep, that is an excellent time to jibe, as the wave will surf you through the jibe.

Generally, I would say that to win a lot you have to have a "seat of the pants" feel for the boat. It is something that requires time in the boat and some natural ability.

The worst thing some people do is always worry about what the "hot skippers" are doing, rather than about themselves. They are always looking for some trick or go-fast, thinking that maybe the hot skippers are using something that they are not. What they should be doing is looking at what they are doing themselves.

If more sailors would work with their own sheet, their own sails, their own helmsmanship, they would develop their own "seat of the pants" sailing technique. That would be better than looking out ahead of themselves and saying, "What are they doing that I am not doing?"

Instead of concentrating on the boat ahead of them, they should concentrate on their own boat.

THE HOBIE 16
Chapter 22

BY WAYNE SCHAFER

Hobie 14 National Champion, 1974, 1976
McCulloch Trophy for best all-around sailor in a Hobie 16, Lake Havasu, 1971
Retired the Ancient Mariner Series trophy at Newport Beach after winning it three times.
Hobie 16 Southern California Divisional Champion, 1979 and 1981
Past runner-up in Hobie 16 Nationals
Runner-up in the Hobie 14 Worlds in the Canary Islands in 1977
Qualified for the 1983 Hobie Worlds.

     Wayne Schafer, silver-haired but still as trim as a teenager, races and wins against skippers twenty and thirty years his junior.

     He considers himself a "seat-of-the-pants" sailor and credits his racing success to a "lot of time in the boat."

     One of the early cat sailors, Schafer's sailing experience actually began back in 1951 in a Rhodes 32. He was converted to multihulls four years later when he started sailing with a friend on a 16-foot outrigger.

     He raced P-Cats for a time before getting into the Hobie 14 in 1968 and the Hobie 16 in 1971. He still races both boats and recently began trying his hand, with his usual success, on the Hobie 18.

     Schafer's home waters are off Capistrano Beach, California.

TUNING THE HOBIE 16

MAST RAKE

I almost always sail with my mast raked aft. There is the rare occasion, say a drifter on a small inland lake with smooth water, that I might get the mast up there more. But ninety-eight percent of the time I will sail with the mast raked aft.

How much it should be raked is kind of hard to say, since it depends on your style of sailing, your crew weight, the wind and wave conditions. I just know where to rake it from the feel of the helm.

To find the right spot for your own boat and conditions, I recommend starting with the mast perpendicular. Sail with it that way to see how it feels; and then start gradually raking it back one hole at a time until you find the point where your boat performs best.

Basically, three things happen when you rake the mast aft.

First, the weight aloft in the length of the mast itself makes the mast act as a levering tool. When it is straight up and down and you add wind power, it forces the leeward bow down with all that power. The aft rake acts to take that leverage off the bow and frees it up some. In choppy situations, hobbyhorsing will be even more pronounced with the mast straight up and down. If you move that weight back, the boat will balance much, much better.

Second, with the mast back you somewhat depower the sail. You allow the wind to strike the sail in a less powerful way, allowing the boat to be more controllable.

Third, you are moving the center of effort aft toward the lateral resistance supplied by the rudder, letting it act much like a daggerboard. The boat then becomes much more efficient to windward, sails through the chop better, and will point higher.

Some of what you gain going to windward, you will lose when you begin your downhill run, especially in light to moderate air. However, it has been my experience that you won't lose as much downwind with an aft-raked mast as you would going to weather with a perpendicular mast. And if you are sailing well enough, you should be able to hold onto what you have on the downwind leg.

The harder the wind blows, the less disadvantage you will have downwind. In heavy air the aft-raked mast helps to keep the bows from digging in.

Ideally, you would like the mast aft upwind and more forward downwind. The Hobie 14 can be sailed that way, but you cannot do that in the Hobie 16.

Crew weight is an important factor in mast rake. We try to stay at around or under 300 pounds overall (minimum weight on the Hobie 16 is 285 pounds), and we feel that we can handle both light and heavy air with our mast aft.

However, if the crew weight starts getting up there, like 310 or 320 or more, then you want more power and can move the mast more forward. Still, those same guys will sail with their mast back in heavier air. It is a matter of style. You should go out and experiment with it.

If you do rake the mast back, you definitely will have more weather helm, but you will go to weather better. If your helm is really excessive, then your rudders probably are out of alignment. You shouldn't get an overwhelming helm. Some guys say that if you have helm, you have a lot of drag; but I think some helm is good on the 16, and it doesn't seem to slow down the boat.

But helm also can be corrected now with the new adjustable rudders that can be raked forward under the boat. By raking them under the boat, you eliminate almost all that controversial helm, anyway.

Before the adjustable rudder, a lot of guys used to plug the holes of the rudder axis points and then redrill them to rake the rudders forward, thereby eliminating helm. But others just didn't want to go to the trouble of doing all that, and they still did well.

With the new adjustable rudder, however, Hobie has opened up whole new terrific avenues for tuning. The combination of rudder rake with mast rake probably will have the boat going a lot faster in the near future. If you can get the combination that fits your style of sailing and your crew weight, it's going to make a world of difference in the performance of this boat.

MAST ROTATION

How far you want to rotate your mast is a matter of taste. The stock rotation is fine, but it gives you a stiffer mast to work with, one with less bend. If you overrotate the mast, you get a much wider range of sail shapes to play with. You will have a bendier mast, and then it depends on your sheeting as to what kind of sail you will have. And, of course, downwind the overrotation gives you a much better entry into the wind. So I go with the overrotation.

When I want a fuller sail, I do not sheet as much. When I want the sail flatter, I sheet more. With the bendy mast, I can do these things with the sheet.

You have to be careful, though, when cutting off the mast rotation stops. Take off very little at a time; otherwise, you will have overdone it, and you will not be able to build it back up very easily. And you know you cannot use a wishbone maststop like the Hobie 18 has.

I wouldn't overrotate to more than 60 and 80 degrees. A good way to see what is happening is to put telltales on your mast and note the wind flow around it. The best way is to shave a little bit off at a time and sail a little bit. See how it does, check the telltales on the mast to see what they are doing. The telltales should be placed right at the front of the mast, a little to each side. You should see an eddy on the windward side; the leeward side will tell you a lot.

MAINSAIL

People ask me whether I want my mainsail draft full or flat, forward or aft. I'll tell you, I have been all over the map with those questions.

At first we started sailing them as they were, with the draft cut way forward at about 33 percent. They seemed to be fine that way.

But then we got to fooling around with the untapered battens and getting the draft back to 40 to 45 percent. And theoretically, that should work great; the air should attach longer to the mainsail; it opens up the slot; and just generally it made a lot of sense. But the catch was, it didn't work any better than with the draft farther forward.

So now we are back at the original 33 percent, and we are using tapered battens. This configuration, to me, seems to give a little more power; it seems to get through the chop better and generally has a little more punch. It also gives me a wider range of sail shapes. Off the wind it seems to have more power as well.

Of course, that is just my opinion at this time, and it may well change next year.

As for the fullness or flatness of the sail, here in California we usually sail in medium air, and we shoot for the optimum weight of 285 to 300 pounds. In these cases we want a moderately flat sail.

If the wind blows hard, we depower the boat somewhat by loosening the rig. The slack allows the mast to fall off to leeward a little and helps the lighter crews hold the boat down. In this heavy air you do not need power at all; you want to get the boat to where you can control it. So you want the sail flat, mast aft and rig loosened. All these things are depowering the boat to the point where you can handle it better in wind over 20 knots.

Some guys play around a lot with battens, weighing their poundage and tapering them very finitely to a point where they are a perfectly balanced, matching set. And that is fine, if you have the time and the desire. But all I do is try to play around with them once in a while so the sail looks good. I taper here and there, but I do not make a science of battens.

Generally, I put the battens in with enough pressure to take the wrinkles out. Then, to get sail shape, I use the downhaul, outhaul and sheet. If it looks as though there may be some uneven battens, then you can either tighten or loosen a batten or so, to get a smooth mainsail.

On the downhaul: Once I set the luff, I leave it. In the morning when I first raise the mainsail, I won't put a lot of tension on the luff. I don't want to honk it down yet; I prefer to let it gradually start stretching. I go out on the water with it that way.

Then after the wind hits it and stretches it, and after I see what the actual conditions are in which I will be sailing, then I tension the luff for the conditions. Basically, I am just taking the wrinkles out; and if the sail looks good, that is where I leave the luff tension.

I usually use a tight outhaul going to weather because the Hobie 16 needs to have a tight leech. Leech tension is what makes the boat go to weather. By helping the wind, and therefore pressure, adhere to the windward side of the main to as far back on the sail as possible, more load is put on the rudders, so they can help resist leeway and keep the boat pointing higher and driving nicely.

The leech and rudder work together in very close partnership to get you to weather. This partnership can easily be destroyed by either oversheeting or undersheeting — the two major sins on the Hobie 16. It is really hard to find the perfect sheeting spot.

If you are undersheeted, your rudders will not be loaded enough, and you will tend to sail a lower course and maybe make more leeway.

If you are oversheeted, you will still be going to weather, but the boat will feel a little doggy, your rudders will be overpowered, you will have too much helm, and you will make more leeway than you would normally.

Because it is easier to feel oversheeting than undersheeting through the helm, I start out sheeted tightly. If I feel the symptoms of oversheeting I let off a little bit and I am right on the money.

Leech is an area that's very hard to read; telltales don't read very well there. The only way you can tell what the leech is doing is by what you feel on the helm, but you have to have enough tension on that leech, and there's no way to tell anyone how to set it. You have to feel it and learn this by time on the boat.

It is hard to decipher and coordinate all this, and it takes a lot of experimentation. As a matter of fact, I am still playing around with it myself after all these years of sailing.

THE JIB

I like my jibs cut a little on the flat side. If the jib comes to me on the full side, I take it to a sailmaker and make adjustments within the rules to get it flatter. A fuller-cut jib does not do as well on the 16. In fact, the jib is usually just in the way, despite the fact that you do need it. So a fuller jib probably won't work well for you.

In the 16 we just try to get upwind any way we can. The boat is a reacher, and weather work is a struggle. With a full jib you won't point as high; and if there is wind, you probably will have to sail a lower course in order to carry the weight of the crew on the trapeze. The flatter jib seems to have a better entry angle into the wind; it allows the boat to drive better and is more controllable.

Another advantage of the flatter jib is that you can now taper the jib battens, giving you a wider range of sail shapes for your jib. The fuller jib, with tapered battens, comes off looking like a big sack.

The draft location of the tapered-batten sail will be up around the 33 to 35 percent area. If you prefer, you can extend the taper farther back on the battens, or you can just thin the battens out for their full length and let the sail cut dictate to the battens where the draft will be located.

Jib sheeting is very tender on the 16. I use a low-profile set of blocks, which can be bought through the "Hobie Hot Line," and attach them to the lowest or next to the lowest hole in the clew plate. This pulls the jib more on the foot than on the leech. If you were to put the jib blocks in a higher hole, you would be pulling tighter on the leech and the sail will cup more, throwing the wind into the main, closing off the slot.

As for the traveler: Going to weather, I leave the jib leads in pretty close to the mast in lighter air. If the air begins to come up, you can move them out a little; it doesn't hurt, as you can always sail on the main alone.

And if it is really blowing hard, I'll just move the traveler all the way out and not worry about the jib. After all, you have so much air blowing through there, anyway. Backwinding your main and blowing your mast out of column — that's worse.

You cannot be too dependent on the jib going to weather. The main is the big engine.

Off the wind, however, the jib is everything. The boat won't do anything on this point of sail until the jib is set all the way out.

As for the luff tension, I put quite a bit of pull on her. If the luff is too loose, the sail will curve off and will not present a good entry into the wind and will not be an efficient profile for the weather leg.

HELMSMANSHIP

TO WEATHER

Going to weather I usually sail with my main traveler set out at about 3 to 6 inches, depending on the wind condition. That allows for the loaded hook of the leech. If you have a tendency to oversheet, then certainly leave the traveler off a little bit. If you want to sail a higher line but do not mind sacrificing some speed, then you can pull the traveler in to the center.

The leech is what is getting the boat to go to weather (through its effect on the rudders), but if it is pulled too tight, it will hook back to windward and will slow your speed a bit. It will point higher, but you are looking for the ability to go high and yet as fast as possible.

In heavy air, put the traveler out to the point where you can make the boat controllable. If you keep flying a hull,you must still spill some wind up high by easing the sheet. The Australians put a lot of mast rake in and sheet block to block. When you're in that position, you main is not full sheeted and wind will be spilled up high, keeping the drive down in the lower section of the sail. They are very good at doing this.

Air spills off the upper part of the sail because it twists to leeward more than the lower section of the sail. The top does not offer as much drive as the bottom, anyway; but it does try to heel the boat over, which is something you just don't need in heavy air.

I prefer not pinching, because otherwise you create so much leeway. If you drive off more, you get to the same place and much quicker. Occasionally, when it is just too heavy for me, I will be forced to feather up.

As a steering guide, I do have a bridle fly, but I only use it to get general directions of the wind. Mostly I sail by what the other boats are doing. Of course, I look at my jib, the telltales, and the bridle fly; but mostly I just sail in relation to the competition. If they are pointing higher and going faster, then I adjust. I really do key off them.

TACKING

Tacks can be difficult if a person doesn't work on smoothing them out. The first thing to do is alert the crew of the tack, so he or she can get off the wire and get the sheets organized. And the crew should know not to cut the jib loose too soon.

The skipper should stay on the wire and put the helm over and come in when the boat comes head to wind. Tension on the main also should be released when the boat comes head to wind. As you cross over, the crew should be watching the bridle fly; and when the fly is past the centerpoint of the boat and 15 to 20 degrees on the other tack, the crew should cut the jib loose from the previous tack and quickly sheet in from the new side.

In other words, for the jib the secret is "Slow to cut, quick to pull." The jib really does all the work in getting the bows across the wind.

During the tack the crew also should come aft on the trampoline as far as possible without impeding the skipper's progress across the boat. That can take some practice. If the crew comes back too far, you will collide. If the crew is too far forward, the boat will stay into the wind. By getting the weight aft, you are shortening the water line, allowing the boat to pivot on the back part of the hulls.

Once the bows are about and the jib brought in, then you can sheet in on the main. However, if the wind is heavy, both the jib and the main should be brought in together. The main should never be brought in ahead of the jib, as it will cause the boat to weathervane right back head to wind, and you will be in irons.

DOWNWIND SAILING

On the downwind leg I generally put the main traveler out to near the hiking straps. The jib traveler goes all the way out. I do not want the main traveler all the way out, because I want some twist in the sail. If the boat feels good to me (balanced without too much helm), then I begin concentrating on the waves. If the helm is too great, I probably will ease the sheet some. Occasionally, I will let the traveler out more. It all seems to depend on the feel of the helm.

I usually try to sail as deep as I can, but not so deep as to sacrifice speed. The lighter the air, the closer to the rhumb line I sail. I figure that the wind is shiftier and less predictable, and it is very difficult to make up the extra distance with the speed. The more the air is blowing, the more you want to sail by that apparent wind. That is what catamarans are all about. Apparent wind must be made use of, and so you will sail a higher course.

Good downwind sailors will work closely with that apparent wind; and when they are getting too high a line, they will jibe. They will not sail down into a stall. But jibes hurt, too. They are faster than tacks, but you still lose a lot of distance on a boat that is moving.

I sail wing-and-wing only in winds of 5 mph or under. In that kind of condition, by sailing straight for the mark, you are assured of not making any mistakes. It's not much fun sailing straight down there, and you may feel like a dunce, but you may surprise yourself. When the air lightens or dies, aim at the mark or as close to it as you can.

The big telltale downwind is my bridle fly. I use it exclusively. Sometimes I sail with it pointing between 85 to 90 degrees. Do not let the fly point any further forward than that, as you will stall the boat and will have a hard time getting it going again.

It takes a lot of concentration to keep the fly just where you want it, but that is the big fun on the Hobie 16. That is really what it is all about.

Downwind is my favorite point of sail on the race course.

THE HOBIE 17 (unirigs)
Chapter 23

A Q&A INTERVIEW WITH CARLTON TUCKER

Back in the 1960s a number of unirig designs enjoyed a brief popularity — the Sea Spray, the Unicorn, the Isotope and the Dingo, among others. They all but disappeared from the scene during the early '70s when the limelight was taken by the Hobie 14, which has certainly earned its place in the Catamaran Hall of Fame (if anyone ever starts one). But even the 14's momentum ran out in the early 1980s. In the mid-1970s development began on the 18-square-meters. But their appeal has always been limited because they must be disassembled to trailer due to their 10-foot width.

Then in the mid-1980s along came the Hobie 17, just in time to fill a need for numbers of sailors who, for one reason or another, could no longer find crews for their two-person cats. It can be single-handed by a woman as well as a man. It has wings which effectively extend the width of the boat so even lighter-weight people can handle it. And it is almost as fast as many of the larger, sloop-rig boats.

But sailors new to unirigs quickly discovered that having less sails to handle does not necessarily make a boat easier to sail.
In fact, it can make it more difficult. To help take some of the pain out of the learning process, we interviewed current Hobie 17 World Vice-Champion Carlton Tucker to find out what makes the 17 tick.

One of the best and most versatile catamaran sailors in the world, Carlton has won national championships in the Hobie 14, Hobie 18 (three times), Stiletto 23, and Prindle 19 (two times), and he won the worlds in the Nacra 5.2 in 1986. He has placed third in a Tornado Nationals.

Carlton also is a master at long-distance races. He has raced the Worrell (later World) 1000 four times, winning it once. He took a third in a Hogsbreath 1000, a first in the 500-mile Rally of the South China Sea and a close second in the island-hopping Tahiti Mondiale World Cat Challenge.

1991 was a great year for him. In addition to taking a second at the Hobie 17 Worlds, he won the Prindle 19 Nationals (for the second time), took the overall season trophy for the Topsail professional sailing circuit, and won his third Alter Cup (the national multihull championship regatta sponsored by United States Sailing (USS, formerly USYRU).

Carlton and his father Jim Tucker run "The Boat," a sailboat dealership in Ft. Walton Beach, Florida.

Although this chapter is specific to the Hobie 17, most of the general principles will apply to all unirigs except the Hobie 14, which is unique in many ways.

IS THE HOBIE 17 REALLY MORE DIFFICULT TO SAIL THAN A SLOOP-RIGGED BOAT?

I think so, yes. For one thing, it seems like there is more to do on the boat because there is only one of you doing it. It is harder to tack without a jib to help get it around. And it requires more finesse on the helm — because it is a lightweight boat and has less crew weight on it, it does not have much momentum and can stop very easily if you don't steer smoothly.

If you don't really concentrate on your steering, it's easy to go into irons — and harder to get out of irons without a jib.

And it is a less forgiving boat to sail. It's harder to find the groove and stay in it. There is no jib to "carburete" the mainsail. In addition, the jib sees the wind first, and it gives you the first indication of changes in the wind. If you don't have a jib, you don't have that early warning system.

Most jibs are not fully battened, so if you're luffing, you can actually see it in the cloth. If you don't have a jib, your mast doesn't luff. And your fully battened mainsail may luff, but you won't be able to see it as easily or as soon.

WHAT IS YOUR TECHNIQUE FOR TACKING THE HOBIE 17?

It is a little different for light air and for heavy air.

In light air I stay on the old windward back corner all the way through the tack, carving a nice, smooth turn. Right before the boat goes head to wind I release about an arm's length of mainsheet and then continue to ease out more mainsheet as the boat goes through the wind until I have eased from 3 to 5 feet of sheet. I recleat the sheet, come across to the new side and go forward. By now the boat is pointed on a close reach. I begin sheeting SLOWLY, so the boat won't try to weathervane into the wind, build up speed and start heading back up to close-hauled as I am continuing to pull in the sheet.

When I tack in heavy air, 15 mph and up, when I'm out on the trapeze, this is what I do: I uncleat the mainsheet and put it in the same hand with my tiller. As I start putting the tiller over for the turn, I come in off the trapeze onto the wing. The mainsheet is going out at the same pace as the tiller is going over, since they are in the same hand. Now I take the mainsheet again in my other hand, while still steadily pushing the tiller. I move to the center of the boat, mainsheet still going out. As I transfer the tiller and cross to the other side, I cleat the mainsheet. By now I have eased 8 to 10 feet of mainsheet and the boat is around onto a close-reach angle on the new tack. Then I begin sheeting in and heading back up to close-hauled.

The two major differences in tacking a unirig as opposed to a sloop rig are, one, that you need to let out more mainsheet and, two, you need to turn farther through your tack so that you are bearing off on more of a reach to build up speed before coming back to close-hauled. This is due to the fact that there is no jib to help pull the bows down and accelerate forward.

I try to postpone my movement to the new side as long as conditions allow. The boom is often over to the new side before I slide under it.

IF YOU GO INTO IRONS, HOW DO YOU GET OUT?

I first of all decide which tack I want to be on — it may be the tack I was on before; but I may want to go onto the other tack. If I was on starboard tack when I went into irons and I want to stay on starboard tack, I stay toward the starboard side and push the boom away from me (to port) and push the tiller away from me (to port). If I want to come out on the opposite tack, I move toward the port side and push the boom away from me (to starboard) and the tiller away from me (to starboard). This maneuver is actually backing you around so your bows will be pointed in the direction you want to go.

It will speed things up if you also use weight distribution by getting over as far as possible to the same side the boom is out on.

HOW DO YOU STOP THE BOAT AND HOW DO YOU PARK IT, LIKE BEFORE THE START, TO KEEP IT FROM GOING INTO IRONS?

When I am maneuvering like that, I will have my traveler about half-way out. When I want to stop, I jam my rudders over and let the main out, but I am careful to never let the boat go above a close-reach angle. Parking is the same thing, keep the bows pointed toward a close reach, with the main out.

You have to really concentrate on your steering so you don't let the boat start heading up to close-hauled, or you can easily go into irons. If that occurs (as often happens), push the boom and the tiller away from you to back the boat onto course again, as described above.

HOW DO YOU THINK A UNIRIG WOULD COMPARE WITH A SLOOP RIG OF COMPARABLE SAIL AREA, IN TERMS OF SPEED AND EFFICIENCY?

It depends on the point of sail. Upwind, I think the unirigs will point higher and go faster than sloop rigs with the same sail area. Downwind, I think the sloop is faster and can sail deeper.

HOW DO YOU EXPLAIN THESE DIFFERENCES?

I'm not really sure, but I think the primary reason the unirig can point better and go faster upwind is that a jib actually disturbs the air somewhat and also changes its direction before it gets to the main. On a unirig, the main is meeting undisturbed air from its true direction, so it can point higher.

Perhaps the other reason is that unirigs in general and the Hobie 17 in particular can sail with a flatter sail because they are lighter than comparable sloop rigs. Just in crew weight alone, they are at the very least 100 pounds lighter, because there is only one person aboard. So they don't need as much power in their sails and can flatten them out. This lets you point higher and go faster.

Downwind the unirig has to sail a higher course than sloops to keep the air flow attached to the back side of the main. A jib helps sloop rigs to develop more apparent wind, so they can sail deeper faster.

HOW DO YOU RAKE YOUR MAST ON THE HOBIE 17?

On a unirig, helm is less sensitive to mast rake because there is no jib pulling on the bows that could, for instance, give you lee helm if the mast was too straight up and down.

In general, mast rake is not too important, so what I would do is set up the mast the same way as the people in my area who are going fast so I am sailing a same or similarly adjusted boat. Then all I can say is, the more the wind blows, the more I rake the mast back, especially if you can't keep your bows up, which is a rare situation for a Hobie 17 and for most unis other than the Hobie 14. The 14 takes more rake by far, and this improves its performance greatly as well as compensating for the unforgiving nature of its small bows.

WHERE DO YOU PUT TELLTALES ON YOUR SAIL AND HOW DO YOU USE THEM?

Up to this point I have basically used just two sets of telltales on the main, and they are the same as the ones I use on my sloop rigs. I put a set up in the top 25 percent of the sail and another set halfway down the sail. They are located at the deepest point of draft, which is about 40-50 percent of the way back on the sail on my boat.

I use the upper set of telltales for sailing to weather and the middle set for sailing off the wind. The reason I place the upper set so high is that we know there is a different wind velocity between the wind that's on the water and the wind that's, say, 20 or 30 feet up. So if there's a different velocity, there's a different apparent wind, so to speak, so you can adjust your sail to that — you can put the twist that's necessary to account for that difference in speed and angle between what's on the water and what's aloft. Those top telltales are up there where the most power is and where the different angle is. So they are what I have always used for going to weather.

When I am going to weather, I strive to keep the upper windward telltale from flowing back flat. In other words, I want it acting up a little to keep my sail a little "soft." If the windward telltale streams back flat, I know I am on the verge of a stall, even if the back telltale has not yet started to act up. So when the windward telltale streams back flat, I immediately either head up or ease my sail a little. I do not focus on this continually — just when the boat doesn't feel good.

The reason for the middle set is that is where my sail twists off to leeward when I am reaching or running.

On a reach I will use the middle telltales as a reference for adjusting my sail in and out, keeping the windward telltale just acting up a little. Again, I am sailing primarily by feel and speed.

Downwind, I sail primarily by my bridle fly — but we'll be talking about that in a few minutes.

I also put a couple of telltales on the leech of my sail. I rarely look at them, but if they start curling forward or wrapping around the back of the sail, it probably means I am hooking my leech and am sheeted too hard.

Recently I have begun experimenting with putting some additional telltales a few inches back from the mast, both at the top and in the middle. The theory behind this is that they are helpful for tuning the amount of rotation for the mast. They're the indicators for your leading edge. I don't trim the main to those telltales, but I would trim the mast to them.

So the fore, the aft and the center telltales can all tell you different things, but they are ONLY references. Forget striving for perfection.

I would advise people not to get wrapped up in putting too many telltales on their sails or paying too much attention to them, although they are good indicators of what the wind is doing. Try to sail more by feeling the boat than by watching telltales. Get your head out of the boat.

LET'S TALK ABOUT THE START OF A RACE. HOW DO YOU GET THE 17 MOVING AND ACCELERATING?

At the start everyone tends to have a burst of adrenalin and enthusiasm and want to sheet in hard, head up and go. But if you do this on a 17, you probably won't go anywhere but into irons —if you do get moving, it will be slow. The fastest way to get going fast in a 17 is to start out slowly.

Let's say you're parked, as explained before, with your bows pointing onto a close reach and your main out. Approximately 30 seconds before the start you will center your traveler and take your position on the boat where you are going to be for going to weather, being very careful not to let your boat point above that close reach angle.

When you are ready to start accelerating, begin bringing your sheet in slowly to the point where it begins to move forward on the close reach. Then continue to sheet slowly and, simultaneously, slowly steer the boat up to a close-hauled angle. This will let you build speed AS you are heading up.

HOW DO YOU SAIL THE HOBIE 17 UPWIND?

In heavy air I point high and feather the boat a little. Of course, chop and the angle of the waves will be a factor in my pointing angle. In light air I will point as high as the attached flow will allow. In all wind conditions I sheet the 17 harder than the main on a sloop, because, again, the boat is lighter and can go with a flatter sail. Make sure your leech is tight, but not hooking to weather. The exception is very light air, where I will ease the sheet a bit.

Mast rotation principles are the same as on any cat, but because the sail is so flat and it points so high, you can probably rotate a little less, to keep the mast entering the wind at the proper angle.

In light air I will have the traveler centered. In heavy air, as with all the cats, I will start easing it out to the point where the boat is under control.

I try to get the feel of the boat when it is going high and fast and the front telltale is acting up a little. Then I will only glance occasionally at the telltales.

In light air I keep my weight inboard and forward far enough to keep the sterns from dragging and making noise. Usually I am just behind the main beam and maybe leaning forward with one hand on the hull ahead of the beam. As the air picks up, I move back and outboard as necessary.

After a tack or whenever you slow down for any reason, it is very important to get up speed before trying to point too high. If you don't get water flowing over the centerboards before you start pointing, you will have too much leeway. The faster you go, the higher you can point.

WHEN DO YOU USE THE WINGS?

Going to weather the only reason for using the wings is to get your weight out to balance the boat if necessary. You should stay on the deck going to weather as long as possible. If the boat is just starting to fly a hull a little bit once in a while, stay on the hull and lean back against the wing if necessary to keep the hull from flying. If it starts flying a little more, get on the wing but lean in toward the boat. You want to keep that windward hull "light." As the wind builds, you may be sitting up straight on the wing, then leaning out a little and, finally, getting out on the trapeze. But the object is to go only as far as you have to, so you can keep the windward hull skimming the water.

Going downwind you never get on the wings. On a reach, as in going to weather, they are there if needed to get weight farther out or back to balance the boat.

HOW DO YOU SAIL THE HOBIE 17 DOWNWIND?

Downwind I run the traveler all the way out, which is about to the inside of the hull. I ease my mainsheet until the sail is just touching the side stays but not being dented by them. My mast is rotated all the way, as far as I can get it. Then I sail by my bridle fly or telltale on the bridle, keeping it pointed at 90 degrees to the boat.

The 17 will have to sail a slightly higher angle than sloop rigs because it is harder to keep the flow attached to the back side of the main. However, I am still sailing at a 90-degree angle to my apparent wind, keeping the telltale perpendicular to the boat.

It is important to remember that the course is not a straight line, as you will have to steer to changes in wind angle brought about by true wind shifts and apparent wind angles due to boat-speed changes. It may assist in steering to raise the windward rudder.

The most important thing is to do what feels fastest and watch your competitors — clear air is a commodity worth investing in! If they come up and increase speed to drive over you, you must act accordingly. Work for POSITION at the next mark.

And remember that the angle you sail downwind is a variable that can change from one day to another due to wave angle, chop height, current, land effects, etc.

MAST ROTATION

It has to be rotated as far forward of the main beam as you can get it. The 17 now is allowed to use a simple, positive mast rotation device available from the factory. But before this was available, I handled the problem by sitting on the tramp right behind the mast, reaching around the front of the mast and pulling the mast rotater bar forward. Doing this caused my weight to be a little farther back than is ideal. But with a device to take over the mast rotation job, I will be able to get forward on the windward hull in light air.

HOW DO YOU EXECUTE A JIBE?

Jibing is pretty much the same as on a sloop rig, except that your S-turn will be more exaggerated, just as your turn is more exaggerated when tacking upwind. When the sail has jibed over, you will continue your turn up to a faster reaching angle and then come back down to your normal course. This is to expedite the return of attached air flow to the sail after the jibe.

WHAT IS THE BEST ADVICE YOU CAN GIVE PEOPLE ABOUT SAILING?

If I could say something to everybody out there, sailing all these different classes, it would be to get your head out of the boat and think about what you're doing on the race course. The biggest problem I see with people is they get too concerned with this technical stuff. Meanwhile, they're starting at the wrong end of the line. Think about going the right way instead of worrying about how tight your diamond wires are.

The best advice I can give is to get back to basics. This means sound tactics; boat-handling through practice; boat feel through practice (and even night sailing); and true sportsmanship.

THE NACRA 5.8
Chapter 24

A Q&A INTERVIEW WITH LARRY HARTECK

Larry Harteck knows Nacras, literally, from the inside out. He worked for the company for several years, primarily in research and development. He created some of the designs as well as some of the equipment innovations.

Now 33, he has been sailing since he bought an 18-foot Alpha cat — the predecessor to the Nacra — when he was 15.

His most recent accomplishment, after a few years away from the racing scene, was taking second place at the 1991 Nacra 5.8 Worlds in Australia.

Prior credits on Nacras include winning the 5.8 Nationals in 1983 and the 5.2 Worlds in 1983 and 1984. He also is a four-time winner of the Pacific Multihull Association Championships and was Nacra California State champion four years in a row.

He sailed the Worrell 1000 in 1985, placing third; and the Pacific 1000 in 1986, taking a second.

WHAT ARE THE ADVANTAGES AND DISADVANTAGES OF A BOOMLESS MAIN?

The advantages are that, number one, obviously, you can't get hit on the head accidentally by the boom. But there is one less piece of equipment to break or to forget when you are going to a regatta. And it means cheaper production costs.

The first question that comes to mind is: How do you inhaul and outhaul to make the sail flatter or fuller when you do not have a boom?

You do not have as much adjustment on the boomless rig; however you do not really need it. The original 5.8's had a series of holes in the clew plate, and the main blocks attached to the clew by means of a hook through one of those holes. It was possible — but not very feasible while sailing — to change the angle at which the blocks were pulling on the clew by moving the hook to different holes.

Now we have a track which is an integral part of the clew of the main, so the block attachment can be easily moved forward or back. However, this is still not a critical adjustment.

The sail is cut so that it is basically flat at the bottom. The track adjustment makes it possible for you to fatten this up for light air and for going downwind.

What the track does is a little different than what an outhaul on a boom does. With the clew track, when you move the sheeting angle farther forward, as you would do in heavy air, it pulls back more on the foot of the sail and opens up the leech, letting it twist off and spill wind, even though your mainsheet continues to be tight.

In light air and downwind, when you move the sheeting angle back on the track, it tightens up the leech and fattens up the bottom of the sail, which is what you want.

The only disadvantages to a boomless sail are not so much disadvantages as they are differences in sail-trimming that must be learned if you are used to sailing with a boom. We'll get into that in a few minutes.

WHAT DO YOU DO WITH TELLTALES?

I put three sets on the jib. Dividing the jib into quarters vertically, I put one set a fourth of the way down from the top, another set a fourth of the way up from the bottom, and one set in the middle. These are only to help the crew in adjusting the jib downwind.

I don't use telltales on my main. I tried it a long time ago, and I could never make any sense out of them. And the sound of them slapping against the sail drove me nuts, so I took them off. When I get a sail from the factory with telltales, I take them off.

I go by what the sail looks like and what the boat feels like and the feel of the wind on my body and by watching my competition.

If you practice sailing with your eyes closed, you can learn to feel a windshift by the change in pressure on your helm.

There are times, in light and fluky conditions, that the telltales on the jib can help you react to lifts and headers. But, I think people put too much emphasis on telltales.

Going downwind I use a bridle fly or cassette tape on the bridles as an indicator for how deep to sail my course.

TELL US MORE ABOUT GETTING THE FEEL OF THE BOAT.

I will fly a hull with my eyes closed — maybe 20 seconds or so — just to get the feel of the boat. You can tell when the hull is getting higher, because the pressure on your feet gets more and the pressure of the trapeze harness on your body gets less. When the boat is coming down, the pressure on your feet will decrease and you will again feel more pressure on your body from the harness.

WHAT DO YOU DO TO KEEP IN PRACTICE?

When I go pleasure sailing, which I do often, I don't go reaching out and back for three miles like most people do. Instead, I do a lot of drills.

I may only go 300 yards off the beach. Where I sail there are a bunch of little buoys just offshore. I just keep doing tacks and jibes and race around these buoys until I'm winded.

HOW DO YOU RAKE YOUR MAST?

I definitely want some aft mast rake. Normally the tip of my mast is 1 foot to 18 inches aft of vertical. But in heavy air conditions, I will rake it as much as 3 1/2 feet back from vertical.

Aft rake does two things: It helps relieve the pressure on the leeward bow on reaches; and it moves the center of effort back, loading up the rudders so they can help with lateral resistance.

WHAT DO YOU DO WITH RUDDER RAKE:

As you rake the mast farther back, you may need to compensate for increased weather helm by raking the tips of your rudders more forward of the line down from the pivot point, which in this case is the rudder pintle. You do not make this measurement in terms of the transom.

We adjust the rudder rake with the boat on the trailer and the rudders in the down position. Take a straight-edge and hold it vertically, lined up with the pintle, and draw a line down through the rudder. You don't want more than 1 1/4 inch, and preferably no more than 3/4 inch, of the rudder's leading edge ahead of that line.

If you put it too far forward, you can get lee helm. The steering can get pretty squirrelly and the boat may dive off to leeward in a puff, which can be pretty scary.

WHAT ABOUT RUDDER TOE-IN?

I think rudders should be slightly toed in. The reason behind this is that you are going to have a little bit of weather helm, and the leeward rudder is going to be going through the water angled slightly to weather because you are tugging on the tiller. This can be helpful. However, the windward rudder, which is going up and down, in and out of the water, is a surface-piercing foil, and you want it to go straight through the water. This is accomplished by toeing the rudders in slightly rather than having them perfectly parallel.

WHAT BASIC SAIL SHAPE DO THE NACRAS HAVE?

You are restricted to the factory sails, which you can get in either mylar or dacron.

I would say the basic Nacra sail shape is in the medium range. You have spreaders you can rake and diamond wires you can adjust and the clew track, all of which allow you to fatten up the sail pretty well if you want to.

I think the mylar sails can be made fatter than the dacron sails, so all things being equal, I think the mylar sails are faster downwind.

WHAT ARE THE NACRA 5.8'S BEST AND WORST POINTS OF SAIL?

The best point of sail in general is upwind.

Upwind in 8-12 knots with relatively flat water, the Nacra 5.8 can beat almost anything — maybe even a Tornado.

The boat doesn't like chop unless it gets really rough.

It has the most problems in winds between 12 and 18, with chop, because the bows are very full and have a blunt entry, tending to slow the boat through waves.

But when the wind gets over 20 and you have 2-to-3-foot chop, and your bows are going through the waves and under the water, the round shape and overall smoothness of the top of the bows is better than the hard angular decks of most of the other boats.

Although downwind is not the Nacra 5.8's forte, the same reasoning applies for its performance off the wind. It does best in light air and flat seas or in heavy air and rough seas, while it does not like the middle range with moderate wind and chop.

SAILING TO WEATHER

WHAT DO YOU DO WITH YOUR MAINSAIL GOING UPWIND?

Going to weather in light air I have my traveler centered and I sheet just enough to firm up the leech. A big problem on boomless rigs is that people have a tendency to oversheet.

You have to realize that on a boat with a boom, part of that sheeting energy is transferred down the boom to the gooseneck. On a boomless boat, that energy goes into the leech, instead. So it is easy to end up getting your leech too tight.

If in doubt, let it out.

My mast is rotated to 45 degrees (a little aft of the sidestay) for light air, and that is adequate. Because we have no boom to help keep the mast rotated, we cleat the positive rotation line so the mast will stay in that position and not keep flopping around. My philosophy of mast rotation is that I want to keep the leading edge of the mast pointed into the apparent wind.

For light air I will move my clew track out to get a little more fullness in the sail.

HOW DO YOU DEPOWER THE BOAT?

As the wind picks up, my procedure for depowering is to first trapeze.

The second step is to rotate the mast. As the wind picks up, I rotate more until the wind reaches about 18 knots, when the mast should be rotated to 90 degrees. This is not the ideal angle for the mast into the wind, but it flattens the sail while keeping the slot open and giving better air flow around the back of the sail.

I sail with loose diamonds, so my technique is to flatten the sail by bending it on its minor axis. We tried using prebend on the Nacra 5.8, and it hasn't seemed to work.

Even at the Worlds in Australia, where they refer to the wind as so strong it's "blowing dogs off chains," they were using the loose-diamond-wire technique rather than prebend.

The third step is to tighten the main downhaul, in conjunction with sheeting tighter.

The fourth step is to drop the traveler down. In a breeze it is not inappropriate to drop it 12 to 18 inches.

The last thing we do is move the clew track on the main forward.

WHAT IS THE RELATIONSHIP BETWEEN DOWNHAUL AND SHEETING?

It is very important to tension the downhaul in accordance with sheet tension, so that you pull the whole sail down vertically.

The leech is controlled by which has the greater force, the downhaul or the sheet. So if you change one, you have to change the other to compensate. If you pull down too hard on the sheet without downhauling enough, your leech will be too tight. If you downhaul to a greater extent than you are sheeting, your leech will fall off.

You and your crew have to work together on this. If the skipper sheets harder, the crew downhauls harder, and vice versa, to keep the boat driving.

But if you get hit by a puff, instead of releasing the sheet, the crew can whale in on the downhaul. This flattens the sail even more and also opens up the leech to let the air blow off.

It's pretty easy to work the downhaul in this way, because we use 12-1 purchase on it; some guys are using 16-1.

WHAT DO YOU DO WITH YOUR DAGGERBOARDS UPWIND?

In heavy air I will pull my daggerboards up 9 inches to a foot. At high speeds you don't need the board all the way down to prevent leeway. Pulling them up will reduce wetted surface, and it will also prevent "daggerboard plane." This is something that used to happen with the original Windsurfers. The daggerboard would try to rotate out of the water to weather and capsize you. This problem stopped after they started using a smaller daggerboard.

WHAT DO YOU DO WITH YOUR JIB GOING UPWIND?

Our jib leads are on fore-and-aft tracks on the inside edges of the hulls. In light air I will keep the jib car on the forward part of the track, and as the wind increases we move it to the aft part of the track. If it is windy with flat seas, I will put the cars very far aft; but if there is chop, not as far back.

The jib luff is tightened just enough to get the wrinkles out. We tighten it more as the wind increases. It helps flatten the sail.

WHAT IS YOUR WEIGHT DISTRIBUTION GOING TO WEATHER?

In light air the crew will be forward on the leeward hull, and I will be sitting as far forward as I can get and still steer. Usually I am forward of the main beam on the hull.

In heavier air the crew will have his forward foot in front of the main beam, and I will have my forward foot in front of the shroud.

WHAT IS YOUR PROCEDURE FOR DOING A ROLL TACK?

As I start into the turn, my crew and I move aft, even if we are still on the wire. This lifts the leeward bow a little bit and makes it easier for the boat to turn. We don't come in off the wire too quickly.

My crew goes in first and backwinds the jib.

I stay out until the very last minute, which isn't very long on a Nacra, because it tacks very fast. I will get as far back as I can, so my foot is way back by the rudder, helping to push the sterns down so the bow can come around faster. By being that far aft on the trapeze, I am actually a little more vertical, so it is easier to come in off the trapeze from that position.

As the boat is coming into the eye of the wind, I come off the trapeze, uncleat a foot to a foot and a half of mainsheet, and cross to the other side. I immediately move forward — both my crew and I will go forward a little farther than our normal positions to help get the bow down so the boat can drive off.

I head the boat to a few degrees low of the ideal upwind setting. The crew has already sheeted in the jib but has set it a little soft. I sheet in the main, and then we accelerate and head back up to a normal heading, sheeting in the jib and main the rest of the way. And we move back to our normal positions.

The crew has to handle the mast rotation as well as the jib. The rotation is released right before the tack, and the crew gets it cleated on the new side as soon as he gets the jib in. If he is going out on the trapeze, he gets on the trapeze first and then does the mast rotation.

DO YOU TACK YOUR RUDDERS?

I think it's a little bit of a waste of time going upwind unless you have a very long course and are going to be on tacks for a long time. I do raise my weather rudder sailing downwind.

HOW DO YOU ROUND THE WEATHER MARK TO GO DOWN-WIND?

Before rounding, we pull up the weather board and kick up the weather rudder. As we round, I ease the sheet and dump the traveler a little, but not too much. I don't turn too deep right away. You generate a lot of apparent wind in the turn, and I like to use it instead of dumping it and heading immediately down. I'll carry it maybe as much as 75 yards beyond the mark. As I start to lose the apparent wind, I will head down to my normal course and sail settings.

HOW DO YOU SET YOUR BOAT UP FOR DOWNWIND SAILING?

I move the clew traveler to its aft position and move the traveler out to the inside of the hull. I sheet the main fairly firm — the lines between the blocks will be angled more toward the vertical than the horizontal. The reason for this is, again, the fact that we don't have a boom to maintain leech tension. Another common problem new Nacra 5.8 sailors have is that they sheet too loosely going downwind. You don't have a boom to maintain leech tension by maintaining a fixed distance between the tack and the clew, so all control of your leech is dictated by mainsheet tension.

Once I set the main, I don't touch it unless there is a change in wind velocity or I am surfing down a wave. In both cases, I would sheet in some.

The crew rotates the mast to 90 degrees, eases the jib luff until there just a few wrinkles, eases the main downhaul and sets the jib by h
the main beam and his feet are ahead of it, and he will be holding the jib so the clew is approximately above the end of the main beam.

Another thing I do is pull up the weather daggerboard so it is flush with the bottom of the hull, and I leave the leeward board down 5-6 inches. If we are not going to have time to tack boards when we jibe, I will just leave both boards down that amount.

The reason for this is that the boat is so round-bottomed, it will slide when you turn to bear off or head up. Having a little bit of board down will give you some lateral stability and gives you a mini pivot point.

WHAT IS YOUR DOWNWIND SAILING TECHNIQUE:

I sail by a bridle fly or telltales on the bridle, and I try to keep them pointing at 90 degrees to the boat ánd also surf the waves.

My crew plays the jib and also uses the telltales on the jib to keep the shape uniform from top to bottom.

The boat goes deep downwind, but it pays to heat it up a little bit. It sits on top of the water, and it is quick to accelerate, so it pays to head up and get some apparent wind going and then head back down and bleed it off.

But surfing waves is what really pays off in this boat.

I definitely recommend pulling your weather rudder up for going downwind and for reaching. Ideally, your rudders should be toed in slightly for going upwind, as we talked about earlier. But going downwind you have no weather helm, and the toe-in is just going to offer additional resistance by both rudders. If you pull up the windward rudder, the leeward one can track straight through the water. In addition, it reduces some wetted surface by pulling it up.

HOW DO YOU EXECUTE A JIBE:

As I start into the turn, I also ease my mainsheet because I am going deeper. At the same time, the crew is holding the jib farther forward and out.

Just before the main goes over, I go back and put the weather rudder down. I help the main across, go to the other side and raise the rudder and go back forward.

I handle the mast rotation, because it is controlled from the windward side. So before the jibe, I release it. And when the jibe is completed and I am back in position on the new side, I adjust it on that side.

What I like the crew to do is hold the clew of the jib, easing it forward and out. When it is ready to come across, the crew stands on the main beam, crosses in front of the mast, holding onto a diamond wire along the way, and then sets the jib in position on the new side.

WHAT DO YOU DO TO PREPARE FOR THE LEEWARD MARK ROUNDING?

The crew tensions the jib luff, cleats or barber-hauls the jib, puts down the leeward board and goes to the weather side, where he sets the mast rotation for upwind and tensions the main downhaul. He then prepares to go out on the wire (or may even be out on the wire before the actual rounding), and releases the barber hauler and prepares to sheet in the jib.

The skipper sets the clew track back forward, centers the traveler and sheets in the main.

WHAT IS YOUR TECHNIQUE FOR REACHING?

I keep my leeward board down halfway, because the boat tries to fly a hull less, and I pull my weather rudder up.

My goal is to keep the weather hull off the water at all times on a reach. We play the sails to try to achieve that.

But if the wind gets up over 25 knots, then it pays to keep the boat flat so both hulls can absorb the pressure of the sails.

I think a mistake a lot of people make on a reach is not trapezing low enough. You should be getting slapped by the waves once in a while. We trapeze literally flat with and maybe lower than the trampoline.

WHAT IS YOUR ADVICE FOR OTHER SAILORS:

People get too wrapped up in their own boat instead of looking around at what other people are doing.

After someone wins a race, go over and look at their boat and see how it is set up. Ask them what they are doing and how they do it. Have your crew look around, too.

A key mistake people make is not trying hard enough to learn from others.

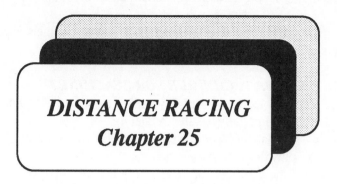

AN INTERVIEW WITH ROY SEAMAN

Long-distance races for small catamarans have become increasingly popular during the last several years. The trend was begun by the handful of trailblazers who could and would race grueling events like the Worrell 1000 (more recently the World 1000), the Pacific 1000, and the Hog's Breath 1000.

And riding their coattails, several smaller long-distance races of around 100 miles came into being at locations around the country. These appeal to the many hundreds of sailors who just want a weekend taste of the adventure, challenge and danger of the thousand-milers.

To get the real scoop on what it's like being out there on a thousand miles of ocean and why anyone would do it, we talked to the guy who has done it more than anyone else: Roy Seaman.

Seaman raced the Worrell (World) 1000 five times and won it twice. He raced the Pacific 1000 twice, taking a second and a third. He raced as crew in the Tahiti Mondiale in 1990. These are just in the small cats. He has been racing large cats, 36 to 75 feet, in offshore and distance races for many years, setting numerous official and unofficial speed records.

We asked Roy Seaman why he likes long distance races. We were expecting an answer about the challenge of doing battle against the elements and the sea, man against nature, one on one.

Instead, he said: "It's a good way to get a lot of sailing in. Think about it — in the Worrell you went a thousand miles in 10 days."

We thought about it, and it did not really seem to answer the question. So we asked, "But WHY would you want to get that much sailing in?"

Then came the real answer: the search for speed. "Even in a thousand miles, you're lucky to get one good day or even one good hour where you really get a great speed run. It's a very rare thing, and it is very difficult to get when you go out daysailing on a weekend.

"What makes it possible to achieve this kind of ultimate speed on a long-distance race is when you start downwind in the morning with a big chute up, and then it starts blowing harder and harder and harder until you really fly. You get to sail with your chute in winds you would never normally be able to do, because if you started out in winds like that you would never be able to even get the spinnaker out of the bag. But when it's already up, you just keep going faster and faster and fly it all day.

His best long speed run was in a Worrell 1000 when he averaged 19.5 knots for three hours, covering 65 miles in a total of 3 hours and 15 minutes.

Another time he had his finest hour — the one that made all those long-distance races worthwhile — he was hitting speeds of 28-30 miles an hour in a 35-knot wind.

"Speed is everything," he said, "— to get the most out of a boat."

The adventure and challenge, although secondary for him, are probably the biggest attractions the long-distance races hold for most people, Roy admitted.

As compared to sailing around the buoys, "you can see yourself going somewhere, and you are always exploring new waters rather than being confined to a few square miles for triangle races.

"And you are more on your own most of the time. After the first one or two hours, you may never see another boat the rest of the day. Of course, this is more desirable to some people than to others."

"The races can be grueling, but it's not too bad if you are stopping every night and can walk from your boat to your hotel room, take a shower and get a good night's sleep.

"These high-performance cats can cover 80 to 100 miles a day very comfortably. I can go 8, 10, 12 hours on the helm, and it doesn't really bother me at all. I guess I get sort of mesmerized, and the time seems to pass really fast."

But he admits it wasn't always so comfortable. Until he started putting hiking racks on his boats (wings that extend out an additional 10 feet on each side of a 10-foot-wide boat), he and his crew had to trapeze on the side of the boat all day every day. "When I got in at night, sometimes I could hardly walk, and my sides would be very sore where the trapeze harness pulls against you. I never have found one that is really comfortable.

My neck would be really stiff and sore from having to trapeze with my head turned forward the same way all day. As I got wiser and older, I had to come up with something better.

"With the racks you can turn your whole body and move around and change position or let your legs dangle — they're a lot more comfortable, and you hardly ever get wet.

"Another advantage of the racks is the leverage. With my crew and I both out on the racks, it adds a tremendous amount of leverage. If you put 100 pounds out 10 feet farther, it becomes like 1000 pounds, so you can imagine what it is with two men out there. With that much leverage, we seldom have to ease the mainsheet even in heavy air."

Without racks, too, the races can be really hard on your hands from playing sheets all day. Roy said, "I've seen guys come in with their hands all torn up, right through their gloves."

One minor disadvantage to the racks is that it is hard to see the compasses (built into the deck) from out there — "you're too far away and not at the right angle. But now they have those hand-held digital compasses; that makes it a lot easier."

He could only think of one other slight disadvantage to the racks. "I didn't think about it until we tipped over one time. I had never figured how long the fall would be. The boat is 10 feet wide, and I was out another 10 feet on the rack, so that put me 20 feet above the water when the boat was on its side. I fell and went right through the sail like it wasn't even there."

HAZARDS OF LONG-DISTANCE RACES

"Without question, the greatest danger out there is falling off the boat and becoming separated from it. If your crew can't get back to you fast enough, he can lose track of you. Or, worse, with one person on the boat, it may capsize. One person cannot right it, and the boat will drift away faster than you can swim to it."

In the Tahiti Mondiale race, competitors were required to be attached to the boat by a restraining line, and Seaman says this probably would be a good idea for all long-distance races. "In Tahiti I did fall off the boat when a trapeze buckle broke, and I was glad I had that line attached to me."

Another, closely related hazard is fatigue. "When you're wiped out and tired, it causes you to make mistakes. You're more likely to capsize or fall off the boat. And the worst thing is that after a while you can get to the point where you just don't care anymore.

"One time it was 10 o'clock at night. I had a really bad headache, I was tired, and it was heavy air. I was under a lot of stress just trying to keep it together, mentally and physically.

"I saw a bunch of waves breaking up ahead over a shoal. I was too tired to care, so I just went right through them. Luckily, I made it across."

Storms are another hazard that can be much more fearsome when you are at sea, unable to seek safe harbor and out of sight of other boats. The dangers are from lightning and from the winds that can come out of them, according to Roy. "I got a shock once on the boat, and it has happened to other racers."

A storm capsized him once. "We were trapped-out in heavy air and all of a sudden the boat came right over on top of us. The wind switched around to the other direction so fast we didn't even make it to the hull before it went over."

Although it doesn't happen often, fog can be a real problem for the racers, especially when they are trying to find their checkpoint to come in for the night. "One time we were in heavy fog, and my chart said there were three piers before the checkpoint. We didn't know someone had put in another pier, so we sailed up on a beach behind somebody's house and had to ask where the hotel was. You could hardly see the beach from the surf line."

Another competitor in a Worrell 1000 had a more serious problem with fog when his boat was sucked into an inlet on a rising tide and smashed against a bridge.

Fog or no fog, getting lost has been a problem at one time or another for most competitors in long-distance races. Everyone has a story about himself or someone else who has had to sail in to a beach and ask directions. "One time we went in to ask directions from some people playing volleyball," Roy said.

A remote hazard is collisions with animals or debris in the sea. Especially a problem on the east coast are sea turtles up to 4 feet long floating lazily on the surface of the water. They usually don't try to move out of the way fast enough, so the boats have to avoid them. "They're not really a problem," Roy said, you usually can straddle them if necessary. But one time I saw the water turn all dark up ahead and it was wider than the boat. I tried to straddle it, and both boards hit, and then the boat lunged forward almost throwing us both off the rack. It was a giant ray at least 12 foot wide.

"And one time off the coast of Florida we sailed through jellyfish for miles and miles, thousands of them.

"The biggest danger on the East Coast is hitting sandbars and shoals — you have to watch for them."

"I've never worried much about sharks. In all my races I've only seen one — a hammerhead. I know Randy (Smyth) had a shark following him for a while in one World 1000."

For many competitors, another hazard can be the surf they often have to sail out through when leaving the beach and back in on when arriving at the checkpoint.

"It is definitely harder to get out through the surf than get in," Roy said, adding this is where people are most likely to break their boards or rudder assemblies.

"Coming in is not very difficult, if you know how to ride the waves" — easy for him to say; he's been a surfer all his life.

BREAKDOWNS

One of the most potentially serious problems is breakdowns. If a boat is dismasted or holed or loses its rudder system, or for some other reason is unable to continue under its own power, it is at the mercy of the wind and sea until help arrives.

Unfortunately, in most long-distance races, there is not a crash boat nearby to render assistance. In fact, there is not a crash boat at all.

"We carry a radio and a EPIRB (a radio distress signal device that enables rescuers to locate the boat). If we get in trouble, we can radio the Coast Guard as well as activating the EPIRB."

One time during the Worrell, Roy's boat broke down and he was able to limp to a small island. "A plane would fly the course twice a day. So when the plane flew over, we radioed to them and told them where we were and to tell our ground crew at the next checkpoint.

"The ground crew had to drive back down the coast, find a little motorboat to get out to the island, and then they had to wade through swamps and everything else to bring parts and repair materials and work on the boat."

Tahiti was an exception to the every-man-for-himself attitude that prevails at some long-distance races. "There they had two powerboats, a Navy cutter and a sightseeing boat accompanying the racers. It gave us a very secure feeling."

Because of the length of the race, the variety of conditions and sustained stresses, breakdowns of some sort must be anticipated. While some racers may go so far as to bring along enough components to make a whole new boat, Roy brings only extra daggerboards, rudders and all the rudder assembly components, including castings, tiller bars, crossbar and tiller extension. His ground crew also has basic repair materials like body putty, fiberglass cloth and resin.

To make minor repairs on the boat, he takes a vice grips, screw driver and knife, extra shackles and "lots of lines, fat lines, thin lines, long lines, short lines, for jury-rigging."

But what he brings the most of is sails. "In fact, I carry four or five extra sails right on my boat. I always take three spinnakers — two big ones and a small one. Spinnakers are such light material, they can easily get torn. And I always want to make sure I have the right sail aboard for the conditions."

When preparing for a long-distance race, if he plans to use a stock, production boat, Roy said the most important thing he does to it "is make sure it is very waterproof. I install hatches and put in positive flotation. As long as your boat stays afloat and you don't get too cold, you'll be okay until someone finds you. When I designed and built my own boat for the last World 1000, I put three watertight chambers in each hull so it absolutely could not sink."

"In general, production boats do not have too many breakdowns. The boats most likely to have problems are 'designer boats,' that people have built themselves. You don't know what or where the problems are until something breaks. A long-distance race is going to find all the problems."

SAFETY EQUIPMENT

"I take all the usual safety stuff, flares and a throwable as well as the radio and EPIRB. We have flashlights for sailing at night. I don't take an anchor — too much extra weight."

"We wear life jackets. Probably a restraining line to connect you to the boat should be added to the list.

"We also take a strobe light, but we don't usually use it unless we want them to be able to see us at night coming in to the checkpoint. The light can be very distracting flashing in your eyes at night.

"For the Tahiti race, they required us to use the strobe at night, but we could put it up high, near the hound on the mast, so it didn't bother us too much."

Another safety item Roy carries is a water bag to assist in righting the boat.

TAKING CARE OF THE BODY

Surviving days of being at sea in the hot sun, requires attention to the little things.

"I am real careful to protect myself from the sun and stay covered up as much as possible," Roy said. "I use a good, waterproof sunblock and reapply it frequently. I keep it on my person, so it's easy to get to.

"To protect my eyes, I use dark-tinted, polarized ski goggles. I treat them with Rainex to keep them from spotting. Sunglasses don't always work very well — you still get wind and water and sun in your eyes.

"One time before I started using the goggles, I actually had to drop out of a race because my eyes were so badly burned."

Another important thing is to stay warm and dry. "I try to dress in the morning for the conditions I expect that day, because it's real hard to change clothes out on the water.

"Usually I wear drysuits. Occasionally, if I expect it to be too hot for a drysuit, I'll wear white foul weather gear — it helps keep me dry but reflects the sun so I don't get too hot.

"Sometimes I will start out in a bathing suit and later in the morning if it looks like the wind is starting to pick up, I'll put on my drysuit.

"One time when we capsized after dark in heavy air, we were in the water quite a while, and after we got the boat up, I was really glad I was wearing my drysuit. It is pretty miserable to be cold and wet at night. It's great to come ashore comfortable and dry."

"For food we just take along sandwiches and granola bars and candy bars in ziplock bags. For liquid I take mostly juice — those little juice cartons with the straws. I'll take as many as 10 of those and maybe a quart of water.

WHERE TO STORE ALL THE 'STUFF'

After making note of a huge pile of stuff, including sails, jury-rig repair materials and tools, safety equipment, food and water, we asked Roy where people put all of it.

"Most people have it piled on the deck, tied down, or in bags or tramp pouches.

"But I make hatches in my boats so I can store most of it —in fact all of it, if necessary — in the hulls, so I can sail with a clean tramp. This also cuts down on windage and gets the weight down lower in the boat."

CHOOSING A CREW

Two people are confined on a small boat together — in fact, confined on a rack together — for a thousand miles of empty sea. How do you go about finding someone you can get along with in those conditions?

"I want someone with good mental strength as well as physical strength, someone who is quick and agile, and, hopefully, someone with a winning attitude. It also is important to have a crew who knows navigation.

"Although I have never specifically tried to get someone who is also a good helmsman, I can see how that could be an advantage, having someone to take turns with you on the helm and give you a break."

"Several times I have sailed with people I did not even know before the race. Sometimes it works out well; sometimes not so well. But I've never really had any problems getting along with my crews, as far as compatibility.

"I think the most important thing you need in a crew, though, is mental toughness — so they're not going to psych out on you in adverse conditions. I had that happen once. My crew got so mentally and physically exhausted, he totally lost it. I had to put him on the trampoline and sail the boat myself."

NAVIGATION

"Knowing navigation is very, very important. You have to know how to read charts, how to use a compass, how to identify navigation marks, etc.

"We waterproof our charts and seal them in plastic. We carry with us the chart for that day's leg of the race. Every time you sail that same race you add more things to your chart to help identify where you are by landmarks along the way."

THE GROUND CREW

Every crew on the water in a long-distance race has a support crew on land, meeting the racers at each checkpoint. But what exactly do they do?

"My ground crew usually consists of my wife and one other person," Roy said. "They drive the vehicle, bringing along the spare parts and repair materials.

"The ground crew takes care of checking in and out of the hotel, carrying our gear when we get in to the beach, helping with any repairs that might be needed to the boat, and hopefully giving my neck a massage and, in general, rendering some TLC.

"They also take care of preparing our food to take on the boat and stop to pick up anything we may need before the next checkpoint."

THE COST FACTOR

"Cost is a big variable — it can be quite cheap or as expensive as you want to make it.

"If you already have a boat, you could probably keep your expenses to a minimum of $6,000. That covers things like your entry fee, travel expenses, food and lodging for sailors and ground crew, and extra parts.

"To be safe, I usually figure a maximum of $10,000 for the basic expenses.

"Of course, if you have to buy a boat, you have to add in that cost, too.

"And if you are building a boat, it really gets up there. The boat I designed and built for the last World 1000 cost me $20,000, and that did not count my two months of labor. And that was with a traditional-construction mast. One of the other development boats in that same race spent $10,000 for the mast alone, because it was made of exotic materials.

SPONSORSHIP

We asked how he or anyone else could afford to participate in these races.

"I have been sponsored for all the races but one," he said. "Without sponsorship, it is very, very difficult.

"Unfortunately, sponsorship is very hard to get — not just for the participants but for the races themselves. That is why the races are dying out.

"The last World 1000 was held three years ago, and they have not been able to get a race sponsor since. It looks like it won't happen this year, either. The plan for the new Hogsbreath 1000 from New Orleans to Key West was dropped for lack of a race sponsor.

"I think the big problem is there is no good way to get network TV coverage of the events. You can make a film and show it afterwards, but it's difficult to do it live. If we had TV coverage, sponsorship would be easy."

For those who really love the long drag races, and who want to do it just for fun, maybe the only answer is to go back to the simple and informal way the Worrell first started: Start at one end, finish a thousand miles later, and do whatever you want in between.

After all, the Worrell 1000 reputedly got started in the first place in a bar when someone bet Mike Worrell that he couldn't sail a Hobie 16 from Virginia Beach to Fort Lauderdale.

NEW IN SAILS
Chapter 26

BY DAVE CALVERT

Dave Calvert established his racing and sailmaking reputation originally in sailboards, winning two nationals and one world championship in the early-to-mid-1980's.

He began expanding into the multihull market in the last half of the '80's. Calvert and his sails won the Stiletto Nationals two years in a row - - the Stiletto One-Design 27' Nationals in 1990 and the Stiletto Modified Class in 1991.

His sails helped win first place and set a course record for the cruising multihull class in the 45-mile Miami-Key Largo Race in 1989, with Rick White on the helm and Calvert as a member of the crew.

Calvert Sails on a Hobie 18 won the Key Largo Steeplechase, a 110-mile distance race, in 1991 and set a course record of 1 hour and 3 minutes for the 22-mile Interlake Yachting Association Deepwater Race from Sandusky to Put-in-Bay, Ohio, also in 1991.

DACRON OR MYLAR, WHAT IS BEST FOR YOU?

Your old sails are starting to complain. The leech flutters, the nice smooth shape that was once there won't return, no matter what the trim. To make matters worse, a friend whom you often sail against shows up on the water with a bright new set of sails and smiles as he motors by you to windward.

Thoughts of new sails come to mind. What's new and hot in sails? What about mylar? Is it very expensive? You want something that will last. How important is the sail cloth?

Once the sailmaker has decided on the outline profile and three dimensional shape of a sail, he is faced with the decision of what sailcloth and cut to use. Often as much time and consideration is spent on selecting the proper cloth for the job as designing the sail itself.

It's fair to say it is easier for an engineer to build the right shape into the wing of an aircraft than it is to build a sail. The wing is made of metal and does not change shape in use. So it can be counted on to perform as designed.

Sails, on the other hand, are made of material which is not only flexible but stretches under pressure. the amount of stretch also varies from one type of cloth to another. The way the cloth stretches alters sail shape in various wind strengths.

If the wind increases and trim is not altered, a sail will ordinarily become somewhat fuller with more draft aft as a result of fabric stretch. Optimum boat performance in a rising wind would call for a flatter, more-draft-forward sail shape, exactly the opposite of what we get.

There is nothing we can do about the characteristics of a sailcloth once it has been used in the construction of a sail, (short of replacing the sail). The sailcloth literally is the sail.

So now we can see the importance of selecting the right sailcloth for the job.

MYLAR VS. DACRON

Almost all working sails today are made up of either woven dacron or one of the various mylar laminates. With each of these materials there are definite advantages and disadvantages. At this time we will look at characteristics of various cloth suitable for multihull sails.

Let's first start by getting a clearer picture of how the two types of cloth are made and how this affects the performance of each.

DACRON SAILCLOTH

Dacron is extruded out of a round nozzle to create a filament which becomes a dacron yarn. These polyester yarns are then woven in large, high speed looms to construct the basic cloth. The raw fabric is then finished in a number of ways.

"Finishing" is a complex, multi-step process which extensively alters the fabric. The cloth is chemically cleaned, then treated with resin and heat. The two cloth finishes that are most used are resin-impregnated and resin-coated. A fabric that has been impregnated has been dipped through a solution of resin prior to heat setting. This resin soaks into the fibers and during heat setting it chemically bonds those fibers together. An impregnation can be thought of as inhibiting the stretch of a fabric as opposed to trying to eliminate all stretch. Most dacrons used fall under this category.

A coating, instead of seeping into the fibers, is an actual film of resin which sits on one surface. An example of coated cloth is yarn tempered. These cloths are the firmest and highest performance of dacrons. Intended strictly for racing, these fabrics have a very hard, firm coating, which provides the lowest stretch characteristics available in a dacron sailcloth.

MYLAR LAMINATES

Mylar laminated sailcloth is made by laminating a clear mylar film onto dacron or kevlar cloth.

Mylar was used as sailcloth as early as 1964 but when used on its own, it lacked sufficient tear strength to be usable. In 1977 America's Cup boats tried sails of mylar laminated to dacron cloth, but poor adhesion resulted in delamination.

In 1978 development of new bonding formulas produced the first high-strength, low-weight mylar laminates. Since then sailcloth manufacturers have been able to laminate mylar films to polyesters, kevlars, and spectra substrates with virtually no delamination problems.

Mylar laminates came in a wide range of different styles of mylar/dacron and mylar/kevlar laminated cloths. Some are designed for horizontally cut sails and some for vertical or radial cuts. The two most commonly used laminates are scrims and taffetas.

Scrims are 3-ply laminates of loosely woven substrates (woven yarns) with mylar film laminated to both sides.

Taffetas are tightly woven substrates with mylar laminated on one side.

Scrims, with their higher percentage of mylar film to fabric, often offer less stretch than single-sided laminates. But they may have less tear strength and durability as well.

SAILCLOTH SPECIFICATIONS

Now with a working knowledge of how dacron and laminates are constructed, let's see how performance characteristics differ from one to another.

Sails for small performance multihulls are usually made from one of three types of sailcloth: all-purpose, colored dacron; yarn-tempered dacron; or mylar/dacron laminates.

Below is a list of sailcloth specifications for various cloths suitable for use in small cat sails. To determine how sailcloth will perform under load, tests are made to evaluate the amount of stretch. The numbers shown represent 100s of an inch of elongation at various loads in the warp (the length of the panel), the fill (the width of the material), and the bias (45 degrees to the thread line).

To measure this a strip of fabric is cut from each of these directions. The strips are then clamped into a tester which measure the elongation in 100s of an inch at 10 lb. loads.

TYPE OF CLOTH	WARP	FILL	BIAS
5.3 oz. colored all purpose dacron	8.0	8.0	28.0
5.4 oz firm finish dacron	–	2.5	12.0
5.4 oz yarn tempered dacron*	–	2.0	4.0
4.4 oz firm finish dacron	–	3.0	15.0
4.4 oz yarn tempered dacron	–	2.0	4.0
4.5 oz colored GTS scrim mylar	3.3	3.8	5.4
4.6 oz colored GTS taffeta mylar	4.3	4.5	5.7
3.6 oz Bainbridge 3-ply scrim mylar	–	3.0	5.0
4 oz Bainbridge woven mylar	2.5	–	6.0
3.7 oz Bainbridge kevlar weave	0.8	4.4	4.8

*Treat them with Rainex to keep them from spotting.

From these spec comparisons we can easily see the large differences in stretch from one type of cloth to another. The 5.3 oz. all purpose dacron has by far the most stretch, but offers good durability and a wide range of colors. The yarn-tempered dacrons have performance characteristics similar to the mylar laminates, but have poor tear strength and durability, and come in white only. Mylar/dacron laminates offer very good stretch and performance, are quite durable and come in a wide range of constructions and colors.

ADVANTAGES VS. DISADVANTAGES

So how does all this affect the average small catamaran sailor? Let's look at the main factors to consider:

PERFORMANCE

In light air and choppy water a soft dacron sail may have a slight edge over a firm finished sail. Here a bit of stretch is not a problem. As the wind increases though, a sail that stretches easily will become fuller and the draft will begin to move aft. This changes the designed shape and will result in less speed and pointing ability as well as more heeling and weather helm.

In gusty conditions less stable sails will lack acceleration. As a puff hits, the sails will stretch more, causing the leech to twist and distort. A stable sail that holds its designed shape in a puff will convert the puff into power and accelerate forward.

Some one-design classes have allowed both dacron and mylar to be used. In these cases, sails made with the firm, yarn-tempered dacron show similar top end speeds to the mylar ones. In light air the less stiff mylar sails seem to fill better, giving slightly better speed than the yarn tempered ones. The 5.3 oz. colored production sails were the worst, holding their own only in light air, but loosing their shape soonest as the wind increased.

DURABILITY

Durability is certainly a big consideration when buying sails. As with most aspects of sailing, there must be compromises. Only all-out racers, without regard to price, can buy sails for performance only. The other extreme may be sails on boats used for beach rentals. In this case, longevity and price are major considerations.

Most of us fall somewhere in between these two extremes. The majority of sailors use their boats for recreational sailing and part-time racing. Here is where the most compromises between performance, longevity and price are required.

The major factors affecting sailcloth durability are chafe, effects of ultraviolet rays, and delamination. The soft dacrons have good tear strength and resist chafe fairly well. Yarn-tempered dacron is so stiff that if creased it can break the fibers. Once a tear starts, it is hard to stop it. Most new laminates have good tear strength. Some have heavier threads running on one direction than the other, giving better tear strength across those heavier threads.

Most sail repairs on fully battened mainsails occur at the batten pockets, especially where the sail lays across the shrouds. Dacron here would probably wear better than mylar, although mylar sails will have dacron batten pockets.

Exposure to ultraviolet rays has very strong effects on all synthetics. Tests made by Howe & Bainbridge, the largest U.S. sailcloth manufacturer, showed that 6 oz. dacron lost up to 70% of its strength after just six months of continuous exposure to the intense sun in South FLorida. Mylar/dacron laminates seem to suffer about the same, with nylon and kevlar the worst. So minimizing your sail's exposure to the sun is very important, be it mylar or dacron.

Delamination obviously is not a problem with woven dacron cloth, but can occur in laminates. The adhesives and laminating techniques of today have greatly reduced this sort of problem. The heavy open weave scrims have very little delamination problems. With an open weave, the mylar films on each side can make contact with each other, greatly increasing the bond.

Some problems may occur in areas of high loads as the sail gets older. Areas to watch are each end of batten pockets, especially the inboard ends, and the inside of corner patches. Excessive downhaul can also cause problems along the luff.

PRICE

How do sail prices differ from dacrons to laminates? This can be a real deciding factor when choosing a new sail. Surprisingly enough, the price of mylar/dacron cloth is about the same as dacron, and in some cases less. Mylar/kevlar, on the other hand, is usually about 150% more than dacron.

A large determining factor in sail cost is the construction. Sails made from laminates may require special construction techniques. The lightweight scrims need special 2-sided reinforcing tape in the seams, windows, pockets and where corner patches are sewn on. In some cases complex panel layouts are used to reduce weight and stretch. These extra steps in construction can add greatly to the price of sails.

This brings us to another question. Which sort of cut is best for each material?

HORIZONTAL VS. VERTICAL CUTS

The term "cut" refers to the panel layout. The three most commonly used cuts are horizontal, vertical and radial.

Why different cuts? In order to answer this question, we must first understand how sails and sailcloth are loaded when in use.

Sails are not loaded equally across their entire surface. The greater loads are along the edges of the sail, especially along the leech. The loads follow curvo-linear or catenary-like paths from one corner of the sail to the other. These curved lines create a topographical view of the loads within a sail. *(See Figure 1.)* Modern sail designs are using elaborate panel configurations in an effort to keep the primary yarn direction of the fabric in line with these loads. The better the yarn and load alignment, the lighter the fabric you can use.

Most sailcloths have heavier threads or yarns running in one direction than the other. Sailcloth is referred to as fill-oriented or warp-oriented. Fill threads run across the width of the fabric, warp threads along the length. Since the highest loads on a sail are along the leech, care has to be taken to align the heaviest cloth yarns in this direction. Sailcloth with heavy fill threads should be used in horizontally cut sails. Care should be taken to lay the panels 90 degrees to the load from head to clew. *(See Figure 2).*

When using a vertical or radial cut, warp-oriented cloth must be used. An example of a vertical cut as used for small performance sails is *Figure 3*. This design uses continuous panels along both leech and luff. This aligns the warp yarns with the loads in these two directions. The vertical luff seam is also used to position the "draft")amount of curvature) of the sail.

In this cut composite construction works well. The leech and center of the sail can be mylar with the vertical luff panel dacron. The more stretchy dacron luff gives better adjustability to downhaul, as well as helping to keep the draft forward as the wind increases.

The third and most complicated cut is the tri-radial. *(See Figure 4).* With this sail cut an attempt is made to keep cloth yarns tangential to all

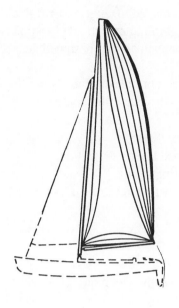

Figure 1

Figure 2

Figure 3

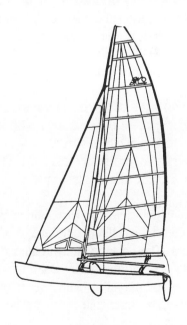

Figure 4

load lines. Panels radiate out from each corner, following the load lines that radiate out in the same direction. This cut minimizes stretch to a point that lighter cloth can be used, as well as maintaining the designed shape longer.

Our experience with larger boats like the Formula 40s has shown this to be the most functional cut for lightweight sails under high loads.

Advantages of vertical or radial construction:
- facilitates alignment of yarns with load lines.
- reduction of the number of load-bearing seams.
- vertical luff panel and composite construction to help lock in the draft.
- lighter-weight sails.

Disadvantages of vertical or radial construction:
- new methods of horizontal sail shaping are required -- either through vertical broadseaming or by inflicting horizontal broadseams after assembly.

Advantages of horizontal construction:
- the only real advantage of horizontal cuts is the ease of construction. It is much easier to shape the three-dimensional sections of a sail with horizontal seams. Batten pockets can be made by using extra wide seams. This reduces labor and sail price.

Disadvantages of horizontal construction:
- alignment of yarns only with leech loads, allowing for more distortion and bias stretch.
- heavier or firmer cloth needed to help reduce the bias stretch.
- more load-bearing seams.

In conclusion, modern laminates are becoming widely accepted. They offer an excellent combination of performance, durability and range of colors. The delamination problems have been all but eliminated, and strength greatly improved. Dacron does still offer a good choice for economy and durability with reasonable performance. With sail cut, as a rule, the more complicated it is, the better the performance and the greater the expense.

The choice is yours.

WIND & WEATHER
Chapter 27

BY BOB CURRY

Bob Curry is a meteorologist with the United States Air Force. That is what he does for a living. But what he does for fun is win sailboat races.

He has won the worlds and five nationals on the Hobie 14, two nationals on the Hobie 17 and one on the Hobie 14 Turbo. For the past year he has been sailing a Prindle 19 and will probably add this class to his string of successes.

Currently, he is teamed up with Randy Smyth on a Tornado in an active campaign to represent the United States in the 1992 Olympics.

He attributes his sailboat racing success partially to his ability to read the wind and play the clouds, and he was generous enough to pass some help-ful weather and windshift information along to our readers.

GENERAL CIRCULATION

FRONTS AND HIGH-PRESSURE AREAS.

Picture high and low pressure areas as hills and holes on an otherwise flat plane. The high pressure area is a hill or mound of pressure, while the low pressure area is a hole or depression.

And like all things in the universe, mother nature wants things to be on a smooth plane. So, the hill tries to move into the hole. In doing so, wind is created as the flow of air pressure moves clockwise and outward from the hill. On the other hand, the hole is being filled up by air pressure circulating counterclockwise and inward toward the center of the hole.

When you flush your toilet you are creating a low pressure area of water, and the new, incoming water flows inward and counterclockwise as well. This is all true, if you live in the northern hemisphere. It is just the opposite in the southern hemisphere.

You can locate the low pressure area by putting your nose directly into the wind, raising your left arm out and a little aft. At that time you will be pointing directly at the low pressure area.

A front is a trough of low pressure, or a dip in the air mass, trailing behind the actual low pressure area, and is the leading edge of high pressure area. And if you are looking at a weather map, generally looks like tail trailing behind a low pressure area. Fronts are troughs of low pressure. *(See Diagram 58.)*

Cold air always goes toward warm air — and with a cold front, you have colder air behind a front and warmer air in front of it. The warm air rises, and cold air comes in to replace it, causing wind.

No matter where you are in the northern hemisphere cold fronts will generally move from the northwest to the southeast, with a high pressure area behind.

As the front approaches, the wind will turn more southerly, and keep gradually clocking.

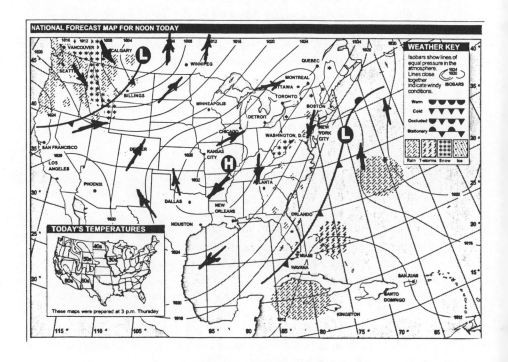

DIAGRAM 58

If a race course is set up to the south of the front, as the front approaches, the wind will gradually clock around to the right, making the right side of the race course favored.

You want to work the outside of the course on the right side going to weather, and the opposite side going downwind.

If the wind has been gradually clocking to the right on Saturday and you get up on Sunday and the wind is out of the southwest or west, that front is close! You better start looking for clouds or thunderstorms and a windshift that is going to come out of the opposite direction

When the wind is out of the west, you know the front is real close. Expect a sudden, big wind shift to the northwest as the front passes over. Usually it just bangs right in, although I have also seen it go dead calm before the shift.

If the wind is shifting to the right, you want to go over to the right side so you will be on the inside of the shift. You will sail a shorter distance by going over to the right and the outside of the course. If you sail over to the left side on starboard tack, you will be getting lifted, lifted, lifted, and you will be sailing a much longer distance to the mark.

After the front has gone by, the wind is going to primarily come out of the northwest, and it is going to continue to clock as the center of the high pressure area continues to march from northwest to southeast.

You can pretty much figure on it going to the right — but you can't always bank on it. That's why you have to get out there on the water and do your homework before the race — see what's going on.

Check out the weather map in the paper before a regatta and see where the front is. If you're really good, you'll be doing it for a week in advance. The Weather Channel on TV will have all the fronts drawn out for at least three or four days in advance. And if you do that prior to a racing situation, you can get kind of a feel for where that wind is going to shift and about what time.

After every weather station in the country reports their own barometric pressure, lines are drawn connecting areas with the same barometric pressure. These lines end up looking like big swirls and some circles on the map. They are called isobars. When these isobars very close together, they indicate the high pressure hill is very high, and, by contrast, the low pressure hole is very deep. So, the air rushes faster to flow off the top of the hill and into the deeper hole.

When the hills and holes are slight, the air pressure moves slower, and the isobars are further apart.

Look at the weather map to see if the isobars are close are far apart in your area. If close together, you will see a lot of wind. If they are far apart, there will not be much wind.

In the very center of the high, there is no wind. If the center of the high passes over the lake you are on, there will be dead air, and it will be very variable — it can come from any direction.

You can tell from the isobars whether there is going to be wind behind the front or whether it is going to be light air. Isobars are the more or less concentric circles on the weather map around the high and lows, and they indicate the differences in barometric pressure. If the isobar lines are close together, it means wind; if the circles and loose and wide apart, it means light air.

Since highs rotate clockwise and lows rotate counterclockwise, where the outer edges of the two circulations converge, you will have a lot of wind going in the same direction — heavy-duty downhaul and trapeze weather. If a high and low are very close together, you will have a lot of those isobars packed close together — wind!

Wind will always blow in the general direction of the isobars. The wind will never blow perpendicular to the isobars. When you have loose isobars (meaning light air), that is when you can usually count on another phenomenon called a sea breeze (or a lake breeze).

SEA BREEZE

This is based on two important concepts:

● Cold air always flows toward warm air. Warm air rises, and cold air comes in underneath to reinforce it.
● Land heats and cools three times faster than water — water holds its temperature constant for a longer period of time than land.

During the evening and night or when there is no sun, usually you have a land breeze — an offshore breeze — because that's when the water is warmer than the land. The cooler air from the cooler land mass blows toward the warmer air over the water.

This will persist during the morning after the sun comes up until we reach a point where the temperatures of the land and water become equal and you will have dead calm, sort of a slack tide of the wind. Temperature contrast is what drives wind — when there is no temperature contrast, there is no wind.

As the day progresses, usually around noon, you will notice these little puffy clouds developing right along the coast — not over the water; right over the coastline. That is the initiation of the sea breeze. What we call a "steam engine" has just begun.

In the northern hemisphere the prevailing winds aloft are from west to east. The hot air off the land rises up and forms a cloud as it gets into the cooler air above. The upper west-to-east winds push the rising air to the east, out over the water, where the air is even cooler. As the air cools, it begins to sink, and it then moves back toward the land to attempt to move in beneath the rising hot air.

As this goes on through the day, the wind strength keeps increasing because this steam engine just keeps going around and around and around.

So in coastal areas and even on lakes, start looking for a sea breeze right when it starts getting really hot, around noon or 1 o'clock, and it will persist until about 4 o'clock. The sun will reach its maximum heating between 3 and 4 o'clock.

When the sun begins to go down, things start to cool off, and the engine starts slowing down, and the wind starts getting lighter.

An important thing for the racing sailor to understand about this sea breeze, in addition to when it is likely to occur, is the wind shift that will accompany it.

In the northern hemisphere the sea breeze will always try to follow the sun, which means it will clock to the right from the direction where it originally filled in. Between noon and 1 o'clock when it begins and 3 or 4 o'clock at its maximum velocity, the wind may shift 20 to 30 degrees to the right. It will have reached its maximum point of shift between 3 and 4 o'clock, and it will not shift any farther to the right.

But as soon as the steam engine starts to cool down, the wind will shift back again to the direction it started from — it will shift back to the left.

As I said, wide isobars allow the sea breeze to develop. If the isobars are tight, the front will dominate the wind direction and velocity.

Even for an inland lake there is usually a dead spot in the middle of the lake. There will be a sea breeze coming in straight onshore at every point around the lake. You could theoretically sail all the way around the lake on one tack. There usually will be more wind near shore with a sea breeze because there is more temperature contrast closer to shore. Again, this effect will only happen when the isobars are widely spaced. If the front is dominating, you will get a more consistent air flow across the lake in the direction of the isobars.

If you have a weak high pressure system, the closer you are to the center of it, the lighter the air. Sometimes there is more wind at the outer ends of the high.

SEA BREEZE SUMMARY

1. Land heats and cools three times faster than water.
2. Cold air goes toward hot air.
3. Little puffy clouds will tell you when the sea breeze is going to appear — usually between noon and 1 o'clock.
4. It will last until 3-4 o'clock.
5. It will clock with the sun to the right until 3-4 o'clock, and then it will shift back to the direction it started from.

6. The greater the contrast in temperature between land and water, the more breeze you will have.
7. If you have a cloudy day, you will probably not see a sea breeze, because the land is not going to heat up enough.

GEOGRAPHICAL SHIFT

If you are sailing or racing near a shoreline, you can take advantage of Mother Nature's 90-degree rule: Wind likes to cross the division between land and water at a 90-degree angle — whether it is blowing onshore or offshore. This results in a geographical shift near a shore. How close to the shore this bend will occur is something you must find out by going out to the race course early and sailing it.

Let's say there is an offshore wind that is coming from the right as you face the land. This means that as you approach shore on starboard tack, going toward the left side of the course, you will eventually run into a header, because the wind has shifted to the left to make its perpendicular exit from the land. Therefore, you want to go to the left side of the course. And generally, the person who starts at the port end of the line, no matter which end of the line was favored, will get the header first and will be first to the weather mark.

On the other hand, if the basic wind direction is coming from the left as you face the land, you will get the header as you approach shore on the right side of the course. Therefore, you want to go to the right side and start at the starboard end of the line.

You will probably be lifted for a while until you get into the perpendicular bend in the wind, when you will get the header. You know there is going to be a shift somewhere in relation to the shore, but you don't know how close to the shoreline it is going to happen. So here again you must do your homework and get out early to find out where the "normal" wind direction is and where that shift begins and whether you are going to be able to take advantage of it. Sometimes this shift is very close to shore and you can't get much use out of it — other times it may extend out well into your race course.

The wind is always going to TRY to turn and exit or enter the land at a perpendicular angle. However, in light air you are more likely to see it happen. In a strong sea breeze, it is more possible that it might turn and go parallel with the shore instead of crossing it at a 90-degree angle. In this case, the geographical shift would be in the opposite direction from the one we have been talking about. Again, do your homework and find this out before the race.

THE CAPE EFFECT

Most sailors are familiar with the windy reputations of places like Cape Canaveral, the Cape of Good Hope, Cape Cod, Cape Horn and Cape Fear.

Capes are humps in the shoreline, and off a point of land like this, large or small, you have an area of convergence. When a front is dominating the wind pattern and you have fairly strong winds to begin with, paralleling the shoreline, the wind accelerates as it makes the bend to get out around the promontory, and then it bends back to its former direction as it joins the wind a little farther offshore that was just going to straight. Right off the end of the "cape," you have an area of convergence, creating a lot of wind. In addition, the accelerated wind curving back out toward sea as it bounces off the windward side of the cape will cause a windshift that will give you a header as you sail to weather toward the point of land.

So from the starting line, you want to head toward the point of land. But be careful not to get into the lee of that point, because there will be no air there. Go to the point or just beyond it.

The side of the course away from the point will not only have less wind, it will not have that favorable header.

To bring together your knowledge of circulation patterns and geographical shifts, get a chart of the area and get the weather map and try to bring the big picture into focus on your little map and figure out what the wind is going to do.

In addition, ask someone from the area (preferably not your competition) what the wind is likely to do. If you REALLY want to win races, these are the kinds of things you have to do.

Remember that when the wind parallels the shore, it usually is generated by a front rather than a sea breeze effect.

Of course, there are other geographical factors that influence the wind's course, including trees, buildings, channels or rivers that cut through the land.

Again, you have to do your homework before the race — I can't stress this strongly enough. I go out before the skipper's meeting and immediately after the skipper's meeting.

CLOUD STREETS

When you have clouds above you over the water, you can play the "cloud streets".

When you are directly beneath the cloud, you will have a lull in the wind. When you are between the clouds, you will get a puff.

Rising, hot air under the clouds causes a lull; sinking, cooler air between the clouds causes a puff.

If you play the cloud streets, you will be easing downhauls and easing sheets; then pulling downhauls, pulling sheets and trapezing.

OSCILLATING SHIFTS

MEDIAN WIND AND THE 2-HEADER TACK

Whether you have a steady wind or a wind with a persistent shift, you will have oscillations back and forth from the median direction of the wind.

But let's talk about the steady wind with oscillating shifts.

First of all, the wind is never perfectly steady. It will always be going back and forth from one side of the median wind to the other. If you are going to sail the oscillations, the two-header tack is the way to do it.

First of all, you have to know what the median wind direction is so that you will know when you are on a lift or a header in relation to the median wind. This means spending some time on the water before the race to find out the angle at which the shifts and headers average out so you know the median angle.

After the race begins, when you are sailing what you believe to be the median wind direction, when you get a header, tack. Now you are on the opposite tack. When you get a header, do you tack again? No. Because the first header is just the wind going back to its median angle. Wait for the second header, because that is when the wind is shifting to the opposite side of its oscillation away from the median wind.

By waiting for the second header, you have gained that much more leverage on the boats behind you.

Depending on how long the time period is between oscillations — and you usually can't nail them down to a nice neat schedule — on catamarans you may want to do a four-header tack or a six-header tack, but it should be in even increments.

Of course, if you start off on the wrong foot to begin with, you are going to be out of synch all the way up the weather leg.

For better overall finish results, check the weather patterns, but mostly, go out early and check out the shifts on the race course. Get to know the race area.

OLYMPIC CLASS
Chapter 28

AN INTERVIEW WITH RANDY SMYTH

In 1972 the Tornado became the first, and so far the only, multihull to be accepted as an Olympic class. It first participated in the Olympics in 1976.

When the Tornado was accepted as an Olympic class, the aim was to make the Olympics a goal attainable by anyone. It was to be a boat that you could build in your back yard, and in the early years some people even tried that.

But things have changed — the level of competition, the Olympic political climate, the cost of competing, and the boat itself. A backyard boat is no longer a viable option; and getting to the Olympics takes a major commitment of time, effort and money.

We talked to 1982 silver medalist Randy Smyth, who is currently campaigning for the 1992 Olympics, about what has happened to the boat since it acquired Olympic status, what the future holds, and what it takes to make it to the Olympics.

DO YOU THINK OLYMPIC STATUS HAS HELPED OR HURT THE TORNADO CLASS?

That depends on your viewpoint, I guess. You don't see many boat manufacturers pushing to get their boats accepted as an Olympic class because it doesn't make commercial sense. They would sell a lot less boats. The level of competition and the cost of competing gets so high, the weekend sailor feels obsolete. That has happened to the Tornado class.

But on the other hand, it has resulted in the Tornado becoming the most competitive racing class in the world, and it has been leading the way in technology and innovations that eventually filter down to the other catamaran classes. That benefits everybody.

WHAT CHANGES HAVE BEEN MADE TO THE BOAT OVER THE YEARS, AND WHAT ARE SOME OF THE INNOVATIONS THAT HAVE COME FROM THE TORNADO CLASS?

The sails have become much more versatile and easy to adjust. It used to be that you had to be a weather man and second-guess the wind before you went out to a race. You had to have the right sail and the right battens and have your diamond wires set right. But now you can adjust your sail right on the water just with the downhaul.

The mast has gone from a teardrop shape to more of a wing shape, longer fore and aft.

The main beam and rear beam have gotten bigger to reduce flex. The boat used to be very flexy; now it is very stiff.

Although the Tornado is a one-design boat, as far as sails, hulls and mast and other basic components, you are free to do what you want as far as barber haulers, inhaulers, outhaulers, mast rotation, jib luff tensioner, jib-lead arrangements, travelers, cleats and block systems. So people are constantly experimenting with new equipment and new ways of doing things on the boat, as well as developing new sailing techniques to increase speed.

The most significant innovation of recent years is the pre-bent mast. As described elsewhere in this book, this refers to tightening the diamond stays very tight so the mast bends fore and aft rather than sideways. This keeps the mast from bending into the slot between main and jib. It also means you have full adjustment of the mainsail with the downhaul alone.

We used to have to change the battens, the diamond wires, the mast rotation — some of which you can't do on the water. Now all you have to do is downhaul more to flatten out the sail or downhaul less to get it fuller.

Another innovation was the change in the sheeting point for the mainsheet. On the Tornado we used to sheet the main from the rear beam just as is done on most boats. Now we are sheeting from the middle of the trampoline. We bolt a plate to the tramp for the block a few inches behind the jib-lead cable.

This gives the crew (who holds the mainsheet) more leverage, because it comes more directly to him, and he can keep his legs straight. He used to have to bend his aft leg to brace himself when sheeting.

In addition, because the skipper does not trapeze on the current Tornadoes, the sheet used to come across his legs — with the new sheeting point, this is no longer a problem.

Barber haulers, which used to be attached to a free-running ring on the jib sheet, are now attached directly to the pigtail from the clew of the jib. This sometimes eliminates the need to cleat the jib sheet downwind.

There are probably hundreds of little things that have been developed by the Tornado class that everyone now takes for granted in all the classes.

"Wild Thing" is a very recent Tornado innovation, and the technique is described in detail in the chapter on Sailing the Prindle 19. This is still being perfected.

(Editor's note: Randy both invented and named the 'Wild Thing.')

WHAT DOES THE FUTURE HOLD FOR THE TORNADO?

After the 1992 Olympics, Tornadoes will be going through their first major modifications since the boat was designed in 1967. In the fall of 1991, the International Tornado Association approved adding a second set of trapeze wires, increasing the sail area by 18 percent and permitting roller-furling for the jib.

The sail area increase will be entirely in the jib. There will be no change to the mainsail or any of the boat's other basic components.

The present boat has 235 square foot of sail. The new rig will have 276 square feet of sail, adding 41 square feet to the jib.

WHAT IS ACCOMPLISHED BY THESE CHANGES?

For one thing, they will help the Tornado retain its throne as the king of the one-design catamarans, speedwise. Some of the newer boats, like the Prindle 19 and the Nacra 5.8, have more sail area AND double trapeze wires, and in certain conditions are capable of beating a Tornado.

But while staying No. 1 in the speed department was a factor in the decision to approve the modifications, it was primarily aimed at enticing more sailors into the Tornado class. We had to get current so we can attract sailors from other catamaran classes. It's hard to get someone interested in a boat when they find out they are going to have to sit on a hard deck and hike out, when they are used to being on a trapeze.

It was archaic to have a single trapeze, and although everybody has wanted this rule changed for years, they could not figure out an equitable way to do it. If they simply added a trapeze, it would be an advantage to the lighter-weight teams, who can use the extra leverage. Some of the heavier teams currently sailing would no longer have been competitive.

The problem was resolved by adding sail area to compensate for the additional leverage, so the change will affect all teams equally, and it will not give any teams more advantage or less advantage than they had before. The same teams will be able to continue sailing together.

There is no minimum crew weight, but it seems to sail best with a crew weight of 300 to 310. The range among the top racers is from 280 to 335. These figures should stay pretty much the same with the changes.

Fringe benefits are that adding the sail area in the jib will lower the center of effort, while adding a trapeze will give the boat more righting moment.

Another advantage of adding the sail area only in the jib is that people will not have to buy all new sails — only new jibs.
The jib sheeting points will remain the same, and no rigging changes will be required.

This is the boat we will see at the 1996 Olympics.

CAMPAIGNING FOR THE OLYMPICS

FIRST OF ALL, WHAT IS AN OLYMPIC 'CAMPAIGN'?
This just means you and your crew have decided to dedicate your lives for the next four years to the goal of trying to be the one team that will represent your country in the next Olympics.

HOW DO YOU GO ABOUT DOING IT?
You should be in the class for at least four years prior to the Olympics.

Just having experience in another catamaran is not good enough. A lot of dinghy sailors actually have made the transition into the Tornado class better than Hobie sailors. But it takes time in the boat to reach the necessary competitive level.

The Tornado is without doubt the most competitive racing class in the world. If our best Hobie sailors went to the Tornado Worlds, where 87 boats are on the starting line, they probably wouldn't stand a chance of being in the top 20.

I would say you should allow three years of training at a level you can fit in while continuing to work.

But for the last 12 months, if you are going to do it right, you have to quit your job, and you should spend 200 days out of that year on the boat. In other words, you should spend half of your time or more training and racing.

Not many people in this country do it right; you can't make it by sailing in two international regattas a year and expect to be able to compete against the Europeans.

At last count there were 41 Tornadoes in Canada, 800 in the United States and 3500 worldwide. But only a small percentage of these race competitively.

As far as how many United States sailors are campaigning seriously for the 1992 Olympics, it's hard to say. There probably will be around 30 at the Olympic trials. But there were only eight who cared enough to go to Italy for the Worlds in the fall of '91.

HAVE THERE BEEN CHANGES IN THE WAY YOU HANDLE AN OLYMPIC CAMPAIGN?

Yes, there have been two very important changes.

For one thing, the days when you could get a boat and go out on your own and try for the Olympics are gone. These days you have to associate yourself with a strong team-training approach, if you want a chance at the Olympics.

The second major thing that has happened is that we now are permitted to have sponsorship and we can actually be professionals, getting paid for sailing.

The Tornado Class Association, and at least half of the other Olympic boat classes, allow sponsor advertising to be displayed on the boats. We can advertise on the mast, boom and hulls — not the sails.

We will not be permitted to carry advertising on the boat during the 1992 Olympic races in Barcelona, but that could change before the 1996 Olympics.

This was a major breakthrough in making it possible for people to afford to commit to an Olympic campaign.

HOW MUCH DOES IT COST TO WAGE AN OLYMPIC CAMPAIGN?

The cost of an Olympic campaign depends on where you live. You have to be able to race as often as possible against good competition.

If you live in Europe, it's relatively inexpensive. The top competitors are there; there are a lot of boats; and there are many regattas. If you live in Holland, for instance, you can go to a regatta every weekend for the price of a tank of gas. Europeans can probably wage an Olympic campaign for 50 or 60 thousand dollars a year.

If you live in the United States, it is going to be a lot more expensive. The only way to do it right is to have two boats — one here and one in Europe — and make it to as many races over there as you can.

And if you happen to live in New Zealand, it will be really expensive — you would have to either move to Europe or commute.

If you want to get into a campaign for an Olympic berth, you do need a competitive boat. Right now the competitive boats are the Marstrom boats from Sweden. He has the highest quality control, and as a manufacturer he really has made the Tornado a true one-design class, with a very high level of quality.

One of the Marstrom boats new costs $18,000. You're on your own for sails. A set of sails costs $1,000 to $1,500, and you need a lot more than one set of sails. That's something you should probably think about more in terms of dozens.

When you get down to 12 months before the Olympics you need everything you think is fast, in the way of sails. When you go to an Olympic training regatta, or any major regatta, you are only allowed to check in with one main and two jibs — so you had better be sure you have the best sail for the job.

The cost of the boats is not really lost money, because Tornadoes hold their value pretty well — especially the Marstrom boats.

But the big expense of an Olympic campaign is not in the boats, and it's not in the air fare and food. It is the investment of your time and the expense of having to quit your job and lose your income.

That is why sponsorship is so important, if you can get it. In addition to your travel and lodging and food costs and the price of the boats, you have to figure in salaries for you and your crew to make up for your lost incomes.

WHAT DO YOU DO TO TRAIN FOR THE OLYMPICS?

Because Tornado regattas in the U.S. are few and far between, almost any of the small beach cats are good training boats. What I do is pick the most competitive boat in my area and the one which has the most similarities to the Tornado. In my area, that happens to be the Prindle 19, so that is what I have been racing for the last couple of years.

For this last training year before the 1992 Olympics, I have set up an "open door" training camp, inviting European sailors to come here to train with us. We race against each other and pace against each other and when we learn things, we all learn them, and we help each other get faster.

It's what I was talking about earlier — the team approach. You just can't do it by yourself.

You also have to get into condition physically. The best thing you can do is sail all the time. In addition, it helps if you can find a sports training center where they can get you on a training program with weights and exercises that strengthen the appropriate muscles.

For instance, on a Tornado the skipper doesn't trapeze, so he has to hike hard — therefore, his program includes doing a lot of situps. Both skipper and crew need exercises that strengthen the muscles that are specifically used when you are pulling from a low angle — sheeting from the trapeze.

HOW DO THEY DECIDE WHO IS ACTUALLY GOING TO THE OLYMPICS — AND WHO IS "THEY"?

Every country has its own elimination process for finding the best team to send to the Olympics. In the United States it is based on one, and only one, Olympic qualifying regatta put on by USS (formerly USYRU).

WHO CAN PARTICIPATE IN THE REGATTA; IS THERE SOME WAY OF QUALIFYING?

Anyone can go and participate. That's the whole philosophy of the Olympics — to make it accessible to anyone. Whoever wins that regatta goes to the Olympics.

Of course, you would probably have to join the class association and USS before the regatta. But there are no other restrictions on who can sail in it.

During the years prior to the Olympics, the class has a series of regattas each year, and the boats that race get points based on how they finished. At the end of the year, they rank people based upon the points they accumulated during the year. Any money that is available from various Olympic fund sources is divided, based on the rankings, to help cover expenses for X number of people to go to the Worlds, for instance.

Money also is allocated (if it is available) for things like research and development within the class.

But the rankings people get every year have no bearing on getting to the Olympics. It all comes down to that one regatta.

It's sort of like a class in college where the professor is going to base your grade for the quarter only on the final exam. It's a lot of pressure. And the pressure is another important factor, because you have to be able to handle it. A lot of great sailors have fallen by the wayside on the road to the Olympics because they couldn't take the pressure.

ABOUT THE AUTHORS

Rick White and Mary Wells are both pioneers of catamaran racing in this country. Mary's family began racing a Shark catamaran in the early 1960's when fleets were first developing on the East Coast and the Great Lakes, and Rick joined the catamaran movement with a Shark a few years later.

Since then he has won over 50 championships including Nationals, North Americans, Mideasterns, Midwesterns, Southeasterns and numerous State championships in Sharks, Tornadoes and Hobies. He and wife Mary Wells are Hobie 18 Masters National champions. Rick holds records in three long-distance races.

This is White's third book on catamaran racing. The first, "The Complete Manual of Catamaran Racing," was published in 1976, and the second, "Catamaran Racing: Solutions, Secrets, Speed," was released in 1983.

In 1989 the couple founded Rick White's Sailing Seminars and have since been traveling the country putting on the only regularly-scheduled, on-water-oriented, race-training programs available for catamarans in the United States.

Currently, they are working on a teaching videotape based upon the seminars and a booklet of drills that sailors can use alone or with a group to improve their sailing skills.

Now living in the Florida Keys and in Put-in-Bay, Ohio, the White-Wells team still race the Hobie 18 competitively, as well as a MacGregor 36 catamaran, but are spending most of their time putting on seminars to help others get faster and promote the sport of sailing.

INDEX

This school is a *pool-of-knowledge* gained from our many Guest Experts—a star-studded lineup of the World's Greatest Sailors.

You can *learn all their secrets* in a few intense days, filled with on-the-water drills, on-the-water coaching, video feedback, and chalk talks.

Rick White's Sailing Seminars are now on the *cutting edge* of technology and technique: You will learn:

✔ The **Wild Thing**, a new, faster way to sail downwind

✔ The **Catamaran Roll Tack**, the newest, fastest trick to cut your tacking time down to only 5 seconds

✔ **Power Righting**, the fast way to right your capsized catamaran

✔ Plus, gain tons of ability in **Boat Handling, Strings to Pull, Starting, Sailing to Weather/Downwind/Reaches, Finishing, Windshifts, Tactics, Tuning/Sail Trim!**

You will do over **200** crowded starts, **300** crowded mark roundings, and over **500** tacks and jibes (more than most sailors do in a decade); you *HAVE* to improve dramatically.

Videos of each day's drills will by analyzed in evening sessions, along with written tests, and chalk-talk lectures.

NO CREW? NO PROBLEM! Team up with a buddy!

Seminars are limited to only 20 catamarans,
So Hold a spot! Sign up now! Call/Write for info or..,
Send a deposit check in the amount of $100 to:
Rick White's Sailing Seminars
PO Box 2060
Key Largo, FL 33037
or use Visa/MC/Discover, and Call **1-800-484-2075**, then 'SAIL' at the prompt, or **305-451-3287** and charge your deposit.

Get a copy of this great, all-new book

CATAMARAN RACING: *For the 90's*

by Rick White and Mary Wells

Written by the founders of Rick White's Sailing Seminars, this book is on the cutting edge of technology and technique:

✓Learn the **Wild Thing**, a new, faster way to sail downwind

✓Learn the **Catamaran Roll Tack**, the newest, fastest trick to cut your tacking time down to only 5 seconds.

✓Learn **Power Righting**, the fast way to right your capsized catamaran.

✓Plus, gain tons of information on **Spinnakers, Prebent Masts, Distance Racing, Mylar/Kevlar Sails**, and much more.

This book is a pool of thoughts of the World's greatest sailors. Just look at the star-studded lineup of world-class sailors that have contributed:

*Randy Smyth on the Prindle 19, Spinnakers and Olympic Class

*Carlton Tucker on the Hobie 17 and other unirigs

*Hobie Alter, Jr. on the Hobie 18

*Wayne Schafer on the Hobie 16

*Larry Harteck on the Nacra 5.8

*Bob Curry on Wind and Weather

*Roy Seaman on Distance Racing

*Dave Calvert on Sail Designs and Materials

And look at some of the chapters:

Boat Handling, Weight Distribution, the Mainsail, Battens, the Jib, Mast Rake, Strings to Pull, Telltales, the Start, the Weather Leg, The Downwind Leg, the Reach, the Finish, Windshifts, Tactics, and the Revival of Sailing.

And, for the *crew*, highlighted notes throughout, as the subject appears in the book!

"It doesn't matter what kind of multihull you sail, or what size — this book will make you better at it..," says National Outdoor Journalist, Eric Sharp.

With over *60 diagrams*, this 352-page book is the ultimate catamaran sailing book.

— —

To order, fill out the following coupon:

Name:

Shipping Address:

City, State, Zip:

Telephone No. & area code

Send To:

RAM Press

PO Box 2060

Key Largo, FL 33037

To use credit card, call 1-800-484-2075, then 'SAIL' at the prompt (or 305-451-3287)

Please send me____copies of *Catamaran Racing:For the 90's* @ $29.95 + $2 shpg

Cash___Check___Charge(Visa/MC/Discover)#_____

exp date_____